Juvenile Del
and Young Peop
in an Open Envir

CW01065569

Dr Willie McCarney has been a lay magistrate in Northern Ireland for 20 years and is a justice of the peace for the City of Belfast. He is a past Chair of the Northern Ireland Juvenile Courts Association (NIJCA), a past Chair of the British Juvenile and Family Courts Society (BJFCS) and a member of the Executive Committee of the International Association of Juvenile and Family Court Magistrates (IAJFCM). He is the author of many articles on youth justice and juvenile welfare and editor of NIJCA's *Lay Panel* magazine, editor of the BJFCS *Newsletter* and editor-in-chief of *The Chronicle* - the journal of the IAJFCM - which is published bi-annually in English, French and Spanish.

He is a member of the Probation Board for Northern Ireland and Chair of its Practice Committee. He is a member of the Licensing Review Committee at St Patrick's Training School, Belfast and Chair of the Independent Representatives Committee. He has been Chair of the Board of Directors of Glenand Training Agency for ten years and Vice-Chair of Worknet (two agencies involved in youth training). He was Chair of the Intermediate Treatment Association for Northern Ireland for three years.

Dr McCarney was president of the Ulster Council of the Racquetball Association of Ireland for 15 years and Irish President on two occasions. He was also manager of the Irish racquetball team at the European Championship and the World Championship.

Juvenile Delinquents
and Young People in Danger in an Open Environment
Utopia or Reality?
Legal Frameworks and New Practices
Comparative Approach

Edited by Willie McCarney

Contributors

Frieder Dünkel
Dilly Gask
Ruth G. Herz
Annina Lahalle
Martine Mérigeau
Horst Schüller Springorum
Alenka Selih
Collette Somerhausen

Translated from the French by Liam McCarney

WATERSIDE PRESS

in association with the

International Association of Juvenile and Family Court Magistrates

Juvenile Delinquents and Young People in Danger in an Open Environment

Utopia or Reality?
Legal Frameworks and New Practices
Comparative Approach

Published 1996 by
WATERSIDE PRESS
Domum Road
Winchester SO23 9NN
Telephone or Fax 01962 855567
E-mail INTERNET:106025.1020@compuserve.com

In association with the International Association of Juvenile and Family Court Magistrates

ISBN Paperback 1 872 870 39 2

Editor Dr Willie McCarney, MA(Ed), JP
St. Martin, 175, Andersonstown Rd
Belfast BT11 9EA, Northern Ireland.
Telephone 01232 615164; fax 01232 618374

Translated from the French by Liam McCarney

Foreign edition Published in French by Erès, Toulouse (1994)

Cover design by John Good Holbrook Ltd, Coventry

Printing and binding by Antony Rowe Ltd, Chippenham

Juvenile Delinquents and Young People in Danger in an Open Environment

CONTENTS

Members of the International Network for Research into Juvenile Law

Frieder Dünkel
Professor of Criminology, University of Greifswald, Germany

Dilly Gask JP
Magistrate, Member of the Council of NACRO, Great Britain

Ruth Herz
Juvenile Court Judge, Cologne, Germany

Annina Lahalle
Researcher, CNRS: A Centre of Interdisciplinary Research in Vaucresson (CRIV), France

Martine Mérigeau
Researcher, Max-Planck Institute of Foreign and International Criminal Law, Freiburg-in-Breisgau, Germany

Horst Schüler-Springorum
Professor of Criminal Law and Criminology, University of Munich, Germany

Alenka Selih
Professor of Criminal Law and Criminology, University of Ljubljana, Slovenia

Colette Somerhausen
Director of Courses, Free University of Brussels, Belgium.

Preface to the English Edition

The International Association of Juvenile and Family Court Magistrates (IAJFCM). Who or what is it?

The IAJFCM is a Non-Governmental Organization (NGO) with consultative status at the United Nations. It was founded in 1928 and registered in Brussels, Belgium. It represents world-wide efforts to deal with young offenders, to take action against juvenile delinquency and to improve youth protection. Its membership is comprised of national associations and committed individuals from all parts of the globe, who exercise functions as juvenile court judges or within professional services directly linked to juvenile justice or juvenile welfare.

For many years the IAJFCM has been active in the Council of International Organisations Directly Interested in Children and Youth. Members have been appointed by both the United Nations and the Council of Europe as 'leading experts' and have contributed to the drafting of international conventions relating to the rights, interests and welfare of children and young people including, for example, the preliminary draft for the European Convention for the Protection of the Rights of the Child and the draft for the Minimum Standard Rules for the Administration of Juvenile Justice. The IAJFCM:

- holds an International Congress once every four years;
- holds regional seminars in various parts of the world - generally two per year;
- works with international organisations and NGOs - e.g. ECOSOC, UNICEF, ILO;
- has been involved in the drafting of legislation affecting children at both UN level and for the Council of Europe.

Association meetings

The Executive Committee of the IAJFCM generally meets twice each year and, because members have to come from all over the world, tries to combine meetings with a regional seminar, so that members have an added incentive to travel. The General Purposes Committee, a much larger group, generally meets once every two years. It must meet at least once every four years to agree the date, venue and theme for the next World Congress.

Objectives

The Objectives of the IAJFCM are :

1. To establish links between judges, magistrates and specialists all over the world who are attached to a judicial authority of whatever nature which is concerned with the protection of youth or with the family.

vii

2. To study, at international level, all problems raised by the functioning of judicial authorities and bodies for the protection of youth and the family; to ensure the continuance of the principles governing those authorities and to make them more widely known.

3. To examine legislation designed for the protection of youth and the family and the various systems existing for the protection of maladjusted children and young people, or children and young people in social or moral danger, with a view to improving such systems both nationally and internationally.

4. To assist collaboration between nations and competent authorities with regard to foreign minors, especially with a view to their repatriation or treatment.

5. To collaborate with international associations which are concerned with the protection of youth and with the family.

6. To encourage research into the causes of the criminal behaviour or maladjustment of youth, to combat their effects and to seek a permanent prevention and rehabilitation programme; to concern itself with the moral and material improvement of youth's destiny and, in particular, with the future of youth in moral or social danger.

The present research

The replacement of deprivation of liberty by measures designed to retain children and adolescents in their natural environment is to be found as a point of orientation in all the international texts adopted in recent years: recommendations of the United Nations and of the Council of Europe. These recommendations reflect the evolution in tendencies of criminal policy regarding juvenile delinquency and policies designed to protect children and young people who are particularly vulnerable. Addressed to all member states, the recommendations enumerate the basic principles which must be interpreted and applied in the general framework of the Universal Declaration of Human Rights and other international conventions relating to the rights, interests and welfare of all children and young people. The best known of these international conventions are: the Minima Rules on the Administration of Juvenile Justice, 1985 (the 'Beijing Rules'); the Directing Principles for the Prevention of Juvenile Delinquency, 1990 (the 'Riyadh Guidelines'); the Minima Rules for the Protection of Minors Deprived of Liberty, 1990 (the 'Havana Rules'); and the Convention on the Rights of the Child, 1989.

Arising from these international instruments the retaining of the young person in the family and in the community is becoming a primary objective in most new (national) legislation. A greater priority is being given to all measures which can be used as substitutes for deprivation of liberty, in the case of young offenders, or for placements in institutions, in the case of young people in difficulty.

The aim of the research

The 'utopian' situation raised in the sub-title of this work is the 'treatment' of young people in an open environment. The aim of the research was the study, in a comparative light, of new forms of treatment in an open environment both for young delinquents and young people in danger or in difficulty. Answers were sought to the following questions :

- Are there notable differences, from one legislation to another, in the treatment of juvenile delinquents and of children and young people in difficulty?
- What place is given to measures in a 'secure environment' and measures in an 'open environment' among the range of measures which can be taken concerning minors?
- What kind of change and real expansion of measures in an 'open environment' is taking place?
- What is the influence of the recommendations of international texts on new legislation? What new measures result from them?

I am not aware of any comparable research on this topic which embraces all of Europe. The original report was published in French in 1994. Resources did not allow for publication in any other language. I believe that the results of the research are extremely important and should be made available to the widest audience possible. Consequently I appealed to the Human Rights and Democratisation Unit of the European Commission to fund the translation and publication of the report in English. I am happy to say that they agreed to do so and I thank them for it.

I am confident that readers will agree that this is a very valuable piece of research and that the findings should be made available to all. Also that readers will be heartened, as I am, by the findings which are almost impossible to dispute: deprivation of liberty concerning juveniles is in the process of decline, although this decline is not proceeding at the same speed or by the same route everywhere. I trust that this research will play a role in accelerating that decline.

The International Network for Research into Juvenile Law

The research reported in this text was carried out by the International Network for Research into Juvenile Law. The Network was established in 1989 by the Executive Committee of the International Association of Juvenile and Family Court Magistrates in pursuance of Objective 6 above. The members of the Network are listed on page *vi.*

Dr Willie McCarney

Belfast
March 1996

Foreword

The International Association of Juvenile and Family Court Magistrates (IAJFCM) proposes in article 2, point 5 of its statutes: 'to favour research on delinquency and lack of social adaptation of youth and likewise their causes, to combat their effects, and, in particular, to create a permanent program of prevention or re-education . . .'

It is therefore in the general context of the constant concerns of the IAJFCM that the International Network for Research into Juvenile Law has deployed its activities since 1990 and arrives today at the publication of this much anticipated volume *Juvenile Delinquents and Young People in Danger in an Open Environment.*

Therefore we must greet with enthusiasm the completion of this work and express profound gratitude to the authors and researchers who have given us the product of their reflections; they have conquered the real obstacle course represented by any research carried out on an international level, especially where the people involved are obliged to sacrifice leisure time, where distances reduce the possibility of meeting, where different judicial systems impose obligatory passages of comparative law, without even speaking of the inconvenience of translation and the problems of material and financial resources. Therefore, here is a challenge well met. The merit should be attributed totally to our friends from the International Organisation, to Willie McCarney, who has prepared the text for publication, and to his son Liam who translated the text from the original French. They will find here very modest thanks.

Beyond the wording of its statutes, the IAJFCM professes a permanent interest in the cause of children. For several years, it has been resolutely involved in several directions:

• in the area of *International Adoption,* it has never ceased to condemn the traffic of children between rich and poor countries and has devoted several of its international events, notably the 1986 World Congress of Rio de Janeiro to this question; it co-operates, with other non-government organisations, in preparing a convention of global scope on adoption; the urgent need for draconian measures is becoming more and more evident, even if the limitations peculiar to such a treaty of private international law are known;

• in the area of *Rights of the Child,* it has taken part, either as an entity or through some of its members, in the advent of the true body of rights conferred to the child by large international treaties: the United Nations Convention on the Rights of the Child, the Beijing Rules on the Administration of Juvenile Justice, the Riyadh Directing Principles on the Prevention of Juvenile Delinquency and the Havana Rules on Minors Deprived of Liberty. This very extensive work carried out by international instances during the past decade represents, in the domain of the protection of childhood, a remarkable advance, which the IAJFCM intends to defend and not permit to be emptied of its essence by excessive formalism or by a return to purely repressive measures;

- in the area of *Deprivation of Liberty,* the IAJFCM has always campaigned for 'less prison and more education'. A permanent support for permanent measures, an invitation to use prison only as a last resort, respect of the principle of not separating children from their family background, such are the key points which juvenile magistrates have unceasingly supported and to which they have dedicated numerous national, regional and international seminars.

Therefore, in these last two areas of protection of children and deprivation of liberty, it was logical that the IAJFCM should devote a great deal of international research to *current forms of treatment of juveniles in an open environment.* Such a study, which could give a clear and objective view of national situations and which could serve as a summary of various tendencies, was lacking until now.

The importance of international instruments which, in many instances, have already been modified or are in the process of modification and their influence on national legislation, supposed likewise that it is possible to enlarge the field of vision usually limited by our traditional frontiers. It is therefore a wide panorama which the authors have painted for us, thanks to the complementary colours of their rich palette, law certainly, but also criminology, history, sociology etc. From this interdisciplinary approach emerge, like in a cubist landscape, the multiple facets of intervention in favour of this juvenile population which is disadvantaged, in danger, delinquent, ill-treated or abandoned, and which cries out, often in a clumsy and disordered manner, its need for help.

One of the prime goals of this work is to examine in two prominent chapters the situation of juvenile delinquents on the one hand and the situation of young people in danger on the other and to establish links between these situations. Too often we limit ourselves to one or other of these categories, forgetting that it is in fact the same children, the same questions, the same dramas; here, thanks to the complete opening of the angle of view, we obtain a global representation of reality and can therefore understand that there exists, between different judicial systems and different modes of treatment, passages - often narrow and difficult - connecting two worlds which we must stop contrasting as they are only the expression of one and the same reality.

It is therefore along this path traced across national legislation and practices that the members of the International Association lead us, to offer us an objective, global and resolutely modern vision of juvenile law; they lead us, in fact, to a new state of affairs. This does not only have the objective of illuminating our knowledge but should go further: it should first of all awaken general interest in the cause of children, then inspire those who practice juvenile law in the search for innovative solutions. It should also influence politicians at the moment when choices have to be made and answers found in the face of questions as serious as ill-treatment of children, juvenile drug addiction and the explosion of violence.

We must therefore congratulate th e people who have devoted their skills and a large part of their spare time to this eminent task, and it is important to tell them how significant is their contribution to the cause of the protection of minors, not just today but for future generations.

May we also express our gratitude to the public and private institutions which, thanks to their financial contributions, have made this research possible.

And to you, the readers, may the discovery of this book allow you to familiarise yourselves with the different modes of treatment of young people in difficulty and constantly remind you that the best system or most effective intervention is that which takes into account 'the greater welfare of the child' as stipulated in Article 3 of the United Nations Convention on the Rights of the Child, that is, that which does not forget that behind every text there are always human beings.

Jean Zermatten

President, IAJFCM.
February 1996

SECTION I INTRODUCTION

The Research Annina Lahalle

The transformations in family and society, particularly those in law and justice are subjects which have provoked a considerable quantity of intellectual research for several years now. The area of juvenile law is not excluded: Which solutions for which young people? In what families? In what society? Is the theory properly grounded in practice and in particular in the changes in the social fabric of society and the new populations which integrate themselves into it?

To speak of 'evolution' and to define our area of study 'in time and space', in a certain country, is not an easy task for criminologists, judges, sociologists and other specialists in juvenile law and justice. It becomes much more arduous when we wish to widen it to a combination of systems in very different social and economic realities, in the face of evolution of behaviour and attitudes in the area of young people and children and the place which they occupy, both in law and in local societies and populations.

On this subject, there is for the researcher, a primary desire to describe common sources (international conventions) and national regulations. But there is also a wish to compare the legal sphere with the social and with practices. Law is not the only factor to be considered in tackling the problems of juveniles. Law is subject to change and transformation but it cannot be disassociated from other factors. It reflects changes in criminal policies in criminal matters and the evolution of the methods of dealing with the problems of children and young people, new realities identified as situations of danger or risk, new thresholds of tolerance in each society (changes in the concept of ill-treatment, for example).

It is important to take into account that in many systems the differences between juvenile delinquents and juveniles in danger are much less distinct than in other systems. General principles govern policies concerning treatment and protection of these different categories of young people. The respect of fundamental human rights is present in all new national texts and the Convention on the Rights of the Child is certainly the international instrument which goes the furthest in this direction. Signed and ratified by most member states, the Convention is becoming the protective text which takes on value above a national level and which should guarantee 'respect for the dignity and personal value' of all young people in all countries.

But among the questions debated in many countries, we also see that minors can be at the centre of several political and economic interests and the privileged target of social control programmes, animated by interdisciplinary teams, sometimes based on a context linked to local economic difficulties and needs to eliminate unemployment. This is the case even if, in all official

13

speeches and in practice, 'the greater interests of the child' is held to be (at least in theory) of primary importance.

In this way, the examination of different elements connected to the protection of young people and the administration of juvenile justice can cause all methods of social regulation in different judicial systems to emerge and put in evidence the interaction of different professional bodies concerned. Considering this idea can also highlight the peculiarities of judicial systems in mutation in the face of local political changes (former socialist countries) or the divergence between 'modern' law, based on new tendencies in criminal policy and on social and economic realities which constitute obstacles to the application of these principles (developing countries).

This enterprise of research was born out of a desire on the part of an international group of professionals in law and justice who are members of the International Association of Juvenile and Family Court Magistrates (IAJFCM) to acquire new knowledge. Its conception and realisation called for the union of efforts of researchers specialised in juvenile criminology, in juvenile law, in the sociology of law and used to comparative analysis.

The 'Network' - Its Objectives - The Theme of the Research

The international Network for Research into Juvenile Law was established in 1989, at the suggestion of the Executive Committee of the IAJFCM. The names and details of the members of the Network are given on p. *vi*. The members maintained from the Network's conception that the research carried out must focus on themes *of international interest and of primary importance* in the realms of juvenile law and the rehabilitation of juvenile delinquents and young people in difficulty.

The evolution of social and criminal policies with regard to these young people in recent years has emphasised new key ideas: the social responsibility of young people, their search for autonomy, the defence of the interests of society and the victim, among others. The same applies to the idea of 'sanctions', new ideas to replace deprivation of liberty which should be considered a last resort.

Meanwhile, there has been noted in much legislation a considerable change in the definitions of a 'juvenile delinquent' and a 'minor at risk'. The objectives pursued by juvenile law are often the same for both these categories, in particular when children or young adolescents are involved. Because the age limit for entry into criminal justice is different from one jurisdiction to another, it is only by a comparative approach that we can identify common and/or different measures for juvenile delinquents and young people in danger.

The retaining of the young person in the family and in the community is becoming a primary objective in most new legislation and we have noted in national practices a will to renew educational work in open settings. A greater priority is being given to all measures which can be used as substitutes for deprivation of liberty, in the case of young offenders, or for placements in

14

institutions in the case of young people in difficulty. It is important to underline the significance of the movement in favour of all forms of personalised treatment for young offenders (TIG, community service, intermediate treatment, mediation and reparation etc.). For this reason the researchers, in making a comparative analysis of 'current forms of treatment of minors in an open environment' focus on the question of whether or not the theory as outlined above has lead to effective practice—*Utopia or reality?*

The Funding Sources and Organizations Which Have Supported the Research

This project has been made possible thanks to logistical assistance from research departments of the universities to which the researchers of the network belong, and the funding provided to varying degrees by:

* The IAJFCM
* The Fritz Thyssen Foundation of Cologne, Germany
* The Federal Ministry of Justice, Germany
* The Executive of the French Community of Belgium
* The Ministry of Science and Technology of the Department of Slovenia
* The Interdisciplinary Centre of Vaucresson (Associated Unit of CNRS), France
* The University of São Paolo, Brazil
* The Max-Planck Institute of Foreign and International Criminal Law in Freiburg-in-Breisgau, Germany
* The Institute of Criminology, Faculty of Law, University of Munich, Germany
* The Faculty of Law at the University of Ljubljana, Slovenia
* The Free University of Brussels, Belgium.

The Open Environment and International Regulations

The replacement of deprivation of liberty by measures designed to retain children and adolescents in their natural environment is to be found as a point of orientation in the international texts adopted in recent years: recommendations of the United Nations and of the Council of Europe.

These recommendations reflect the evolution in tendencies of criminal policy regarding juvenile delinquency and policies designed to protect children and young people who are particularly vulnerable. Addressed to all member states, the recommendations enumerate the basic principles which must be interpreted and applied in the general framework of the Universal Declaration of Human Rights and other international conventions relating to the rights, interests and welfare of all children and young people.

A combination of three fundamental United Nations texts is of particular interest to us concerning juvenile delinquency:

15

- The Minima Rules on the Administration of Juvenile Justice ('Beijing Rules' Rb), 1985;
- The Directing Principles for the Prevention of Juvenile Delinquency ('Directing Principles of Riyadh' Pdr), 1990; and
- The Minima Rules for the Protection of Minors Deprived of Liberty ('Havana Rules' Rlh), 1990.

These texts are completed by the Convention on the Rights of the Child (CDE) of 1989 which covers all aspects of the protection of children, therefore including the area of criminal law. Its field of action is certainly more ambitious than that of the aforementioned texts. The CDE wishes to see recognised and respected the 'dignity inherent in all members of the human family, in addition to the equality and inalienable character of their rights which are the foundation of freedom, justice and peace in the world.'

In the European context, two recommendations of the Council of Europe are the product of study undertaken by national experts in the field of juvenile criminology from 1983 to 1987:

- on 'social reactions to juvenile delinquency'; and
- recommendation no. R(88)6 on 'social reactions to delinquent behaviour of children of migrant families'.

These are completed by the 'European Rules on Sanctions and Measures Applied in the Community' (recommendation no. R(92)16). These rules are not considered as blueprints but as 'a body of requirements liable to be commonly accepted and observed; and there can be no satisfactory application of sanctions or measures in the community without satisfying these requirements.'

The United Nations Rules Concerning Juvenile Delinquency

The Beijing recommendations, adopted in 1985, lay out minimum conditions for the treatment of juvenile delinquents in any justice system in all parts of the world.

It is stated that they apply 'to juvenile delinquents without any distinction such as race, colour, sex, language, religion, political or other opinion, national or social origin, wealth, birth or other situation' (article 2.1).

The age of criminal responsibility is not indicated in the RB which nevertheless recommend that 'the threshold of criminal responsibility should not be fixed too low in view of the problems of affective, psychological and intellectual maturity' (art. 4.1). As for the RLH, they indicate that a minor is understood as 'any person below the age of 18' (art. 11, a). And the same text indicates that 'the age below which it is forbidden to deprive a child of liberty is fixed by law'. The Convention on the Rights of the Child points in the same direction; it defines the child as 'any human being up to the age of 18 years, unless national law accords majority earlier'. Finally, article 40, 3, (a) of the

16

CDE expresses the wish that 'Member states make an effort to establish a minimum age below which children are assumed not to have the ability to break the criminal law'.

The principal modifications which the United Nations wish to see introduced into existing or new legislation can be divided into two main groups:

- on the one hand, new resources put into place by signatory countries to arrive at effective protection and re-education of young offenders;
- on the other hand, rules for the protection of the young person before the courts.

These rules for protection are chiefly based on:

- the defence of the welfare of minors and their families;
- a productive life for minors 'within the community, such as to encourage in them during the stage of life where they are most exposed to deviant behaviour a process of personal development and education as far removed as possible from any contact with crime and delinquency' (RB, art.1.2);
- the mobilisation of 'all existing resources, notably the family, volunteers and other community groups, in addition to schools, in order to reduce the need for legal intervention and to treat effectively, equitably and humanely the person in conflict with the law' (RB, art 1.3);
- the role of juvenile justice, which must be 'an integral part of the process of national development of each country, in the general framework of social justice for all young people' (RB, art 1.4);
- the development and co-ordination of legal services for young people 'with a view to improving and perfecting the competence of the personnel of these services, in particular their methods, approaches and attitudes' (RB, art 1.5).

In this way, it is recommended that member states find, in each country, taking into consideration their own social realities and problems specific to young people, measures to replace deprivation of liberty. Recourse to these new forms of treatment should take place both before any judicial procedure and to replace provisional detention, short prison terms or placements in a secure environment.

In the case of extra-judicial measures, that is, in the case of measures taken before any juvenile justice procedure, it is considered essential to obtain the involvement of the young person and the family in the measure envisaged by the services for the protection of youth or any other competent authority. The Beijing rules underline the importance of community services and mediation as suitable means of avoiding the placing of the young person before the courts. This role of the community comes primarily from the

17

comments of the secretariat of the United Nations[1] regarding article 11 of the RB ('Recourse to extra-judicial methods'). One reads: 'Recourse to extra-judicial methods, which makes possible the avoidance of criminal proceedings and often leads to a disposition involving community services, is commonly applied in an official and unofficial manner in many judicial systems. This practice allows the avoidance of negative consequences of normal proceedings in the administration of juvenile justice (for example, the stigma of a sentence and judgement). In many cases, abstention would be the best decision. In this way, recourse to extra-judicial methods from the beginning and without referral to other services may be the best measure. This is the case especially when the offence is not of a serious nature and the family, the school or other institutions charged with exercising unofficial social control have already acted as was necessary and in a constructive manner or which are prepared to do so. The article recommends the organisation of valid solutions to replace normal juvenile justice proceedings thanks to community-based programmes; in particular those which envisage the restitution of goods to victims or which allow the prevention of conflict with the law on the part of minors thanks to temporary supervision and orientation. These are circumstances particular to each case which justify recourse to extra-judicial methods, even if more serious offences have been committed (first offence, acts committed under gang pressure, etc.) . . .'

These new measures are also a part of the list of those which can be ordered through judgement, in isolation or in combination, while 'leaving a great deal of flexibility to the judicial or relevant authority'. Article 18 of the RB envisions that a ruling can order, for example, assistance, orientation and supervision; a period of probation; intervention of community services; fines, indemnities and restitution; an intermediate or other educational regime; participation in group activities with a philanthropic purpose or other analogous activities; placement in a family, a community centre or other educational environment; all other pertinent decisions, adapted to the environment in which the young person lives.

Still in the framework of decisions which can be ordered, article 18.2 of the RB stresses the idea that 'no minor will be taken away from parental supervision, partially or totally, unless circumstances render this operation necessary' and again emphasis is laid, in analysis of the article by the secretariat of the United Nations, on the fact that this standard is applicable equally to cases of delinquency and to situations of protection of a child in danger: 'the family is the natural and fundamental element of society. Within the family, parents do not only have the right, but also the duty to take care of and supervise their children. Article 18.2 therefore indicates that separating children from their parents is a measure to be taken as a last resort. It can be taken only when the facts of the case fully justify this serious measure (ill-treatment inflicted on the child, for example) . . .'

1. The comments concerning each provision are official in the case of the RB: they have been approved with each of the rules by the members of the UN.

In the case of young people who have been sentenced, the RLH stress the importance of adequate preparation with a view to 'facilitating the return of the young person into society, into the family, into the school environment or working life after release. Procedures such as early release and training periods must be specially designed for this purpose' (RLH, art.79).

The philosophy which directs the general principles of the United Nations regulations is essentially based on the protection of the personality of the young person, on the search for educational solutions which do not involve deprivation of liberty and on the mobilisation of all existing resources within the community.

The role of the family, the community and new measures in an open environment are even more in evidence in the PDR. In the framework of prevention, 'efforts will have to be made by public bodies and social organisations to maintain the unity of the family, including the extended family' (PDR, art.12) . . . 'It is necessary that the community put into place or reinforce greatly varying methods of community assistance, recreational facilities and services designed in view of the special problems of children in a situation of 'social risk'. (PDR, art.33).

The Recommendations of the Council of Europe.

The work developed by the Committee of Experts, representing 17 European countries, which met from 1983 to 1987, on 'social reactions to juvenile delinquency', had the objectives of:

- studying the evolution of juvenile delinquency in Western Europe during the last ten years, in both quality and quantity;
- studying the evolution of the application of penalties and educational measures envisioned by different legislation, both before and after judgement;
- knowledge of new measures being taken in different countries;
- verifying if specific provisions are being taken in member states when young people from migrant families are involved.

After analysis of the responses from different countries by the experts and on the basis of propositions drawn up by the latter, two recommendations have been adopted by the Committee of Ministers of the Council Of Europe[2]

1. Recommendation no. R(87)20 on 'social reactions to juvenile delinquency';
2. Recommendation no. R(88)6 on 'social reactions to delinquent behaviour of young people from migrant families'.

2 In 1985, during the work of the Group of Experts, the Minima Rules of Beijing were adopted. These rules have therefore, quite naturally, been retained in the remarks and recommendations of the group.

In recommendation no. R(87)20, the Council of Europe particularly recommends that the member states review if necessary their legislation and practice in view of :

- putting into practice a global policy of prevention of maladjustment and juvenile delinquency;
- encouraging the development of procedures of diversion from the (juvenile) court and associating with these services or commissions for the protection of childhood;
- insuring a more rapid operation of juvenile justice, avoiding excessive delays in order that it may have a rapid educational effect;
- avoiding the referral of minors to adult jurisdiction, when juvenile jurisdictions exist;
- excluding recourse to provisional detention for minors, save in exceptional circumstances for very serious offences committed by older juveniles;
- reinforcing the legal position of minors throughout the proceedings, recognising, among other things: the right to the assistance of a legal defender, the right to have parents present, the right to call witnesses, the right to ask for a second assessment and the right to speak out on measures envisaged concerning them;
- encouraging specialised training of all persons who intervene at different stages of the proceedings;
- foreseeing that intervention regarding young delinquents should preferably take place in their natural environment and should respect their right to education and professional training;
- avoiding, on the level of penalties, measures involving deprivation of liberty, giving preference to measures to substitute for imprisonment;
- putting into place a scale of penalties adapted to the condition of the minors and foreseeing measures of semi-liberty and early release, granting and revocation of suspension of sentence;
- requiring a motive from the judge for sentences involving deprivation of liberty; ensuring academic and professional training of minors in detention, preferably in liaison with the community, ensuring also educational support and assistance in reinsertion into society after the end of the incarceration period;
- reviewing, if necessary, legislation relevant to delinquent young adults, in such a way that the competent jurisdictions also have the possibility of taking educational measures, favouring social integration of young people, taking their personality into account.

The recommendations of the Council of Europe place emphasis, like the Beijing Rules, on the role of the family and society in the treatment of young people. The exposé of the motives summarises this orientation: 'Intervention with young people should, as far as is possible, take place in the environment of the young person, with the family being assisted adequately in order that it can contribute to the educational process. In addition, the community, notably on the local level, should favour this process, for example, by giving young people opportunities to acquire an education and a job, while developing their aptitudes in sporting and cultural areas.'

On this subject, the European rules on sanctions and measures applied in the community (rule 44) underline 'the importance of informing the public and private services on the content of sanctions and measures applied in the community in order that they can understand their sound foundation and consider them as adequate and credible responses to delinquent behaviour.'

Recommendation R(87)20 also emphasises new measures which must be taken, either before the intervention of the juvenile courts (diversion from the court) or afterwards (including the educational phase). Among these measures member states should devote particular attention to those which:

- involve probation supervision and assistance; envisage tackling persistent delinquent behaviour of minors by improving their social aptitudes by means of intensive educational action (among other measures, 'intensive intermediate treatment');
- involve the reparation of damage caused by the delinquent behaviour of the young person;
- envisage community work suitable for the young person's age and educational goals.

From the comparative analysis of the various recommendations of the United Nations and the Council of Europe new directions of criminal policy emerge which are characterised principally by:

- *a different relationship between the offence committed by the minor and the measure involving deprivation of liberty:* such sanctions are being considered more and more as having to be the exception. New legislative dispositions instituting new penal and/or educational measures in an open environment have the object of reducing, or avoiding completely, recourse to detention (preventive or punitive);

- *a new status of juveniles* before a criminal justice system which must remain specialised, guaranteeing procedural rights (no unnecessary delays, the right to defence, the right of expression, among others);

- *a new vision of the 'responsibility' of the young person.* On the one hand, new relationships are being established between the young person and the victim, often through a mediator (extra-judicial or judicial), with the participation of parents and other relevant parties present. This meeting is intended to promote both a better understanding of the concept of reparation and the overall educational development of the young person.

On the other hand we have the growth of new organisations wishing to protect young people 'still in the stage of personality development'. A uniformity of age of entry into the criminal justice system and the age of full criminal responsibility is proposed to member states. Measures particular to *young adults* are suggested, measures which would take into account their personality and degree of integration into society.

- *an evolution in the concept of 're-education'*. The idea of re-education often associated with that of 'treatment' of the young delinquents is giving way little by little to a new conception based on the 'insertion' of the young person into society: insertion by new educational measures in an open environment, by a new approach on the part of schools and professional training programmes, by a better knowledge of the needs of the populations concerned (native or immigrant) and by calling on the participation of new social partners;

- *a new role played by the family and the 'community'*. In civil matters, the 1970s saw a significant evolution in the place of the family in the framework of legislation (particularly in Europe): a new notion of parental responsibility, more associated with the idea of protecting the child than that of parental authority.

International recommendations seek today to see the family pay a privileged role in the reintegration of the young person. This new function of the family has been indicated many times and we have underlined it in our analysis of the texts. Let us note that 'family' in the regulations of the United Nations and the Council of Europe is defined as much as the family of origin as the 'guest family' in the case of absence or inadequacy of the 'natural family'.

Analogous roles are attributed to the 'community': the community where the juvenile lives, the local community or the community in the sense of society. This idea calls on the notion of solidarity, on a local, national and finally international scale.

The European rules on sanctions and measures applied in the community emphasise that 'the community dimension constitutes the fundamental characteristic of this type of non-sanction or measure without detention : the implication of civil society is, in fact, the necessary and thoroughly original element in their execution and it is essential for the purpose of enabling the social reintegration of delinquents' (presentation of motives).

Finally, new needs are associated with these new functions of the family and community work; in training, research and results, and in resources (human and economic).

22

International Regulations and Scientific Research

The evolution of society, both in terms of 'rapid and often radical changes in the lifestyle of young people and the forms and dimensions of juvenile crime' and the evolution of 'reactions of society and the courts to crime and juvenile delinquency which are often outdated and unsuitable' is underlined several times, in various paragraphs of the Beijing Rules. The Rules highlight the *importance of scientific research and 'pilot schemes'* as auxiliary measures to policies for the treatment of juveniles and programmes for training professionals who are charged with their care. In this way, the text indicates that it 'invites member states and the general secretary to undertake research and put into place a database concerning policies and effective practices in the administration of juvenile justice.'

The Beijing rules advocate that research should endeavour to periodically review and evaluate not only the problems and the causes of delinquency and juvenile crime but also the different needs peculiar to incarcerated minors. With the same objective the Council of Europe recommends that member states 'promote and encourage comparative research in the area of juvenile delinquency, which can provide a base for policy on this subject (in particular research on substitution measures for deprivation of liberty, participation of the community in the care of young delinquents and measures of reconciliation between young delinquents and their victims.)'.

With this aim, states should 'make an effort to integrate a permanent plan of research and evaluation in the system of administration of juvenile justice' and strive to 'assemble and analyse pertinent data and information which is needed for appropriate evaluation, future improvements and reforms in administration.'.

Both the recommendations of the United Nations and those of the Council of Europe express the desire that research should be 'oriented towards action' and should be 'efficient': 'Research should be defined, conceived and directed according to the problems encountered by the community, the people in charge and practitioners belonging to a particular social and legal system; it must create an intellectual environment continually allowing the analysis and rational solutions of problems. Finally, research must produce results which can be immediately circulated in a form directly usable by those in charge and liable to stimulate other research oriented towards action . . .' *(Appendix to the Beijing Rules on scientific research).*

The Problem Annina Lahalle

Questioning in the Framework of an Ample Comparative Analysis

The problems of treatment of juvenile delinquents have, to be sure, often been raised in many countries and there exists abundant literature on the subject. However there is no adequate comparative work which sums up the recent evolution in criminal policy, and its continual entry into legislation, as well as new forms of treatment to replace custody. Nor has research so far focused on the influence - effective or not - of the recommendations of international rules in new legislative provisions. The research which we are proposing could contribute to compensating for this deficiency.

A profound study of social policies which guide both legislators and practitioners (social protection and legal protection) should permit a comparative analysis surpassing pure and simple examination of texts, and lead to a real understanding of legal protection in the 1990s, putting in evidence common traits and disparities.

The aim of this research is therefore the study, in a comparative light, of new forms of treatment in an open environment both for young delinquents and young people in danger or in difficulty. Consequently a comparison of different legislations and practices turned out to be indispensable as this comparison had to attempt to understand national tendencies in treatment of each category of young people concerned in our study. We sought answers to the following questions:

- Are there notable differences, from one legislation to another, in the treatment of juvenile delinquents and of children and young people in difficulty?
- What place is given to measures in a 'secure environment' and measures in an 'open environment' among the range of measures which can be taken concerning minors?
- What kind of change and real expansion of measures in an 'open environment' is taking place?
- What is the influence of the recommendations of international texts on new legislation? What new measures result from them?

Other questions focus more on minors themselves:

- What place is given to minors during the proceedings? What are their recognised rights?
- Do new measures take into account the word of the child and cohesion of the family?

Finally, with regard to the introduction of new measures in an 'open environment':

- What is the place of the victim?
- What new participation? What new partnerships? What is the place given to the associative sector and voluntary workers? Is there a new role attributed to traditional structures such as schools?

We could only find answers to all these questions from an in-depth knowledge and comparison of different legislations. There was also a need for methodological instruments suitable for expanding the answers to the questions posed.

The Usefulness of the Research

This study undertaken by the International Network of Research on Juvenile Law had to answer a need for knowledge expressed both by practitioners (magistrates, educators, social workers) and decision-makers (ministers) as. well as by different social partners (representatives of the community or private organisations).

One must observe also that the main problem which serves as a directing principle of our study, in a vast international perspective, of current forms of treatment of minors in an open environment, as a substitute for custodial measures, corresponds to the concern expressed both by the United Nations and the Council of Europe.

This research should answer the concern for information on the implementation of the recommendations of the United Nations and the Council of Europe regarding legislative changes, the planning of alternative solutions to incarceration and the results obtained concerning the introduction of new forms of treatment in an open environment.

The research should also answer the specific need for knowledge against the background of the Europe of 1993, thanks to the data gathered in the countries of our choice.

Finally, in the framework of the new Europe, this kind of reflection and comparative work between researchers from different countries and institutions, with common budgetary allocations and means, should be one of the priorities and should be encouraged, since if this step is particularly enriching for each of the participants, it is also the most apt for answering certain questions and new needs for knowledge.

Methodology Annina Lahalle

Methodology and Choice of Areas

In this perspective of comparative work, the choice of areas was important. We wished on one hand to compare the different countries of the European Community and their legislative changes. However we also wished to extend this comparison to other European countries outside the community. Finally, it seemed important to us also to examine new legislation in developing countries which have modern legislation in a very different socio-economic context.

We must point out that significant political events have intervened in certain countries during the research: for these countries therefore our report may represent no more than a 'snapshot' at a given moment.

The Questionnaire [1]

A questionnaire was therefore drawn up by the Network and sent to correspondents of recognised competence in matters of law and the practices in their countries. [2] The questionnaire, divided into five parts, deals with:

- *the political and administrative background of each country, the demographic data most important for our analysis and the history of juvenile law;*
- *juvenile delinquents: the applicable laws, the age brackets concerned and punishable behaviours.* Other questions bring up different procedural problems (extra judicial and judicial phases, rights of the accused, role of experts, etc.), measures and interventions envisaged (objectives, choices, measures involving detention, substitutive measures, etc.);
- *children and young people in danger or difficulty.* As for young delinquents, the questions seek to highlight all problems linked to procedures, measures to be taken and recognised rights of young people and their families;
- the principal concern of our research project, *current methods of treatment in an open environment; the importance of these measures in comparison to other measures, their evolution, and also new partners concerned by their effective administration;*
- finally, *reform bills being planned or studied in each country.* Certain countries have recently changed their juvenile laws, others are considering fundamental reforms. This highlights the importance of comparing legislation still in force with the spirit of foreseen changes.

---

1. The questionnaire is reproduced in *Appendix I*
2. The people who replied to the questionnaire are listed in *Appendix II*

We had fixed a critical path for this first piece of research and for questions linked in particular to this schedule, our analysis covers 18 of the 21 countries which we had proposed to contact, the reception of data having been stopped on the date we had fixed.

- *Countries of the Community:* Belgium, England and Wales, France, Germany, Greece, Italy, Luxembourg, The Netherlands, Portugal, Scotland.
- *European countries outside the Community:* Austria, Poland, Slovenia, Sweden, Switzerland, Czechoslovakia (still a united state at the time of the study).
- *Non-European countries:* Brazil, a country with modern legislation but very different on the level of its socio-economic problems. We devote a specific section of the book to Brazil, hoping in this way to provide guidelines for other developing countries.

Responses and Difficulties Encountered

On the level of responses to the questionnaire it is necessary to note that, apart from the difficulties related to the schedule of dates which we had imposed on ourselves and our national partners, the analysis of the responses makes apparent a certain disparity. Most of our correspondents have truly provided an important and very detailed contribution; others, however, unfortunately limited themselves to inadequate answers. Finally, some countries did not respond to our request, even though asked to do so several times.

Among the gaps in the responses, we would say that the greatest is that linked to statistics. In fact, few statistics on treatment reached us: kind, number, juveniles concerned, etc. The evaluation has therefore been based on the information which was communicated to us by the questionnaires. However, there are a few exceptions, for example the age of majority and of minority for the purposes of criminal justice was a fundamental question which had received insufficient attention from the majority of our correspondents and which made necessary personal research by the authors of this part of the report.

Moreover, we were obliged to take into account the role of 'subjectivism' which often emerges from the responses, according to the function exercised by the editor of the response (university professor, magistrate, member of a public ministry, etc.). In this way, certain 'omissions' (for example on supervision or conditions of incarceration) or the stress placed on the qualitative importance of certain measures which, in fact, are not put into practice are the direct consequences and are visible only to those who know each of the different systems. For this reason the analysis of the reports cannot be considered exhaustive, but rather the expression of tendencies recorded in a particular country on the bases of communicated information.

Several Presentations: Data from Countries Selected for Research

Annina Lahalle, Dilly Gask

Comparative research must take into account the characteristic differences of the countries represented in order to be able to distinguish national peculiarities and regional differences.

For this reason the questionnaire designed by the Network asks three introductory questions:

- the political and administrative background of your country?
- demographic information?
- a brief history of juvenile law?

The Political and Administrative Background and Demographic Information[1]

All the countries which answered the questionnaire are now democracies, of which five are federal republics (Germany, Austria, Brazil, Switzerland, Czechoslovakia), five are constitutional monarchies (Belgium, Luxembourg, The Netherlands, the United Kingdom and Sweden, with varying degrees of power attached to the sovereign (the Great Duke of Luxembourg seems to be the one with the most constitutional power).

Three countries are former socialist republics (Czechoslovakia,[2] Poland and Slovenia): these countries are still in the process of renewing their different legislation.

As for Brazil, after a long period of dictatorship, it has given itself a new Constitution and new democratic structures.[3]

The vast majority of these countries have several administrative elements in common, such as the separation and autonomy of the three powers (executive, legislative and judiciary). Usually the prerogatives and functions of the different political institutions are foreseen in the Constitution (the United Kingdom is the only country which does not have a written Constitution). Generally these countries have a bicameral system : the Chamber of Deputies and the Senate. Exceptions: Greece, Luxembourg and Sweden which only have a Chamber of Deputies. Czechoslovakia had at the time a system of three chambers.[4]

---

1. Responses are quite variable from one country to another.
2. Country still united at the time of the study.
3. The situation of Brazil is treated separately: see *Section IV*.
4. A succinct comparative table is set out in *Appendix III*.

Little information reached us on the distribution of population between urban and rural zones. Portugal is the only country which reports as important the fact that it is still a country with a high rural population (around 70% of the population).

As for foreign populations, despite their importance both in the population of adult workers and the numbers of young people taken into the care of social institutions and criminal justice, only Belgium places emphasis on their presence in demographic statistics (approximately 881,000 foreigners and 9,070,000 Belgians).

Our study thus concerns 18 countries of very different sizes and populations: in Europe, from Luxembourg, a small country with roughly 375,000 inhabitants, to united Germany with almost 80 million.

As for the responses on the young population, the information is quite variable and difficult to compare as they are based either on national population statistics or on the numbers of children and young people who are the subject of protection measures (as juvenile delinquents or young people in danger).

A comparison has been possible however for children under 15 years[5]: they represent between 17% and 18.5% of the population in Germany, Austria, Belgium, Italy and Luxembourg; less than 17% of the population in Sweden and Switzerland; more than 18.5% in France, Greece, Portugal, the United Kingdom and in the former socialist republics, reach the high figures of 24.9% in Poland and 23.3% in Czechoslovakia.

5. Source for those under 15: *The Economist Vital World Statistics 1990.*

Historical Reminder of Juvenile Justice Legislation[6] Ruth G. Herz

The study of the European countries and of Brazil shows that juvenile law, as a full domain of theory and practice, made its appearance in the twentieth century, independently of the importance of the country under consideration, its culture and socio-political structure.

The birth or rather the discovery of 'young people' at the beginning of this century and in particular in industrial societies is linked to social transformations. This has not been limited to law and its institutions but has equally been revealed through the emergence of new disciplines such as paediatric studies and pedagogy. The emergence of juvenile law rests, in many countries, on the initiatives and activities of child protection organisations or those campaigning in favour of juvenile jurisdiction. At the origin of these movements is the aggravation of the situation of young people in large cities and the threat of poverty. For this reason the history of juvenile law is one of preservation, of the protection of minors and the help which can be given them. This conception implies that minors do not necessarily have to benefit from favourable treatment, but due to their peculiarities should be treated in a different manner.

This implies profound differences in legal systems applied to minors. Juvenile law can take the form of a special criminal law adapted to minors. It can also be legislation protecting minors from the interventions of adults and particularly of the family, while at the same time permitting undesirable conduct to be penalised. But this law can also mean that the treatment of juveniles, be it for criminal activities or other undesirable conduct, is taken care of, contrary to the case of adults, not by the legal profession but by social administration.

The different countries which have been studied have adopted a variety of models and solutions to regulate young people and their accompanying problems. Globally three models can be distinguished.

- The extra judicial model, applicable to young delinquents, has created committees coming from local social administration, composed of people expressing an interest in the problems of young people, such as teachers, pastors, doctors, who are to decide the fate of the young person. In this model there is no juvenile criminal law or specialised jurisdiction. From the countries consulted, only Sweden and Scotland have a roughly equivalent system.

---

6 This text was edited on the basis of data communicated by the national correspondents. It was translated from German into French by Martine Mérigeau (and from French into English by Liam McCarney.

30

- The second model makes no distinction between young criminals and young deviants. The specialised juvenile jurisdictions encounter both cases of delinquency and deviancy, in addition to other similar cases such as protection and assistance. Belgium (for a long time), Brazil, Poland, Luxembourg and Portugal have elaborated systems analogous to this model.

- The other countries consulted have adopted a third model. It consists of a two-way system, distinguishing the criminal domain from the area of protection. In criminal matters, competence rests with special jurisdictions (criminal courts for juveniles). On the other hand, the protection of young people will be assured by special judges and administrative committees.

Sweden was one of the first countries to put into practice measures for the protection of youth. It was in 1902 that the first law on imposed correctional measures came into force. Corporal punishment as a corrective measure was abolished. In 1924 a law for the protection of youth, containing the idea of protection, assistance and paternalism, came into force. It remained applicable for 40 years. The reform of 1964 placed stress on preventive and voluntary measures. Since 1982 there has been a social law which has installed a committee for the protection of youth at the community level. This committee, competent in matters of protection, education and delinquency, decides on measures to take with regard to the social situation of the juvenile. The principle of compulsion has been totally abolished.

As there is no special criminal law applicable to young people, serious crime is judged according to general criminal law which has been partially adapted to juveniles. In 1905, the age of criminal responsibility was fixed at 15 years. Prison sentences for minors, introduced in 1938, were abolished in 1980 to prevent incarceration of young people. Recently, a change of opinion has been observed and, since 1989, some people have been advocating the reintroduction of such a penalty.

On an overall scale, the evolution of juvenile law is characterised in Sweden by a reduction in measures of detention in favour of measures in an open environment in the 1960s, but also by more extensive measures of intervention.

Sweden, other Scandinavian countries and Scotland are the only countries to have developed an extra judicial system for the treatment of juveniles. The extra judicial system established in Scotland is different from the system applied in other regions of Great Britain.

In Belgium, the first law for the protection of young people came into force in 1912. It introduced a specialised jurisdiction, competent for delinquent or pre-delinquent minors in addition to minors in danger where visible signs are in evidence, such as lack of school attendance and runaways. Juvenile courts can only take measures of protection, education and preservation. The age of criminal responsibility was fixed at 16 years. The evolution which operated at a legal level consisted in putting together the two situations of deviant and abandoned children into one group and defining them by the concept of 'young people in danger'. In terms of the law in 1965, a two-tier system for the protection of youth was established. The juvenile court had at that time a general competence to deal with all 'young people in danger' aged under 21 years. It could only take educational measures which however involve institutional placements. The committees for the protection of young people play the role of 'buffer' between society and the court. The problems of young people should be solved as much as possible at the extra-judicial level. The committees are charged with intervening in cases of threats to the child's safety, moral welfare or health and ordering preventive measures, but only with the consent of the parents. Belgium has recently been experiencing a profound evolution in institutions, and consequently legislative changes by the terms of which a differentiation has been introduced in the approach to delinquent minors on one hand and juveniles in danger on the other. For the latter, the system of intervention has recently been changed profoundly.

It was in 1911 that the first law for the protection of children came into force in Portugal. It emphasised individual prevention. The first juvenile courts were established. But this law did not have significant impact on practice. In fact it was only with the law of 1962 that new measures such as assistance and guardianship were brought into force. In addition, in Portugal, there is no distinction made between delinquent children and children in danger. The juvenile courts have jurisdiction over minors under 16, which is the age of criminal majority. In 1979, the competence of juvenile courts was widened by lowering the minimum threshold to 12 years, from which age they can intervene. The Commission for the Protection of Minors benefits from a priority of action compared with the juvenile court. The juvenile court will only intervene when the parents are in disagreement with the measures taken by the Commission. Since 1991 a law exists which gives more powers to local administrative services.

A new law which came into force in 1982 envisages some particular measures for 16 to 20-year-olds. Priority is given to the idea of education and treatment. This implies, for this category of young people, an exemption from sentencing in favour of educational measures. In this area the judge enjoys a great deal of leeway in judgement.

In 1921 the first juvenile courts were established in Brazil. The first law on minors came into force in 1927. The threshold of criminal majority was raised to 18 years. The juvenile judge has general competence regarding young people, whether they are in danger or delinquent. However the law remained repressive and the carrying out of judicial decisions worked badly. Since 1967, many reforms have followed one another without translating into an improvement in functioning. Until the new legislation of 1990 came into force, young people, whether they were delinquents or in danger, remained largely the objects of legal proceedings. Only in 1990 did the new legislation abandon the paternalistic judicial device and recognise recipients as the subjects of law, with individual responsibility and with a right to legal guarantees. Since 1990, the law provides that organisations for the assistance of young people should be given the means to improve assistance and protection.

Juvenile courts made their appearance in 1918 in Poland in Lodz, Warsaw and Lublin, followed soon after by the coming into force of independent juvenile law. This text provided for penalties and educational measures. Special procedural arrangements, intended to guarantee the protection of the juvenile, were also created. However this law had no practical importance as juvenile courts were only formed in the major cities. After the interruption of the Second World War, juvenile courts were again established in Poland. In 1969 the Polish penal code was reformed according to the Soviet model. The law currently in force is that of 1982 which stipulates a unique regime for juvenile delinquents and minors in danger. It is educational and preventive in nature.

The legal systems of Belgium, Portugal, Poland and Brazil can be categorised as the model of protection; their legal system calls for educational measures applicable to young people in danger, who are not, however, exempt from institutional placements and therefore deprivation of liberty. In this way young people aged less than 16 or less than 18 are not subject to repressive courts.

The other countries consulted can be categorised as a third model.

In Germany, the first law on juvenile jurisdiction came into force in 1923. This legislation brought into effect an autonomous criminal law, applicable to juvenile delinquents, provided with specialised jurisdictions and its own system of sanctions, procedural regulations diverging from general law, and special penitentiary law. In parallel, a law was promulgated in 1922 which concerned the welfare of juveniles and attributed competence to the jurisdiction of guardians for all forms of maladjustment and deviancy of minors. The juvenile jurisdiction law of 1923 was received and noted as a progressive and modern text. In the Nazi period, the law was perverted in its application by various modifications and the promulgation of a new law in 1943. Today the law issuing from the reform of 1953 is applied almost in its entirety. It envisages different levels of sanctions for young delinquents aged from 14 to 18 and young adults aged from 18 to 21. Since the end of the 1970s, more and more recourse has been taken to arrangements and informal modes of dealing with proceedings, in addition to measures in an open environment. These practices were reinforced by a 1990 law. A new law to assist young people, which came into force in 1991, reformed the old law on the welfare of youth which dated from 1922. This law envisages an improvement in measures of assistance and recognises a new status of the young person, marked by the principal of voluntary adhesion to the measures.

In Austria, independent juvenile law has existed since 1929. In parallel there is a law for the protection of youth. The initial law on juvenile jurisdiction applied, except during the period of German occupation from

1938 to 1945, until 1961, the date of its reform. In 1989 a new text was adopted which gives priority to diversion, mediation and reparation and to measures in an open environment at the expense of repressive instruments, reserved for serious crimes.

It was in 1908 that the first juvenile court was established in Ljubljana in Slovenia. The first penal code of the Yugoslav kingdom was promulgated in 1929; it envisioned preventive measures for minors aged from 13 to 17 years. On the other hand, the 1951 code placed more emphasis on penalties than on the educational measures. With regard to minors aged from 14 to 15, in principle only educational measures were envisaged. A new system of sanctions was introduced where educational measures became the principle. Only exceptionally, for the most serious cases, were penalties involving deprivation of liberty ordered for minors aged from 16 to 18. At the present time a bill of reform, destined to become part of the new penal code, is in the process of being drawn up.

In Czechoslovakia, a law on juvenile jurisdiction drawn up in 1922 only came into force in 1931. It drew on the German law of 1923 and the Austrian and Yugoslav legislation of 1929. The law emphasised education and protection of minors. The juvenile judges benefited from a great deal of leeway with regard to the pronouncement of educational measures, in allowing them to be combined with a penalty or given in lieu of a penalty. Autonomous jurisdictions were created in which juvenile judges were also deemed to be guardians. Then the educational service of the juvenile jurisdiction was established. In 1950 the law on juvenile jurisdiction was abolished. Delinquent minors were subject to repressive jurisdictions of general law. Only a few arrangements provided for a different category of procedure with regard to minors. However this possibility was abolished in 1961. The penal code of 1990 has not introduced special arrangements applicable to minors.

It was in 1912 that the Swiss Civil Code came into force, including measures for the guardianship of minors. The first juvenile court was created in St. Gallen in 1912. Switzerland does not have autonomous juvenile law. However minors aged from seven to 18 are subject to specialised jurisdictions which exist for them. The penalties and measures foreseen which are relevant to them are contained in the Swiss penal code. They include disciplinary sanctions, such as reprimand and community service but also incarceration or placement in an institution of correction involving work. The aim of the law is the education and protection of the juvenile. In this way no criminal sanction can be applied before the age of 15, while criminal responsibility is recognised from the age of seven.

France provided itself with a criminal system specific to minors in 1912. The age of criminal responsibility was fixed at 12 years. The ordinance of 1945 put into place a specific system for juvenile delinquents, with specialised jurisdictions. In the area of legal protection, the ordinance of 1958, replaced by a 1970 law, assures that priority is given to educational measures and gives powers to the juvenile judge to intervene in the case of minors in danger. The juvenile judge plays a primary role in the legal system designed for minors. The most recent reforms attempt to limit the application of detention with regard to minors.

While the necessity for organising special treatment for young delinquents was recognised in Italy since the end of the last century, it was only in 1934 that a law on juvenile jurisdiction was adopted. This law instituted specialised courts, competent to deal with delinquents or minors in danger, aged from 14 to 18 years. The primacy of education dominates in Italy also. However only in 1971 were the conditions provided for an autonomous structure on the level of personnel (judges and prosecutors). In Italy also the same movement in favour of measures in an open environment can be observed, independent of legal reforms, of which the most important is the creation of a specific criminal procedure in 1988, which came into force in 1989.

In England and Wales, the law of 1908 provided for the creation of juvenile courts. The first major law concerning juvenile jurisdiction came into being in 1933. The protection of children and adolescents in danger or abandoned is the responsibility of local social services who are obliged to assist the juvenile by providing advice, care and help. In the event of failure, it is the juvenile court which deals with the case. The juvenile court has jurisdiction over young people against whom criminal proceedings are taken. Until the 1960s, more sanctions involving deprivation of liberty were imposed on juveniles in order to combat increasing juvenile delinquency. In the face of growing criticism against this method of treatment, the 1968 law established measures in an open environment, which were put into place by reforms in 1982 and 1988. In parallel with the rules of criminal proceedings, a particular procedure is to be found in matters of protection, allowing the imposition of measures of detention in either a secure or an open environment. The current situation is governed in a somewhat different perspective, by two pieces of legislation in 1989 and 1991.

Northern Ireland, although politically part of the United Kingdom, possesses its own legislation. The first law which established jurisdiction for minors came into force in 1908. This jurisdiction has a double competence, concerned with juvenile delinquents and juveniles in danger. The decisions however are arrived at by distinct procedures. This 1908 law remained in force until 1950, except for the introduction of non-professional magistrates in 1942, who sit beside the juvenile judge. The reform of 1950 raised the age of criminal responsibility from 7 to 8 years and introduced placements in homes. In 1968, criminal responsibility was fixed at 10 years and the principle of opportunity was extended in order to avoid, where possible, proceedings against a minor.

In Greece, juvenile courts were first planned in 1927, without however any practical repercussions. Only in 1940 were the first juvenile courts created. As in most legislation, the primacy of education is to be found in the Greek law. Nevertheless, placements in institutions exist. An increasing tendency towards measures in an open environment can also be observed.

The historical evolution of juvenile law in the countries consulted, despite their differences, presents some similarities. At the beginning of our century, it appeared necessary to create autonomous regulations concerning the problems of juveniles. This fact and this conviction are generally shared by almost all the countries consulted and have not been questioned up to today, even if certain countries, under the influence of different totalitarian regimes, have temporarily rejected them. This criminal policy has implied the creation of an autonomous system but with varying aspects. The disparity does not however affect the aim of juvenile law of treating juveniles differently from adults and helping them to become honest citizens.

Juvenile law is addressed in all the countries we have looked at to young people who have offended or who are in a situation of danger. An important distinction lay in whether these two categories are or were distinct and whether they are or were subject to specific procedural rules. We found many similarities also in the evolution of special modes of treatment regarding young people, including the specialised professionalisation of personnel responsible, such as judges, prosecutors and members of various commissions who are acquainted with extra judicial models.

The enumeration of common points should not allow us to lose sight of the differences observed in the countries consulted, which have their origin in the culture and history particular to each country. If this is reflected in the day-to-day practice of juvenile law, it is not verifiable in the responses received, at least concerning historical evolution. Evolution in the nature and means of the struggle against crime and deviancy is also a common point in the countries consulted. At the beginning of the century, people believed in the effectiveness of reform in homes, prisons and closed schools. The aim was to instil into the young person a different attitude, far from the harmful influence of the environment. In the last two or three decades it has been realised that the aim cannot be achieved in this manner. The incarceration of young people has been shown to be not just ineffective but harmful. Notwithstanding the legal system in force, there is an ever increasing tendency to resort to measures in an open environment as opposed to institutional measures. Running in parallel is the concern to respect and ensure the rights of minors and to reinforce legal guarantees.

SECTION II JUVENILE DELINQUENTS

Criminal justice concerning juveniles is characterised by dynamism, continual change, pragmatism, experimentation and a driving role regarding the criminal law on which it depends, at least legally. In recent years a certain number of indicators have been observed which reveal a profound transformation, allowing a revolution in the penal system to be foreseen, if not the signs of a new criminal process.

Criminological research has well demonstrated that juvenile delinquency is a ubiquitous and passing phenomenon, linked to age. Continuing to strive for more humane and mild sanctions applicable to juvenile delinquents, legislators have continually tried to limit any form of deprivation of liberty in committing themselves to the road towards decriminalisation. The innovations brought about by the practitioners and especially their positive results, notably the new modes of settling conflicts, both at the informal level (before any judgement) in the framework of diversion from the (juvenile/youth) court, and at the formal level have reinforced still more the pragmatism of juvenile criminal justice.

The object of this chapter devoted to juvenile delinquency is primarily to reproduce as faithful an image as possible of the different legal systems applicable to juvenile delinquents, including the legal frameworks and interventions, on the basis of responses given to the questionnaire in order to be able to appreciate the place currently given to treatment in an open environment.

With this objective, it seemed indispensable to identify in the first section the major trends which are currently emerging from criminal policy in the struggle against juvenile delinquency. These reflections are based on a vast comparative international study made by the author (cf *Dünkel* 1990; 1992, *Dünkel /van Kalmthout/Schüler-Springorum,* 1996).

Current Directions in Criminal Policy

Frieder Dünkel

1. Introduction: Questions and Methodological Problems in Comparing Juvenile Justice Systems

The opening of borders in Europe at the end of 1992 makes one aware of the different legal frameworks of the juvenile justice systems of the various countries. One may ask whether uniform legal principles and especially age limits should not be made applicable in all European countries. In spite of the efforts of the United Nations (one should consider especially the Standard Minimum Rules for the Administration of Juvenile Justice of 1985 and the United Nations Rules for the Protection of Juveniles Deprived of their Liberty of 1990) and of the Council of Europe (see e.g. Recommendation No R(87)20 on 'Social reactions to juvenile delinquency'), the situation remains unclear and the application of specific sanctions for juvenile offenders as well as the competence of juvenile courts varies considerably from one country to the other. Even the existence of juvenile courts is not self-evident, as can be shown by the example of the Scandinavian countries. In The Netherlands 12-year-old juveniles can already be punished in terms of the penal law for juveniles, whereas in the neighbouring country, Belgium, the age of criminal responsibility has been raised to 18 years. A 20-year-old young adult in Germany has to be sentenced by a juvenile court, whereas in the Scandinavian countries 15-year-old juveniles and in England 18-year-old young offenders are sentenced by the courts for adults (the Criminal Justice Act 1991 has raised the age limit from 17 to 18). With regard to these legal differences one may be tempted to call for the unification of the legal systems in Europe. But on the other hand the advantages of such diversity of juvenile justice systems are often overlooked. Every criminologist will agree that variation gives the opportunity to evaluate the efficacy of, e.g., different social and penal reactions to juvenile delinquency. The liberal drug policy towards soft drugs in The Netherlands and in Denmark in comparison to the much more repressive approach in Germany shows, e.g., that the reduction of penal sanctions does not lead at all to the feared increase of drug abuse by juveniles (apparently the opposite seems to be true). If in national experiments, as for example with the increase of the age of criminal responsibility from 14 to 15 in Norway 1987 or with the decriminalisation of petty offences of 14 and 15 year old juveniles in Austria 1989, it can be shown that there are no negative consequences to be seen in terms of crime rates, other countries could also be encouraged to do the same and to follow a 'reductionist' policy in juvenile justice.

Although there are similar tendencies in the reform of juvenile justice systems in an international comparative perspective, especially because of the development of practices like diversion, the so called new alternatives (mediation, intermediate treatment, other non-custodial measures like social training courses, leisure time activities etc.) and the use of custodial sanctions only as a last resort ('ultima ratio'; see Section 2 below), the differences in age limits remained mostly unchanged. This is partly due to the fact that the recommendations of the Council of Europe as well as of the United Nations express themselves extremely vaguely, if at all, on this issue. The so-called Beijing Rules deliberately did not formulate any concrete age limit and instead of that referred to the 'economic, social, political, cultural and legal systems of Member States'. As the commentary to rule 2.2 notes: 'This makes for a wide variety of ages coming under the definition of juvenile, ranging from 7 years to 18 years or above. Such variety seems inevitable in view of the different national legal systems . . .'. However, rule 4 recommends that the age of criminal responsibility should not be fixed at too low a level, 'bearing in mind the facts of emotional, mental and intellectual maturity'. In addition the commentary refers to the links between the age of responsibility for delinquent or criminal behaviour and other social rights and responsibilities (such as marital status, civil majority, etc.). The relative vagueness about the fixing of age limits found in such minimum rules may be regarded as reasonable because of the desire to make the rules applicable to as wide a spectrum of juvenile justice systems as possible. On the other hand, the 'harmonisation' of age limits remains a very important question of juvenile justice policy with respect to developing juvenile justice systems in Europe, which also are oriented towards principles of proportionality and equality, both in law and in practice.

The central question of age limits for the application of specific juvenile justice measures needs some differentiation, especially with respect to the sentencing of juvenile and young offenders. So many countries provide for a relatively low age of criminal responsibility (as for example Ireland or Switzerland with 7 years, England with 10 years), whereas specific custodial sanctions cannot be applied before a certain higher age (see for example England and Switzerland with 15 years as minimum age for youth imprisonment, see section 3 below). The international comparison of juvenile justice systems causes many methodological problems which go beyond the simple comparison of different legal frameworks in the field of penal law (see *Dünkel/Meyer* 1985, p.12). The problem of 'functional equivalents' becomes even more difficult when considering the different legal approaches with respect to the so-called welfare model on the one hand and the justice model on the other. Even comparing systems following the justice model seems to be difficult. For example, sanctions like youth imprisonment, incarceration in a detention centre or even pre-trial detention, which appear to have different functions, may be used interchangeably (see the evidence given by empirical research in Germany by *Dünkel* 1990, 1994; for an international comparison see *Dünkel/Vagg* 1994). This is often done in contravention of the letter of the law (for example pre-trial detention may in practice often be used as a form of short-term imprisonment). It is extremely difficult even to estimate, to what extent comparable offenders are sent into residential care within the framework of welfare models. The following comparative analysis is mostly restricted to actual developments in Western Europe. In most Eastern European countries the extensive social and political changes probably will not leave much of the former legal frameworks in the field of juvenile justice unscathed (possibly with the exception of Poland, where reforms were already introduced in 1983). Actual developments in Middle and Eastern European countries will be described below in Section 3.

It is also clear that in comparing Western systems of juvenile justice we have to consider the different legal and social backgrounds of each society. Therefore we have to be cautious in transplanting 'models' from one country to another. However, it is possible (cautiously) to draw conclusions, which can facilitate certain decisions of the legislature, for example with regard to the abolition (or at least further legal restriction) of youth imprisonment or pre-trial detention for the youngest age groups (under 16). Another example could be the integration of 18 to 21 year old young adults in the competence of juvenile courts, if one can show that some other countries have already introduced such a reform without (dramatic) negative consequences.

2. International Developments in Juvenile Justice Policy

That alternatives to imprisonment should be given priority is recognised world wide and often incorporated in laws such as the German Juvenile Justice Act, which provide for youth imprisonment only as a sanction of last resort (see sections 5 and 17 öJGG). In connection with the educational ideal the principle of 'subsidiarity' of penal sanctions and of criminal procedures (see *Peters* 1985, p.600; *Heinz* 1986, p.538; 1989, p.15) is recognised as well, as can be shown by the above mentioned Beijing Rules of the United Nations of 1985 (see *Schüler-Springorum* 1987). The administration of juvenile justice must provide for the care of juvenile offenders, but must also guarantee that the reactions will 'be in proportion not only to the circumstances and the gravity of the offence but also to the circumstances and the needs of the juvenile . . .'. In this context forms of diversion should be given preference. The principle that youth imprisonment should be a last resort is enshrined in rule 17.1c in the provision that 'restrictions on the personal liberty of the juvenile shall not be imposed unless the juvenile is adjudicated of a serious act involving violence against another person or of persistence in committing other serious offences and unless there is no other appropriate response'. These principles of the Beijing Rules shall be applied independently of whether the framework of juvenile justice is more welfare-oriented or more justice-oriented (i.e. also in sanctioning, for example status offenders).

There is a clear tendency towards strengthening the legal and procedural safeguards for juvenile offenders in the last 15 years. The restriction of intervention by the state to the minimum is a widely recognised principle as well. However, in the past few years, contrary tendencies can be seen in some Western European countries. So the strengthening of punishment by increasing the maximum penalties and introducing secure training facilities is emphasised. This is especially the case in The Netherlands and in England and Wales. In The Netherlands the maximum sentence of detention in a young offenders institution was increased from 6 months to one year for 12 to 15-year-old offenders and to two years for 16 to 17-year-old offenders by the reform of the Juvenile Justice Act in 1995. (On the other hand the scope of alternative sanctions was extended considerably, see *van Kalmthout* in *Dünkel / van Kalmthout / Schüler-Springorum* 1996; concerning the experiments with alternative sanctions see *van der Laan* 1991). In England and Wales the Criminal Justice and Public Order Act 1994 increased the maximum sentence for 15 to 17-year-old offenders from one year to two years and introduced the secure training order which includes a custodial part of the sentence also for 12 to 14-year-old persistent offenders (see *Wasik/Taylor* 1995, p.6; for a critical comment see *Cavadino* 1994).

Despite these apparent setbacks the tendency is still in favour of reducing the use of custodial sentences. The 'reductionist approach' means not only that youth imprisonment must be avoided as far as possible, but also that the length of custodial sanctions must be reduced to the minimum which can be justified. Like the United Nations, the Council of Europe in 1987 has adopted the principle of only using custodial sanctions as a last resort and of minimising the periods of deprivation of liberty (see the recommendation R(87)20, No.13). These principles are mentioned explicitly in the commentary of the European Committee on Crime Problems on the recommendations relating to 'Social Reactions to Juvenile Delinquency' (see pp.44, 48). This implies abandoning the traditional educative understanding of correctional treatment in juvenile institutions. The underlying hypothesis, that correctional treatment can only be successful if the offender spends a certain minimum of time in the institution, cannot be justified anymore. There must be serious doubts about rules which require relatively long minimum youth prison sentences, as for example in Germany and Greece where the minimum is six months (see sect. 18 öJGG and art. 54 and 127 gr. penal law). This tendency seems to be of major importance especially for the so-called welfare models which provide for indeterminate residential care (mostly limited only by the age of civil majority; see Dünkel 1990, p.537). The abolition of the relatively indeterminate youth imprisonment, in the sense in which it was applied in the borstal or the Scandinavian youth prison, in most countries which had introduced such a sanction, proves that the ideas of proportionality and of limiting the severity of sanctions with respect to the seriousness of the offence are gaining importance in comparison to the traditional welfare model, where the sanction is determined primarily by the supposed educative needs of the juvenile (see also the mentioned recommendation of the Council of Europe R(87)20, No.12). In 1990 Germany followed the example of other countries such as Denmark, Norway, Sweden, Scotland, England/Wales, New Zealand, Canada and more recently, in 1989, Austria, which had all abolished (relatively) indeterminate youth prison sentences (see *Dünkel* 1990, pp.508, 537)

Intensive legislative reforms in the area of juvenile justice (for example, in Austria, England, France, Germany, Italy or The Netherlands) often function as 'outriders' for reforms of the criminal law for adults. In this context one should emphasise the reforms in Austria in 1989, which courageously introduced mediation and conflict resolution as a primary reaction for 14 to 19-year-old juveniles. The Austrian legislature is now considering whether to extend this model to the criminal law for adults. The same is true for Germany where the models of mediation and reparation, developed in the practice of juvenile justice and introduced into the Juvenile Justice Act in 1990, are now playing an important role in the legislative considerations with respect to the reform of the system of penal sanctions (proposals for the introduction of community service and reparation orders as independent sanctions; see *Bundesministerium der Justiz* 1988; *Schöch* 1990, p.73; 1992; Arbeitskreis deutscher, schweizerischer und österreichischer *Strafrechtslehrer* 1992; *Rössner* 1992; *Roxin* 1993).

3. Developments in Middle and Eastern European Countries

Developments in Middle and Eastern European countries are strongly influenced by the dramatic increase in juvenile crime since the end of the eighties. The unanimously accepted necessity to reform juvenile justice systems has also been influenced by the political pretensions to abandon former Soviet law (or law influenced by Soviet legislation) and to adopt (Western) European standards as laid down in the standard minimum rules of the Council of Europe or the United Nations. However, as in Western Europe, contradictory tendencies can be identified. On the one hand reform proposals emphasise the introduction of an independent juvenile justice system which is strictly bound to the rule of law and which stresses the special educative needs of young offenders (see, e.g., the Baltic States, Croatia, the Czech Republic, Russia or Slovenia). On the other hand, despite increasing emphasis on community sanctions, including diversion, there are calls for more tough punishments, especially for persistent and violent offenders. It appears that arguments in favour of prevention are being made most strongly. However, the lack of an infrastructure of effective community sanctions taken together with the community's reluctance to accept such sanctions, will probably result in a still relatively frequent use of custodial sanctions.

Whereas in Western Europe the strategy of shock incarceration (like the German 'Jugendarrest' or the English 'Detention Centre') has declined in importance (having been proven to be ineffective), short term incarceration will be introduced e.g. in Estonia and Croatia. The draft of a Juvenile Justice Act in Croatia (in contrast to the Slovenia law of 1995) maintains a disciplinary sanction of short term detention of up to three months (as existed in the former Yugoslavian legislation). On the other hand the traditionally long term maximum penalties of youth imprisonment seem likely to be cut in

42

Croatia to a maximum of five years, or ten years in very serious cases (as is the case in Germany). The maximum sentence in Russia has been cut to seven years (see *Uss* 1989).

4. Comparative Overview of Juvenile Justice Systems

As mentioned above one can differentiate the ideal types of welfare and justice models (see *Kaiser* 1985). The welfare model is characterised by the dominant role of the juvenile judge and his great discretionary power. The educational ideal and individualised treatment in which social workers, psychologists and similar professions are involved, the relatively informal procedures and the uniform point of contact for delinquent (i.e. included specific status offences) as well as criminal behaviour, are essential elements of this model. The justice model replaces the individualised, indeterminate, educational measures by penalties imposed by judges (i.e. specialised judges, see sect. 37 öJGG), which are of a determinate and proportional nature. The procedures are more formal as prosecutors and sometimes also defence lawyers participate in them. The age of criminal responsibility tends to be lower in the justice model. Sometimes criminal sanctions may be invoked against young offenders from the age of ten or even seven years. Criminal sanctions are provided for the same offences as in the criminal codes applicable to adults (i.e. excluding so-called 'status offences').

This differentiation of ideal types does not correspond to the reality of juvenile justice systems. In most countries we find elements of both systems, as can be shown in Germany or France where there are special educational measures on one hand and penalties like youth imprisonment on the other. The penalties in particular are limited by the principle of proportionality.

There is a strong relationship between an emphasis on the welfare model or the justice model and the age of criminal responsibility (see *Table 1*, p. 45)

In the welfare system the age of criminal responsibility is relatively high as can be shown in the cases of Belgium, Rumania (18 years) or Portugal, Scotland and Spain (16 years) and in nearly all Latin American countries (mostly between 16 and 18 years, see *Tiffer-Sotomayor/Dünkel* 1989). In Switzerland the age of criminal responsibility is seven years, but up to the age of 14 only educational measures and in the case of deprivation of liberty only residential care in 'homes' are permitted, which clearly indicates similarities to the welfare approach. Whereas in the Scandinavian countries the age of criminal responsibility is uniformly 15 years, in some of the continental European countries criminal sanctions are already possible at an earlier age. Thus, for example, in Austria, Bulgaria, Germany, Hungary or Italy they may be imposed at 14, or even at 13 years in the case of France, Greece and Poland. In the common law countries the age of criminal responsibility (under certain circumstances) is traditionally seven years (Ireland) or ten years (England/Wales, see for a comparison *Tutt* 1986). However, the example of England shows that, as in Switzerland, the deprivation of liberty in a youth prison ('young offender institution') is not possible before the age of 15 years.

This underlines the significance of the welfare approach towards the youngest age groups in these countries which restricts deprivation of liberty to (mostly open) residential 'homes'. In Ireland, too, the incarceration of juveniles is not allowed under the age of 15 years, and, in the case of 15 to 18 year old young adults, only in exceptional cases. Similar regulations applied in the former Yugoslavia (and apply today in Croatia, Slovenia and Serbia), where, in spite of the general age of criminal responsibility of 14 years, youth imprisonment has only been provided for offenders who were at least 16 years old.

Reforms of juvenile justice legislations in the last 15 years show clear tendencies to raise the age of criminal responsibility. This tendency is independent of whether a welfare or justice approach is adopted. In Rumania the age of criminal responsibility was raised from 14 to 18 years (1977), in Israel from nine to 13 (1977), in Cuba from 12 to 16 (1979), in Canada from seven to 12 (additionally the age for being punished by youth imprisonment was raised to 14), in Argentina from 14 to 16 (1983) and in Norway from 14 to 15 years (1987; see *Dünkel* 1990, p.513). In Switzerland the draft bill introduced by Stettler in 1986 proposed raising the age of criminal responsibility from seven to 12 years, but it also sought to introduce youth imprisonment for up to one year for 12 to 14-year-old offenders. Under the present legislation this is possible only for the age group from 15 to 17 years.

For this latter group the draft now provided for youth imprisonment of two to six years in the case of most serious crimes, i.e. those crimes which can be punished with at least two years of imprisonment according to the criminal law for adults (see *Stettler* 1986, pp.7, 57; 1988, p138). A recent draft bill of 1993 maintains the proposed age limit of 12 years, but proposes limiting youth imprisonment to juveniles of 15 years and older. The maximum penalty will be one year for 15-year-old offenders and four years for 16 and 17-year-old offenders in very serious cases (see *Bundesamt für justiz* 1993).

In France the draft bill of June 1990 maintains the age limit of 13 years, but restricts the application of youth imprisonment, in the sense of a sanction of last resort, to cases where it seems inevitable because of the personality of the offender or the circumstances of the offence. Youth imprisonment for 13 to 16-year-old offenders shall be excluded in the case of misdemeanours (except physical injury, drug traffic and burglary; see *Ministère de la Justice* 1990). The Bill has still not been passed by Parliament. However, some parts of the reform have been successfully introduced like the role of social work in considering pre-sentence reports and the reduction in remand to prison. Furthermore, diversion and reparation (mediation) have become part of juvenile criminal policy (see *Mérigeau* 1993).

In Germany proposals were first submitted at the end of the 19th century, and there was growing pressure during the 1970s, to raise the age of criminal responsibility to 16 (see *Rossner* 1990, p.527). However, these proposals could not be introduced into law, because, in the 1980s, the reservations about the welfare model increased and one realised that the price of increasing the age of criminal responsibility in certain cases would be a growth in indeterminate detention in residential institutions and that, in general, it could result in a loss of the procedural safeguards inherent in the justice model.

Country	Diminished criminal responsibility (juvenile criminal law)	Criminal responsibility (adult criminal law can/must be applied)	Legal majority
Austria	14	19	19
Belgium	16**/18	16/18	18
Bulgaria	14	18	18
Denmark	15	15/18	18
England/Wales	10/15*	18/21	18
Finland	15	15/18	18
France	13	18	18
Germany	14	18/21	18
Greece	13	18/21	18
Hungary	14	18	18
Ireland	7/15	18	18
Italy	14	18/21	18
The Netherlands	12	18/21	18
Norway	15	18	18
Poland	13	17/18	18
Portugal	16	16/21	18
Romania	16/18	16/18/21	18
Scotland	8/16	16/21	18
Spain	16	16	18
Sweden	15	15/18	18
Switzerland	7/15*	15/18	20
Ex-Czechoslovakia	15	18	18
Turkey	11	15	18
Ex-USSR	14***/16	14/16	18
Ex-Yugoslavia	14/16*	18/21	18

*	criminal majority concerning juvenile detention
**	only for road offences
***	only for serious offences

Table 1: Comparison of Age of Criminal Responsibility in European Countries

Consequently the German legislature has maintained the age limits for the application of the juvenile justice system (i.e. the range from 14 to 21 years), but is considering the execution of sanctions which result in the deprivation of liberty for 14 and 15-year-old offenders not in juvenile prisons, but in institutions of the child welfare system ('Erziehungsheime': see *Bundesministerium der Justiz* 1980, 1980a; *Dünkel* 1990, pp.471). A recent draft bill of the Juvenile Prison Act 'Jugendstrafvollzugsgesetz') of 1991 (and again of 1993) does not even mention this problem (see for criticism *Dünkel* 1992b). The paradoxical statement that juvenile prisons are not the right place for juvenile offenders (see *Rössner* 1990, p.523) but rather for young adults, which is the practice in more than 90% of the cases in Germany, seems to be justified when considering the special needs and disadvantages of the youngest persons incarcerated (see *P. A. Albrecht/Schüler-Springorum,* 1993). Furthermore, in Germany more and more scholars argue for limiting the penalty of juvenile imprisonment to offenders of at least 16 years of age (see *Dünkel* 1990; *Deutsche Vereinigung für Jugendgerichte und Jugendgerihtschilfen* 1992; *Dünkel* 1992a). Fourteen and 15-year-old offenders then only could be sent to institutions which are run by the child welfare administration and which normally are open institutions.

The reform of the Child Welfare Act of 1990 in Germany makes it more difficult to impose residential care as it stresses the consent of the parents and in general provides for 'educational help' instead of enforced educational measures of the former paternalistic type (see *Späth* in *Wiesner Zarbock*, 1991, pp.91ff.).

5. Diversion and New Alternative Measures

Since the end of the 1970s diversionary measures and the development of new alternatives for dealing with minor crimes (and, within welfare-oriented systems, especially with status offences) have been successfully introduced in many European countries (see *Eisenberg*, 1989, p.65; *Dünkel* 1990 p.505). The underlying theory was much influenced by the so-called labelling approach. Furthermore, this development was supported by the educational ideal ('education instead of punishment') and the constitutional principle of proportionality which emphasises the necessity of applying to juvenile delinquency the mildest reaction which could be justified. The 'triumphant advance' of the diversion movement, however was probably due to the fact that it proved to be a useful strategy for coping with increasing crime rates and because it stabilised the case loads of the juvenile justice administration. On the other hand, the recommendations of the United Nations and the Council of Europe mentioned above might have had some influence as well.

In this context one could mention the reform of the Juvenile Justice Act in Germany in 1990, which extended considerably the legal possibilities for diversion. The law now emphasises the discharge of juvenile and young adult offenders because of the petty nature of the crime committed or because of other social and/or educational interventions which have taken place. The efforts to make reparation to the victim or to participate in victim-offender reconciliation (mediation) are explicitly put on a par with such educational measures. The legislature has reacted in this way to the reforms which have developed in practice since the end of the 1970s (see *Bundesministerium der Justiz* 1989; 1989a; *Heinz* 1990; 1992). Before the law reform the discharge rates had already increased from 43% in 1980 to 62% in 1991 (see *Heinz* 1990a; 1992a, p.597; 1994). However, the large regional disparities had not been eliminated. The discharge rates varied in 1990 between 53% in Bavaria and 90% in Hamburg. Apparently in all the Federal States of Germany discharge rates in cities were much higher than in the rural areas (see *Pfeiffer* 1989; *Heinz* 1992a; 1994). This contributes to the rather stable conviction rates and case loads of juvenile judges.

The reform of the Juvenile Justice Act furthermore extended the catalogue of juvenile sanctions by introducing new alternatives like community service, the special care order, the social training course (see *Busch/Hartman/Mehlich* 1986) and mediation (see *Dünkel* 1989, *Schreckling/Pieplow*, 1989; *Dünkel/Mérigeau* 1990; *Schreckling* 1990; *Schreckling et al.* 1991; *Pfeiffer* 1992; *Bannenberg*, 1993). In addition, it became possible to suspend juvenile prison sentences of between one and two years (whereas, before, this was only provided for in exceptional cases). The practice again had already preceded this reform to a great extent by suspending not less than 54% of such sentences in 1990 (the ratio in 1993 went up to 56%). The expanding of alternatives to youth imprisonment to young adults, who are more involved in crime than juveniles, particularly in some areas such as robbery, have contributed to the considerable decline of about 40% in the rate of imprisonment of juveniles and young adults from 1983 to 1990 and even reduced crime rates. This decline can only be attributed to a limited extent (5%) to demographic changes. More than 90% of youth prisoners in Germany are young adults of 18 to 25 years of age, whereas less than 50% of the total population of about 3,600 are 14 or 15 years old. That means that demographic changes will play an important role only in the next few years and possibly will contribute to a further decline of the absolute figures of the youth prison population.

If one compares the German Juvenile Justice Act with other justice-oriented legislation it is evident that the alternative sanctions provided by law for juvenile judges (as well as for prosecutors) are relatively well developed. It is, however, surprising that in other countries such as The Netherlands and Sweden, where the law, until recently, provided for relatively few alternative sanctions, custodial sanctions are seldom applied. Where they are applied the terms imposed are shorter than those in Germany. This is the result of two characteristics of these legal systems. In The Netherlands about 80% of all criminal cases are discharged because of the guiding principle of opportunity and therefore do not come before the juvenile courts (see *Scholten ten Siethoff* 1985, p.577). In Sweden the transfer to the welfare boards as a special 'sanction' of the courts (specialised juvenile courts do not exist, as mentioned above) is used in the great majority of cases (see Section 7 below).

Furthermore, judges have to give special reasons for applying custodial sanctions (this section and see *Cornils* 1985, p.501). In The Netherlands, however, since 1985 there has been an increasing tendency not to discharge cases without sanction but to impose certain obligations, such as paying a fine or completing community service, in order to strengthen the sense of responsibility of young offenders (see *Junger-Tass/Kruissink* 1990, p.31). Apart from The Netherlands and Sweden which have especially high diversion rates, the practice in Germany (1990: 61% of all juveniles and young adults were discharged; see, for developments in the 1980s, *Heinz* 1989, p.17, 1990a, pp.213; 1992; 1992a; *Dünkel* 1990, p.64) and France is also that diversion is used extensively. Although in most countries the principle of diversion is accepted for juveniles to a greater extent than for adults, the practice, for example in Denmark or Finland seems to be much more restrictive than in Germany (see *Klages* 1985, p.394; *Lahti* 1985, p.456). On the other hand, available statistical data in this field often do· not provide information about 'decriminalisation strategies' of the police which is not confined to countries like England, where police cautioning is officially legalised. Especially in countries which traditionally place great emphasis on the principle of legality (which excludes prosecutorial diversion) such strategies of non prosecution are inevitable because there is no legal mechanism for declining to prosecute (see e.g. Italy, Portugal or Spain). This is probably the reason for the extremely low conviction rate of juvenile offenders in Italy (only about one fifteenth of that in Germany, see *Dünkel* 1990, p.535). Furthermore, in Italy the juvenile judge has the additional power to grant a 'judicial pardon'. This power is used in about 80% of all cases involving (14 to 18-year-old) juveniles (see *Picotti/de Strobel* 1986, pp.922, 937, 986) with the result that outcomes are similar to those in The Netherlands (on the prosecutorial level) or in Sweden. As in The Netherlands, the tendency in Denmark also is to attempt to increase the sense of responsibility of juvenile offenders. The Ministry of Justice has introduced the possibility to impose community service or other obligations with respect to leisure time activities on juvenile offenders as part of a 'social contract', that the offender has to accept if he wants to avoid criminal prosecution (see *Vestergaard* 1991, p .70).

The generally expanding diversion practice reflects the criminological findings on the petty nature of most juvenile offences and the episodic involvement of juveniles in crime. It is remarkable that quantitatively most of the so-called new alternatives play only a marginal role (see *H. J. Albrecht* 1990; *Kaiser* 1991; *Pfeifer* 1992a). This is especially true for the mediation and reparation projects as they have been developed in England, Finland, France, Germany and Norway (see *Dünkel* 1989; *Dünkel/Rössner* 1989; *Dünkel/Mérigeau* 1990). The reform measures introduced in Austria in 1989 and in Germany in 1990, however, require a much wider implementation of such schemes. Other countries, too, have put mediation and reparation at the centre of penal or procedural reforms. In Italy and Sweden reforms to the criminal procedure legislation of 1988 (see *Dünkel* 1990, p.536; *Cornils*

48

1991), in Portugal of 1987, give priority to diversion and non-prosecution if the juvenile has completed or tried to make reparation to the victim. The draft juvenile justice bill put forward in France in 1990 and in Switzerland in 1993 also emphasise reparation to the victim as a new 'sanction' (see *Ministère de la Justice*, 1990, sect.63 No.4 of the draft; *Bundesamt für Justiz* 1993, p.49, art. 8 No. 2a of the Swiss draft).

In general, however, the function of new alternatives with respect to the widely discussed question of 'widening the net' cannot be answered definitively. There is a growing debate about whether alternative sanctions are compatible with the principle of proportionality. In France community service is restricted to a maximum of 120 hours in the case of juveniles (240 hours for adults). The draft bill of 1990 proposes a maximum of 100 hours (In the framework of 'protection judiciaire') and limits all other educational measures to a maximum of two years (as has already been provided in German law, see para. 11 öJGG). The German Juvenile Justice Act furthermore limits so-called 'social training courses' to six months, and care orders ('Betreuungsweisung', a measure similar to probation) to 12 months. The Austrian Juvenile Justice Act of 1989 limits community service orders to a maximum of 60 hours (see para. 20(2) öJGG; see also *Jesionek Held* 1994, p.132). The Slovenian Juvenile Justice Act of 1995 limits community service for juveniles to a maximum of 120 hours which have to be served within six months. Social training courses must not exceed four hours per day and, in total, a period of one year. There has to be a guarantee that school education, vocational training or work of the juvenile are not hampered by the social training course (see *Selih*, in *Dünkel/van Kalmthout/Schüler-Springorum*, 1996).

In Germany some empirical research has been conducted on problems of net-widening. The results do not sustain the hypothesis of a widening of the net in the sense that juveniles who previously would have been discharged are now included in diversion programmes and other projects (see *Heinz/Speiß* 1984; *Heinz* 1989, p.36). However, Heinz's research does not cover all aspects of the net widening debate (see *Heinz* 1986a, pp.178; 1989, p.37). At least in some cases one could find that diversionary measures interfered more with the constitutional rights of juveniles than the formal sanctions imposed by the juvenile judge. This is apparent in comparing the simple caution and discharge imposed by a magistrate, with 100 hours of community work or a social training course of two to three months imposed by a prosecutor. Furthermore, in comparing custodial with non custodial measures it is not always clear which sanction intrudes more into the life of juveniles: for example, weekend detention or detention for a week of 'Jugendarrest' (detention centre) may be felt as a less severe punishment than weekly participation at a social training course for up to six months (see *Dünkel* 1990, p. 564).

We can observe in several countries the tendency towards tougher alternatives, for example, in the report 'Punishment, Custody and the Community' of the Home Office in England in 1988 which underpins the legislative reforms of the Criminal Justice Act 1991. Apparently, as the scepticism of juvenile judges towards traditional forms of probation and supervision increases, more structured and controlled alternatives are required. That is why in The Netherlands intensive forms of intermediate treatment were introduced as a 'credible' alternative to pre-trial detention (see *Junger-Tas* 1990, pp.196, 201). The next step in this development is electronic tagging and house arrest, which, at this point in time, are used for juveniles only in the United States. Despite the fact that a few pilot projects in England have not shown tagging to be a very effective approach (see *Mair/Nee* 1990) the legislature opened the door for further use of electronic monitoring within the legal framework of the so-called curfew order (see below). These tendencies underline the importance of the efforts of the *United Nations* (1991), the *Council of Europe* (1992) and the *International Penal and Penitentiary Foundation* (1989) to develop standard minimum rules for alternatives to imprisonment which emphasise constitutional rights and procedural safeguards. Furthermore, it is necessary to impose limits on the length of time for which the alternatives can be imposed and to place restrictions on their repressive aspects. We hope that in Europe the constitutional objections to electronic tagging will be taken seriously even if this does not seem likely in the USA at the moment. For example, the family of an offender who is subject to electronic supervision may suffer from an unconstitutional invasion of its privacy. With good reason all European countries with the exception of England and Sweden have refused to use electronic tagging. As mentioned above, the Criminal Justice Act 1991 in England and Wales opened the possibility of electronic monitoring within the scope of the curfew order for juveniles aged 16 and above (see below). The Criminal Justice Act 1994 restricted electronic monitoring to such districts where arrangements for monitoring the offender's whereabouts are available. The area-by-area introduction of electronic monitoring is planned by the Government with the funding of pilot trials with £1.4 million in 1995 (see *Wasik/Taylor* 1995, p22). In Sweden, too, in 1995, some pilot projects started. In Germany this question was never seriously discussed because the problem of prison over-crowding (until recently) was not as severe as in other countries and because those offenders who would be subjected to electronic surveillance in the USA, for example, are not (in general) held in pre-trial detention in Germany.

In dealing with minor juvenile crimes the current reforms in Europe concentrate on the prosecutorial model of 'decriminalisation'. For example, the Italian Code of Criminal Procedure of 1989 has abolished the traditional principle of legality and made it possible simply to discharge a juvenile offender if he or she has made or tried to make reparation to the victim (see the 'Decreto del Presidente della Republica DPR' of 22 September 1988, No.448). In Sweden, too, since 1988 the willingness of the offender to make reparation has to be considered by the prosecuting authorities, especially in the case of offenders of less than 18 years of age (see sect. l(4) of the law on juvenile offenders; *Cornils* 1991; for the development of new alternatives in Sweden see *Bondeson* 1990, p.19). The draft bill introduced by an expert group in 1993 (which is largely based on the previous draft of *Stettler*) in

Switzerland also considers only the extension of procedural possibilities of 'decriminalisation' (see *Stettler* 1986; 1988; *Bundesamt für Justiz* 1993).

It is regrettable that, while one has to approve of the results of such 'prosecutorial' decriminalisation strategies, 'material' decriminalisation is widely neglected. An exception is the Austrian law of 1989 which provides that 14 and 15-year-old offenders may not be tried for misdemeanours unless there is 'heavy guilt' on their part or unless there are 'special reasons which require the application of the juvenile penal law' (for the proposal to introduce similar regulations in Germany see *Kerner et al.* 1990, p.172).

The advantage from the point of view of legal certainty is that the prosecutor in most cases of petty offences has no discretionary power to decide whether to prosecute or not, but instead has to dismiss the case. The Austrian Penal Code provides that when certain conditions are met, an offence need not be prosecuted, or, when a prosecution has been instituted, the judge need not pronounce a sentence, but may simply caution and discharge an offender (para. 42 öStG; 'mangelnde Strafwürdigkeit der Tat'). This provision applies also to 14 to 19-year-old offenders (see the commentary on the new Austrian Juvenile Justice Act by *Jesionek* 1994). The relevant conditions refer to the gravity of the offence (offences punishable with not more than three years of imprisonment may be included), the degree of the culpability of the offender and the willingness of the offender to make reparation for his offence.

Special regulations of the Russian and the Chinese law for 14 and 15-year-old offenders go even further than those in Austria. In these countries only specific crimes, especially violent crimes such as homicide, robbery, serious assault and rape, and also repeated crimes of dishonesty, are punishable offences (see art. 10(2) of the Russian and art. 14 of the Chinese Penal Code). Similar regulations exist in Argentina, where the criminal responsibility of 16 and 17-year-old offenders is excluded for offences such as criminal defamation which may be subject of private prosecution and also for offences punishable with not more than two years of imprisonment (such as breach of the peace, simple assault, theft). In these cases only protective measures can be taken according to the juvenile welfare act.

As a guideline for future reforms of juvenile justice systems one should seriously study the experiences in Austria. In Germany Ostendorf has proposed the decriminalisation of offences typically committed by juveniles, such as shoplifting or travelling without a ticket (see *Ostendorf* 1989, p.334). In these cases it is already the practice for the victimised owners of the shops or operators of the transport systems to impose a 'civil fine' of 40 to 60 DM. This practice has been accepted by the courts. Penal law seems to be superfluous and that is why circulars from the chief prosecutorial offices in most Federal States in Germany provided for the non-prosecution (i.e. dismissal) of theft offences with damages up to 50 DM (Baden-Württemberg) or up to 100 DM (Hamburg, North Rhine-Westphalia).

In the area of more serious crime, probation and suspended sentences play a dominant role as alternatives to imprisonment. Various countries have extended the scope of suspended sentences in the past decade. The preconditions for probation are often less restrictive for juveniles than for adults. Thus, for example, in Germany prison sentences of between one and two years imposed in terms of the Juvenile Justice Act are regularly suspended (para. 21 (2)), whereas, legally speaking, only in exceptional cases is this possible in the case of offenders over the age of 21 years (para. 56(2) Penal Code). However, there is no difference in practice between juveniles and adults. In both cases more than 50% of the sentences are suspended (see *Dünkel* 1990, p. 115; 1993 56% of juvenile prison sentences and 61% of adult prison sentences of more than one to two years were suspended).

The current developments in many European countries show that under certain political preconditions courageous liberal reforms are accepted by society. Good examples are the reforms in Italy and Austria. In Italy the reform of the Penal Code in 1981 introduced the so-called 'semi-liberta' and the 'liberta controllata' as substitutes for prison sentences of up to six months and three months respectively (see *Bosch* 1983, p.346; *Stile* 1984, p.172; *Dolcini Paliero* 1990, p.231). The semi-liberta is a type of work release programme, which obliges the offender to be in prison for only ten hours per day. The liberta controllata is a type of police supervision. The offender has the duty to report regularly to the police. The reform of the Criminal Procedure Act in 1989 extended these 'substitutive' sanctions for juveniles to prison sentences of up to two years. In addition sentences of up to three years for 14 to 18-year-old juveniles, up to two and a half years for 18 to 21-year-old young adults and of up to two years for adults of more than 21 years of age may be suspended. The effect of the Italian penal policy is that juveniles are incarcerated only in the case of very serious (violent) crimes.

The Austrian reform of the Juvenile Justice Act in 1989 and the preceding general reform of the Penal Code in 1987 also made juvenile imprisonment a sanction of last resort. Besides the traditional conditional discharge ('bedingte Verurteilung': para. 13 öJGG, which now can be combined with the supervision of a probation officer, see para. 22 öJGG) there now exist different forms of suspended sentences. Whereas for adults the longest prison sentence which may be suspended is two years, the juvenile law does not establish any time limit (see para. 5 No.9 öJGG). Furthermore, the new provisions of the Penal Code concerning partially suspended sentences apply also to 14 to 19-year-old juveniles. According to paras. 43, 43a of the Penal Code it is possible to suspend partially sentences of up to three years if the negative prognosis does not allow the full suspension. The part to be executed must be at least one month and not more than one third of the total sentence imposed (for the penal law reform of 1987 see *Schwaighofer* 1988, p.592; *Zipf* 1988, p.439). Again juveniles are in a privileged position because the time limit of three years does not apply to them and even longer sentences can be (partially) suspended. The reforms in Austria (regular release after half of a prison sentence had been served was also introduced) led to a considerable decline of the total prison population and especially of the population of the only juvenile prison at Gerasdorf (from about 175 at the beginning of the

1980s to less than 100 in 1989). The total prison population in Austria declined by 30% between 1983 and 1988 (see *Council of Europe* 1988, p.22; *Dünkel* 1990, p.530). The advantage of the Austrian regulation enabling the juvenile court to suspend any prison sentence is that it gets away from the stark choice between either one or two years imprisonment or probation, for example. On the other hand there is a real danger that regional disparities in sentencing practice, especially concerning the length of suspended sentences, will further increase and that the aim of a more equal sentencing will not be achieved.

Important changes concerning non-custodial ('community') sanctions have been introduced by the Criminal Justice Act 1991 in England and Wales. The Act provides for community sanctions for up to 17-year-old offenders (the age limit was extended from 16 to 17 at the same time): probation orders (sect. 8 Criminal Justice Act 1991) for offenders over 16-years-old. The probation order now is applicable as an independent sanction and can be combined with certain conditions (e.g. attendance at a day centre). The supervision can be intensified in cases of certain risk groups or more dangerous offenders. Community service has been extended to a maximum of 240 hours for offenders over 16 years old (sect. 10). A new sanction is the combination order, a supervision of one to three years combined with 40-100 hours community service (for offenders over 16 years old, see sect. 11). Another new sanction is the curfew order, a kind of restriction of liberty which implies the possible use of house arrest (including electronic monitoring, see sect. 12, is restricted to offenders over 16 years old). In general the curfew order contains certain conditions of staying away from particular places for two to 12 hours per day. All juveniles between ten and 17 can be given a supervision order. The attendance centre order can be 36 hours (regularly three hours on Saturday afternoons) in the case of 16-year-old offenders and 24 hours for the younger ones. Of particular interest is the rule in sect. 57 which allows parents to pay fines or compensation orders imposed on a juvenile.

General reforms are the introduction of the day fine system (since repealed: see Criminal Justice Act 1993) and sentencing rules stressing the principle of proportionality. The seriousness of the offence, and not personal preconditions of the offender, like prior convictions, shall determine the sentence in the future (since repealed: see Criminal Justice Act 1993). The influence of the Scandinavian neo-classic approaches can be seen. The declared aim of the reform was to increase the use of community sanctions and to reduce the use of juvenile custody. At the same time there is a clear evidence of a more repressive approach towards the use of 'tough and credible' alternatives which is especially expressed by the terminology of *'punishment'* in the community. This tendency has been strengthened by the Criminal Justice Act of 1994. A remarkable new sanction is the secure training order (sect. 1 to 4), a partially custodial, partially community based, sanction of a maximum term of two years. It can be applied already to 12 to 14-year-old offenders. It can be imposed if the offender has been convicted of three or more imprisonable offences and if he has been found to in breach of a supervision order or has been convicted of an imprisonable offence whilst subject to such an order. The secure training order therefore is provided for persistent serious offenders (see *Wasik/Taylor*, 1995 p.6.; for a critical comment see *Cavadino* 1994). In any case a pre-sentence report is required. The minimum term is six months, the maximum two years, the period of the custodial part to be as long as the supervision part. The Prison Service is planning to establish five centres with about 40 places each, which will be run by private organisations. However, it is uncertain if the necessary centres will be established in the near future (see *Wasik/Taylor*, 1995 p.9). In this case it would be possible to accommodate young, persistent, offenders temporarily in other residential homes, or even in young offender institutions.

The approach of getting tough can also be shown in the area of other custodial sanctions like detention in a young offender institution which will be dealt with in Section 6, below.

The Criminal Justice Act 1991 had made pre-sentence reports mandatory if the court was minded to impose certain community sanctions like probation, community service, a combination order or a supervision order. There was limited discretion only in certain cases. The Criminal Justice Act and Public Order Act 1994 now broadens the court's discretion not to obtain a pre-sentence report in the case of young adult offenders (18-20 year olds).

6. The Preconditions for Juvenile Imprisonment and Similar Custodial Sanctions - Age Limits With Respect to Custodial Sanctions etc.

As mentioned above, the priority of non-custodial sanctions is recognised world-wide as a guiding principle. However, we find considerable legal differences in the application of preconditions and the determination of age groups and time limits. The systematic approach can be differentiated according to two models. On one hand, there is the independent sanction of juvenile imprisonment within the legal framework of juvenile justice. On the other hand - and this is the legal technique which is used most often - there are special rules for juveniles (and/or young adults) which provide for a mitigation of prison sentences within the legal framework of the penal code (see, for example. Austria, England, Denmark, Finland, France, Italy, Greece, Norway, Scotland, Sweden, Switzerland; see *Dünkel* 1993; 1993a). In this a distinction can be drawn between models which provide only for mitigation and those which also set special legal preconditions for youth imprisonment (for example, educational needs or special grounds in the sense of emphasising the principle of last resort). The 'mitigation model' is the predominant model in Europe. However, in some countries one can find that provision is made for both independent youth prison sentences and for mitigated 'ordinary' prison sentences imposed in terms of the penal code (see for example Italy; *Dünkel* 1990, p.514).

If one looks at systems which provide for the mitigation of prison sentences, one finds that in Bulgaria and the Czech Republic as well as Slovakia the sentences for juveniles are reduced by about half. In France, prison sentences for 13 to 16-year-old juveniles *have to be*, for 16 to 18-year-old offenders *can be* mitigated. It is possible that several mitigating circumstances will be taken into account with the result that in practice, for example in 1986, about 85% of all prison sentences for juvenile offenders were of up to four months only. Not more than 3% were longer than one year. Youth imprisonment in France therefore is largely identical with special forms of short-term imprisonment such as the 'Jugendarrest' in Germany or the former detention centres in England. According to the above mentioned draft bill of 1990 youth imprisonment in France, especially for juveniles between 13 and 16, would be reduced considerably. First of all the bill aims to restrict juvenile imprisonment to felony offences ('crimes' in contrast to 'misdemeanours') and a few misdemeanour offences such as serious assault, drug trafficking and burglary. The maximum penalty will be five years in these cases. For 16 to 18-year-old offenders the maximum prison sentence should be three years in the case of misdemeanours and ten years for felony offences. In general, for all juveniles, the sentences laid down by law will be half of those provided for adults. Even before the parliamentary discussions on this draft started, the practice had changed considerably. Since 1981 the number of juveniles imprisoned has declined by 47%, the proportion of 13 to 16-year-old offenders has diminished even more drastically by 81% (from 134 to 26 in April 1990 and to 24 in January 1992, see *Ministère de la Justice* 1990; 1992).

The Scandinavian countries abolished the special (relatively indeterminate) youth imprisonment sanction in the 1970s (Denmark 1973; Norway 1975; Sweden 1980). However, there are special regulations concerning juveniles which restrict the application of imprisonment and furthermore provide for the mitigation of sentences. In Finland the law provides for a mitigation in the sense of reducing the sentence by at least one fourth in comparison to adults (see *Lahti* 1985, p.428). In all Scandinavian countries the courts are not obliged to follow the sentencing provisions of the specific offences (for example minimum penalties) and can choose milder sanctions, such as fines, even if there is no provision in the penal code for such sanctions in the case of adults. The regulations in Sweden are an important example. Prison sentences for 15 to 18-year-old offenders are restricted to cases where 'exceptional' grounds are given and where transfer to the welfare boards seems to be inappropriate. For 18 to 21-year-old offenders, too, 'special reasons' have to be given for imposing a prison sentence (see *Cornils* 1985, p.501). The above mentioned abolition of the special youth imprisonment represents the rejection of the legitimisation of imprisonment by arguments on special prevention (such as educational needs etc.). This change of juvenile justice policy has led to a considerable decline in the imposition of prison sentences on juveniles. Only about 1% of all convicted 15 to 18-year-old juveniles received a prison sentence, whereas the proportion for adult offenders is more than 20%. Furthermore one has to consider that about 70% of all charges are dismissed by the prosecutor (see *Cornils* 1985, pp.502, 506). Similar figures can be found for Denmark. The law provides, in addition, for special mitigation of prison sentences for young offenders between 15 and 21 years and for their placement in residential care instead of imprisonment. In 1983 only 4% received a prison sentence, which was suspended in 70% of the cases (see *Klages* 1985, p.399).

By using special programmes ('extra-judicial conflict resolution') Norway has widely abolished imprisonment for juveniles under the age of 18 years (see *Stangeland* 1985, *Dünkel* 1990, p.553). As has been mentioned above, in Austria prison sentences for juveniles have been reduced significantly. The Juvenile Justice Act of 1989 brought further improvements in this respect. Previously, both the maximum and the minimum sentences had to be reduced by half. Now there is no minimum at all. In some countries there are also provisions for the reduction of sentences for young adults. This group is defined variously as those between the age of 18 and 21 years (see above) or between 16 and 18 or 21 years as, for example in Portugal, Rumania, Scotland, Spain and Hungary. In other countries such as Italy, Turkey and Russia such reductions in sentence only apply to younger offenders - those aged between 15 and 18, 11 and 15, and 14 and 18 years respectively (see also *Table* on page 45).

Examples of countries with separate custodial sanctions within the framework of the juvenile justice system are England, Germany, Ireland, Portugal, Scotland, Switzerland and Yugoslavia (Serbia, Montenegro), Croatia and Slovenia.

In England, the Criminal Justice Act 1991 provides for the application of a custodial sentence when the offence was so serious that a non-custodial sentence cannot be justified. In addition, youth imprisonment is possible in cases of violent or sexual offences when it is required for the protection of the public. The maximum sentence is two years for 15 and 16-year-olds (before the Criminal justice Act 1994 it was one year). Male minors of at least 14 years and female minors of 15 years of age up to 1991 could be sentenced to a term of from 21 days to 4 months in a detention centre. Already the 1988 Criminal Justice Act had abandoned the terminological distinction between being held in a detention centre and youth custody and had replaced these terms with the term 'detention in a young offender institution' (see *Dünkel* 1990, p.532). In 1991 the minimum age for juvenile imprisonment was set at 15 years for males and females. The reform of 1991 has to be seen in the general context of developing principles of sentencing oriented at the principle of proportionality. This meant that previous convictions should lose importance and that the gravity of the offence should play the dominant role in determining the sentence (since adjusted: see Criminal Justice Act 1993). In contrast to the significant increase of the adult prison population the number of juvenile prisoners has decreased throughout the 1980s, particularly since 1984. A disproportionately large decrease has been observed in those communities where intermediate treatment schemes had been introduced as alternatives to various forms of custody (see *Tutt* 1987).

In addition to detention in a young offender institution there exists the possibility of long-term detention (which, under certain circumstances, can last for life) according to sect. 53 Children and Young Person's Act 1933 (CYPA). These possibilities have been extended. According to sect. 53 CYPA 10 to 17-year-old offenders can be sentenced to an indeterminate period if they are convicted on indictment of an offence punishable in the case of an adult with imprisonment for 14 years or more, or if they are convicted on indictment of an offence of indecent assault on a woman (before the Criminal Justice Act of 1994 sect. 53 CYPA was restricted to cases of homicide). Furthermore, 14 to 17-year-old offenders can be sentenced if they are convicted of causing death by dangerous driving or causing death by careless driving while under the influence of drink or drugs. The sanction must be imposed by the Crown Court (i.e. not the youth court - see *Wasik/Taylor* 1995, p.10).

In Germany the period of juvenile imprisonment ranges from at least six months up to 5 years in the case of 14 to 18-year-old juveniles, and up to ten years for 18 to 21-year-old young adults or for juveniles who have committed very serious felony offences such as murder. Juvenile imprisonment is provided for if, because of 'the dangerous tendencies' ('schädliche Neigungen'), in the personality of the offender (non-custodial) educational measures do not seem to be appropriate. Furthermore, juvenile imprisonment may be imposed because of the 'gravity of the guilt' (para. 17(2) öJGG) of the offender. The imposition of youth imprisonment on the grounds of dangerous tendencies has been much criticised, as the concept of educational need may lead to a more extensive application of custodial sanctions than would be the case for adults of over 21 years of age. Furthermore, criticism has been expressed of the fact that the average sentence of youth imprisonment is longer than the average prison sentence for adults. This is due largely to the high minimum sentence of six months set for youth imprisonment (see para. 18 (1) öJGG). Indeed, empirical research has demonstrated that juveniles and young adults also run a greater risk of being detained in pre-trial detention (see *Dünkel* 1994) as well as in youth prisons. More lenient punishment under the jurisdiction of juvenile courts can be seen, however, in the case of most serious crimes such as murder, robbery, felony drug offences etc. (see *Pfeiffer* 1988; 1991; *Dünkel* 1990, *Heinz* 1992, p.393). The reform of 1990 did not amend the legal preconditions for youth imprisonment, but, in the final debates on the draft bill, Parliament decided that before 1992 the government had to submit another reform bill which must include the regulations on juvenile imprisonment (because of other Government priorities another bill is unlikely to be submitted within the next few years). One can expect that (in the long run) youth imprisonment because of 'dangerous tendencies' will be abolished and that youth imprisonment because of the gravity of the offender's guilt will be restricted to certain serious felonies or repeated offences (see *Viehmann* 1989; *Dünkel* 1990; *Deutsche Vereinigung für*

Jugendgerichte und Jugendgerichtshilfen e.V. 1992; *Ostendorf* 1994; *Eisenberg* 1995 for further references). Furthermore, there is also a movement to exclude youth imprisonment for 14 and 15-year-old offenders except in the case of crimes such as murder or other very serious violent offences (*Dünkel* 1992a). In addition there are proposals to reduce youth imprisonment to within a range of from one month (or possibly three months) to two years, or five years in the case of young adults or very serious crimes committed by juveniles (*Dünkel* 1990; 1992a; *Heinz* 1992, p.404; *Pfeiffer* 1991, *Deutsche Vereinigung für Jugedgerichtschilfen e.V.* 1992).

It is almost unanimously accepted that short-term detention ('Jugendarrest') should be abolished since community sanctions have been successfully introduced over the past ten years for those offenders who would previously have been sentenced to juvenile detention. As in England and in The Netherlands the proposal is to restrict deprivation of liberty to the most serious offences (juvenile imprisonment according to para. 17 öJGG).

In spite of the justifiable criticism of the excessive use of youth imprisonment and of the very considerable regional differences between the Federal States (Bundesländer) and even local districts (see *Dünkel* 1990; *Pfeiffer* 1991; 1992; *Pfeiffer/Strobl* 1991), one has to bear in mind that only 4% of the convicted juveniles and 10% of the young adults in the old Federal States (former FRG) in 1993 received a youth prison sentence. If the cases which were dismissed at the prosecutorial level (because of the petty nature of the offence or because the young offender has completed reparation, community service etc.) are included, this proportion drops even further, to not more than 1.5% and 4% respectively. However, short-term incarceration in a detention centre ('Jugendarrest'), introduced in 1940 by the Nazi-regime, still plays an important role in Germany. It can be weekend detention or detention for a longer period of from one to four weeks (see para. 16 öJGG). 18% of all convicted juveniles and 16% of the young adults were sent to detention centres in 1993 (however only 8% and 10% had to serve their time in the form of a one to four weeks detention - see also Section 7 below).

The regulations in The Netherlands for 12 to 18-year-old juveniles are also of special interest. Until 1995, besides short term custody in a detention centre (from four hours to 14 days) there existed a special custodial sentence of up to six months ('tuchtschool'). The reform of 1995 abolished the distinction between these two forms of custodial sanction and introduced the juvenile imprisonment sentence. Twelve to 15-year-old offenders can be sentenced to juvenile imprisonment for up to one year, 16 to 17-year-old offenders up to two years. As previously, it is possible to transfer the young offender 'to the disposition of the government' in the case of very serious crime, which can mean a residential sanction up to the age of civil majority (18 years of age; see *Scholten ten Siethoff* 1985, p.592). In certain cases 16-17-year-old offenders can be transferred to the adult court and, vice-versa, it is possible to apply the specific sanctions of the Juvenile Justice Act to young adults of 18-20 years of age (see Section 8 below).

The Scottish 'children's hearings', introduced in 1968, have received considerable publicity in other European countries. They include informal ('round table') procedures for under 16-year-olds (in exceptional cases under 18-year-olds) (see *Jung, 1985*, p.713). More interesting in the context of custodial sanctions are the special regulations for 16 to 21-year-old offenders. The law does not allow the imposition of 'ordinary' prison sentences. Until 1980 the relatively indeterminate borstal sanction of one to three years incarceration could be imposed. It was replaced by a determinate period of detention which has to be not longer than the proportionate prison sentence for an adult (of over 21 years). Imprisonment for a period of from 28 days up to four months is executed in special detention centres, a longer sentence in a youth prison (where the young adult can stay up to the age of 21, or in exceptional cases up to the age of 23 years: see *Dünkel* 1990, p.519).

In Switzerland, too, there is a welfare approach for seven to 15-year-old children and a justice oriented approach for 15 to 18-year-old juveniles. Whereas children can only be placed in residential care, youth imprisonment of up to one year exists for juveniles. In very serious cases it is possible to send a juvenile to residential care for a minimum of two years, if the crime committed is related to serious deficiencies of education (in practice this educational measure is of no importance).

Only 1% to 2% of all convicted juvenile offenders are sent to youth prison (see *Hein/Locher* 1985, p.25; in 1989: 2%, see *Bundesamt für Statistik*, ed., Jugendstrafurteile, 1989; *Bern* 1990). For 18 to 25-year-old offenders the Criminal Code provides for a special custodial sanction for mentally disturbed or neglected offenders or offenders with considerable problems in finding employment (Arbeitserziehungsanstalt; sect. 111 bis Swiss Criminal Code). The incarceration is relatively indeterminate and lasts for from one to three years (sect. 100 ter). In practice it is seldom imposed because of the high minimum sentence and the other legal preconditions. In 1987 only 58 young adults were sent to such institutions, i.e. 0.3% of all convicted 18 to 25-year-old offenders (see *Bundesamt für Statistik*, ed., *Strafurteile* 1987, *Bern* 1988).

The new draft Swiss juvenile justice bill does not provide for imprisonment based on the educational needs or personal deficiencies of the offender, but seeks to restrict the use of imprisonment by emphasising the degree of culpability of the offender and the principle of proportionality (see *Stettler* 1988, pp.150, 154; *Bundesamt für Justiz* 1993, report to the draft bill, p.170). The draft bill of 1993 maintains the maximum penalty of one year for juveniles. It provides, however, in especially serious cases of homicide, serious assault, robbery, rape, sexual assault, serious bodily harm and arson for a maximum period of youth imprisonment of four years (only 16 and 17-year-old offenders, see sect. 26 of the draft bill).

In general, in most European countries special preventive (educational) needs have been abandoned as preconditions for imposing custodial sanctions. There are examples, and not only in Germany, of young offenders under the jurisdiction of juvenile courts being disadvantaged, in comparison to adults sentenced by the 'ordinary' criminal courts. The educational ideal and concepts of educational needs have led to a broader use of juvenile imprisonment in some cases. That is why the Scottish legislature emphasises that sentences of imprisonment for young adults should not be more severe than in the case of offenders over the age of 21 years. The above mentioned German experiences with the negative effects of the legal preconditions such as 'dangerous tendencies' show that there is always the danger of over reaction which has to be counteracted by strengthening the idea of proportionality as a limiting principle. Therefore one has to agree with *Kaiser* who emphasises that the gravity of guilt and the heinousness of the offence are more appropriate criteria for the decision whether to impose custodial sanctions or not than educational needs which can only be established with difficulty and cannot easily be subjected to judicial control (see *Kaiser* 1990, p.78; *Ostendorf* 1991, Grdl. zu paras. 17-18, note 6; *Dünkel* 1989a, 1992a).

7. Detention Centre, Shock-Probation, Detention for Default of Non-Custodial Sanctions, and Other Forms of Short Term Incarceration

Only in a few European countries are there specific forms of short-term imprisonment. There were certain similarities between the traditional youth detention centres in Germany (in the sense of 'Jugendarrest') and in England, which both emphasised a tough regime and militaristic discipline designed to make the juvenile conscious of the wrong he had done (see *Schüler-Springorum* 1975; *Huber* 1985, p.680; *Dünkel* 1990a; 1991). However, the German and English versions of detention centre differed considerably with respect to the period of incarceration. In Germany - as mentioned above (see section 5) - the maximum period is four weeks, in England the range was from three weeks to four months. Whereas the English legislature in 1988 replaced 'custody in a detention centre' and 'youth custody' by the term 'detention in a young offender institution', in Scotland and Ireland the differentiation was maintained. In England the legislature raised the minimum period of youth imprisonment to two months and by that abolished short term incarceration comparable to the German or the Dutch ('Jungendarrest').

In Ireland the period of short term incarceration for seven to 15-year-old offenders is up to one month, for juveniles, aged 15 to 17 years, up to three months (with the exception of homicide and similar offences, where longer sentences are possible; see Dünkel 1990, p 800).

In The Netherlands, up until 1995, there existed a very short special form of detention - from four hours up to two weeks. The reform law of 1995 replaced youth imprisonment and youth detention by a single prison sentence (see Section 6 above; for the contents of the bill see *Sagel-Grande,* 1986, p. 281; *van der Laan,* 1988, p. 203).

In contrast to the detention centre in England, Germany and (until 1995) The Netherlands, a similar sentence of up to 20 days in the former Yugoslavia has remained totally insignificant in practice (see *Cotic* 1986, p.1086). The same happened with the short-term youth imprisonment (of three to six months) introduced in 1983 in Portugal for 16 to 21-year-old offenders (see *Lopez Rocher* 1986, p.900). A similar very reluctant practice could be seen in the former GDR where youth detention of one week up to three months according to sect. 74 II of the Penal Code counted for only 3% of the convictions whereas about 25% of the juveniles received youth imprisonment of at least three months (see *Dünkel* 1991, p.24). Contrary to the legal provisions these countries in practice never succeeded in establishing special detention centres. The execution of juvenile detention therefore does/did not differ from the youth imprisonment (often because the young offenders are/were held in the same institution).

A special form of short-term imprisonment of from 14 days up to three months was introduced in Sweden in conjunction with a probation order (see Ch.28 para. 3(1) Swedish Criminal Code). However, this combination of a custodial sanction and probation was never of any significance in practice (in 1988 1.2% of all convictions and 13.4% of all probation orders; see *Rättsstatistik arsbok* 1989, table 3.4.9a). The scope of this sanction was further restricted in 1988 by another combination of probation orders: the offender now can sign a contract to undergo specific treatment, for example, drug or alcohol therapy (see *Cornils* 1991). However, the Swedish form of 'shock' probation was not totally abolished, although in the 1960s and 1970s empirical research had already demonstrated the negative effects of 'shock' probation in comparison to 'ordinary' probation (see *Bondeson* 1983, p.157; 1990). In Germany similar results have been obtained for probation in combination with 'shock' pre-trial detention (see *Schumann* 1986; *Dünkel* 1990; p.440).

While specific forms of short term incarceration increasingly become the exception (in Germany, too, there is a strong move to abolish 'Jugendarrest'; see *Pfeiffer/Strobl* 1991; *Deutsche Vereinigung für Jugendgerichte und Jugendgerichtschilfen e.V.* 1992; *Dünkel,* 1992a), one has to realise that most countries regularly provide for short terms of youth imprisonment, as they do not have a high minimum period of imprisonment (such as exists, for example, in Germany or Greece, where six months is the minimum). A remarkable example of restricted punishment is to be found in The Netherlands where the maximum period of youth imprisonment is equal to the minimum period in Germany. Despite the raising of the maximum term of juvenile imprisonment to one year (12-15-year-olds) or two years (16-17-year-olds) by the reform act of 995 the differences between The Netherlands and Germany (and most other European countries which provide maximum terms of juvenile imprisonment of 5 to 10 years) remain considerable.

Even if one arrives at the conclusion that there is no need of, and no justification for, specific youth detention centres, there remains, at least in Germany, the problem of the so-called detention for not responding to non-custodial sanctions. The German juvenile law allows the detention of a young offender if he is guilty of not fulfilling educational obligations imposed by the juvenile judge. Every third offender sent to a detention centre is a member of this group. Indeed, with the extension of alternative sanctions, this sanction has gained in significance (see *Ostendorf* 1983; *Hinrichs,* 1990, *Dünkel,* 1990 p.355; 1991). As the detention does not necessarily replace the former sanction, but is imposed to enforce specific educational measures, there are considerable reservations about whether the constitutional principle of 'ne bis in idem' is being respected (see *Ostendorf* 1983 p.563; *Werlich* in *Schumann et al.* 1985, p.147; *Dünkel* 1990, p.357).

Only in Sweden does there appear to be a similar possibility of enforcing non-custodial sanctions. A probationer who does not contact his probation officer can be detained for up to one week (in exceptional cases for up to two weeks) until it has been decided whether to revoke his probation or not (see Ch.28 para. 11 Swedish Criminal Code). The detention therefore is more of a preventive measure than a means of enforcing non-custodial treatment as in Germany. Instead of enforcing educational measures one should emphasise the legal possibilities of changing the educational measures if they prove to be inappropriate (see e.g. para. 11 II öJGG). There is provision for doing this in practically all juvenile justice systems (including Germany and Sweden). When the offender fails to fulfil his duties, the most common strategy is to continue proceedings after a conditional discharge.

Altogether one should be very cautious about enlarging the repressive forms of enforcing the co-operation of the offender. Often these possibilities are abused by judges who are simply angry that the offender has not responded to the educational 'benefits' which have been provided for him. One tends to overlook the fact that often the judge was at fault in failing to find out what the appropriate sanction would have been. From the point of view of a consistent juvenile policy which aims to avoid any form of imprisonment one should open the door for 'substitutive' detention only in exceptional cases (the same holds true for fine defaulters). Taking the 'educative ideals' of juvenile justice seriously it seems to be reasonable not to enforce educative measures by the threat of incarceration. This was legally provided in Germany from 1923-40. The repressive approach of the Nazi regime introduced juvenile detention where the juvenile failed to respond to educational measures ('education as punishment'). Proposed reforms in Germany, as in Switzerland, are to restrict this kind of detention to fine defaulters or those who do not fulfil other payment (reparation) or working obligations (community service); *see Deutsche Vereinigung für Jugendgerichte und Jugendgerichtschilfen e.V.* 1992; *Dünkel* 1992a; *Bundesamt für Justiz* 1993).

8. Specific Regulations for Young Adults and Problems of the Transfer Between Juvenile Welfare and Juvenile Justice Systems and the Transfer from the Juvenile Justice to the Criminal Justice System for Adults

The question of how to deal with young adult offenders plays an important role in the current discussions on reforming juvenile justice systems. The tenth criminological colloquium of the Council of Europe in November 1991 dealt with that problem (see *Dünkel* 1993; 1993a). What is meant legally by the term 'young adult'? In most countries the age group between 18 and 21 years, sometimes, as in Portugal or Scotland, between 16 and 21, is defined in this sense. The issues of criminal policy in this area concern the question of the extent to which the special educational measures developed for juveniles can also be applied for young adults. In Germany 18 to 21-year-old young adults in practice have been integrated almost totally into the juvenile justice system and legally full integration is required (see *Dünkel* 1990, p.87 and below).

The following description deals with the general problems of transfers between child welfare, juvenile justice and adult criminal systems. Whereas in 'double track' systems of child welfare and juvenile justice there is the prevalent problem of the transfer of juvenile offenders from one system to the other, in 'one track' welfare systems it is the question of under which conditions the criminal law for adults should be applied to juveniles.

In the USA in particular there has been considerable public debate in recent years about the growing tendency in cases involving serious and repeated offences to use 'adult' criminal law against juveniles. The increasing use of decisions to 'waiver' the jurisdiction of the juvenile courts is part of a wider tendency. On the one hand, this tendency has led to milder treatment of status offenders who are diverted from the justice system (see summarising *Handler/Satz* 1982), whilst on the other hand, the possibility has been created of bringing juveniles before the adult courts and exposing them to the full rigours of the criminal law (see *H.-.J. Albrecht* 1986). The minimum age of criminal responsibility of such juveniles (in the sense of being transferred to the adult courts) is set at from 13 to 16 years in most states (in some states there is no fixed minimum age). In some instances this latter development is restricted to certain crimes, for example, to capital offences. Generally, as a result of the decision in the leading case of *Kent v United States* in 1966, there has been a reduction in the discretion to decide in which forum juveniles may be tried. Such discretion may be limited to certain kinds of offences or to juvenile offenders with previous convictions. In some cases certain offences such as murder, rape and robbery are being withdrawn entirely from the jurisdiction of the juvenile courts. Such developments are serving to reduce the hitherto almost unlimited discretion of the juvenile courts (or the prosecuting authorities; see *Field* 1987, pp.505, 512). There are enormous variations in the law and particularly in the practices adopted in the various states. The proportions of 'waivers' of juvenile jurisdiction vary, for example from 0 per 100,000 in the states of New York and Vermont to 435 per 100,000 in Nebraska (see *H.-.J. Albrecht* 1986, p. 1302). In practice the referral of juveniles to adult courts has not led to the heavier sentences which were being sought. Recently therefore there have been calls for the increased use of the juvenile courts, but with the provision that they should impose harsher sentences (see *Tracy/Wolfgang/Figlio*, 1985, p.24).

Similar partial exceptions from the competence of juvenile courts can be found in other countries as well. The differentiated manner of dealing with 16 to 18-year-old offenders in Argentina so that for more severe crimes they may be sentenced by courts which otherwise have jurisdiction only over adults has already been mentioned (see Section 4 above). In Belgium 16 to 18-year-old traffic offenders are regularly sentenced by 'ordinary' courts (see *Dupont/Walgrave* 1985, p.539). In Germany there are similar tendencies to be seen for 18 to 21-year-old traffic offenders, who, according to para. 105 öJGG are mostly treated as adults. The effect is that they can be subjected to a fine based on a summary procedure *(Strafefehlsverfahren)*.

Several general criminal codes have special provisions for young adults. Mostly these are provisions to mitigate prison sentences for 18 to 21-year-old offenders. Such provisions are found in the criminal codes of Austria, England and Wales, France, Greece, Italy, Spain, Switzerland and the Scandinavian countries. Furthermore, there are provisions which facilitate the imposition of alternative sanctions such as suspended prison sentences (see, for example, Finland or Italy). In Finland prison sentences of young adults can be suspended even when, because of prior convictions, this would be impossible in the case of adults over the age of 21 years. In the former Yugoslavia educational measures applicable to 14 to 18-year-old offenders could also be applied to 18 to 21-year-old young adults. The same is possible in The Netherlands in the case of 18 to 21-year-old offenders, whereas, on the other hand offenders between the age of 16 and 18 years can be sentenced according to the criminal law for adults, if this seems to be appropriate with respect to the seriousness of the crime or the personality of the offender. The tendency to apply the 'ordinary' criminal law is evident in the case of traffic offences, as only the criminal law for adults provides for the withdrawing of drivers' licences. A draft bill currently before parliament will introduce such a measure into the juvenile law (see *Dünkel* 1990, p.540). A similar regulation is proposed by the draft bill of 1990 in France (see *Ministère de la Justice* 1990. sect. 41 of the draft).

Whereas in The Netherlands and especially in the former Yugoslavia the application of educational measures for young adults has remained the exception, the development in Germany has been the opposite direction. This may be due to the fact that since the reform of 1953 the juvenile court is competent to sentence all young adults independently of whether educational or criminal sanctions are to be applied (see para. 108 öJGG). para. 105(1) No. 1 of that law provides for the application of juvenile law if in terms of his personal development ('Reifeentwwicklung') the young adult is closer to a juvenile than to an adult. Furthermore, juvenile law has to be applied if it appears that the motives and the circumstances of the offence are those of a typical juvenile crime (*Jugendverfehlung* para. 105(1) No.2 öJGG). In 1965 only 38% of young adults were sentenced in terms of the Juvenile Justice Act, but by 1990 this proportion had nearly doubled to 64% (see *Dünkel* 1990, p.87, 1993; in 1993 the ratio decreased slightly to 59%). This makes it clear that the full integration of young adults into the juvenile justice system has been accepted in practice. The regulations mentioned above have also been interpreted very widely by the courts to provide for the application of juvenile law in all cases where there are doubts about the maturity of the young offender (see BGHSt 12, p.116; BGH Strafverteidiger 1989, p.311). However, there are considerable regional differences in the practice with respect to specific crimes. In the case of the most serious crimes such as murder, rape or robbery nearly all (more than 95%) of young adult serious crimes such as murder, rape or robbery nearly all (more than 95%) of young adult offenders are sentenced in terms of the (in these cases, milder) juvenile law. The reason is that the higher minimum and maximum sentences provided by the 'ordinary' criminal law do not apply in the juvenile law (see para. 18(1) öJGG). Juvenile judges, therefore are not bound by the otherwise obligatory life sentence for murder or the minimum of five years of imprisonment in the case of armed robbery. The German practice seems to be contrary to the above mentioned waiver decisions in the USA, where the most serious offenders are transferred to the 'ordinary' criminal justice system. Only in the case of traffic offences are the majority of young adult offenders (1993: 60%) in Germany sentenced in terms of the criminal law for adults, because in these cases there is the procedural possibility of imposing fines without an oral hearing (*Strafbefehl*, which is excluded in the juvenile penal law). There are constitutional reservations about the regional inequalities which have emerged in practice. In North Rhine-Westphalia, for example, the convictions in terms of the juvenile law range between 27% and 91% of all juveniles convicted (see *Pfeiffer* 1988, p.96). When the (old) Federal States are compared, the range in 1993 was from 42% in Baden Wurttemberg, 44% in Rhenania-Palatinate to 94% in Hamburg and 95% in Schleswig-Holstein. Apparently juvenile judges have different conceptions about the 'typical' personality of juvenile offenders and of the 'typical' nature of juvenile delinquency. Overall, there is a North-South gap, with the Federal States in the north increasingly applying juvenile criminal law, whereas in the south juvenile judges rely to a greater extent on the criminal law for adults.

Special mitigation of penal sanctions for young adults exists in many countries (see above). In some countries there are special regulations for the execution of prison sentences. In Portugal and Spain young adult prisoners (up to the age of 21 or even 25) serve their sentence in special prisons. In Denmark and Germany too, such a concentration is being encouraged by special treatment programmes (see *Dünkel* 1993; 1993a).

Altogether we find many different regulations and models which provide for some flexibility in applying juvenile welfare or juvenile justice law or even in transferring offenders to the 'ordinary' justice system. The transfer from the court to the welfare boards is used extensively in Sweden. In 1988 the age group to be considered for welfare measures was extended from up to 20 to up to 21 years (see Ch.31 para. 1 Swedish Criminal Code). Furthermore, the community service order was introduced as a judicial sanction which could be applied in conjunction with the transfer to the welfare boards (see *Cornils* 1991). As in Sweden the welfare procedure is predominant in England in the case of very young offenders (from 10 to 15, and also from 15 to 17 years). Only the more serious crimes lead to criminal proceedings and possibly to youth imprisonment (if the offender has reached the age of 15 years; see *Huber* 1985, pp.672, 692).

9. Conclusions

Although at first glance it appears that there are significant differences, comparison of the various national juvenile justice systems in Europe reveals that the fundamental philosophies and practices are developing in very similar ways. Criminological insights into the episodic nature and relative insignificance of juvenile delinquency have encouraged a reduction in the use of penal sanctions. Techniques of diversion and new non-custodial measures such as mediation, community service and forms of intermediate treatment (see *Sace van der Vorst* 1989; *Dünkel/Zermatten* 1990; *Junger-Tas/Boendermaker van der Laan* 1991; *Snare* 1991; *Booth* 1992) have been used successfully with juveniles. They are also being considered for young adults in those instances where they have not already been introduced. It is increasingly being recognised that custodial sanctions should be avoided as far as possible and, where this cannot be done, they should be applied for the shortest acceptable period. This approach to juvenile custodial sanctions reflects the current recommendations of the United Nations and the Council of Europe (see United Nations Standard Minimum Rules for the Administration of Juvenile Justice of 1985 and the Rules for the Protection of Juveniles Deprived of their Liberty of 1990 - *United Nations*, 1991). There is a growing tendency to extend the ambit of juvenile justice to include young adults (for example in Austria and England). Finally, constitutional guarantees of due process are being strengthened by, for example, the increasing role of lawyers in supervising the use of pre-trial detention (see the reforms introduced in Germany in 1990 and the draft legislation in France).

The potential for harmonising the criminal law relating to juveniles in Europe is reduced by the enormous differences in the age categories to which such law is applicable. The variation in the age of criminal responsibility between seven years in Switzerland or Ireland and 18 years in Belgium underlines this point. Nevertheless, some similar tendencies can be observed, in that incarceration in a juvenile or adult prison is generally not possible before the offender has reached the age of 14 or 15 years. The *'Leitmotiv'* for European penal policy in the future should perhaps be that incarceration in a prison, however defined, should only be applied to juveniles who have passed the compulsory school going age, i.e. who are older than 15 or 16 years of age.

Juvenile criminal law specifically for those under the age of 21 years would be conceivable, as young people in this age group have not yet developed their full potential and educational measures are therefore still appropriate. It can be argued from a sociological perspective that persons under the age of 25 are still in the same position, as they are not yet fully integrated into society and as they have often not yet joined the labour market or started their own families. However, in the face of the more intensive

66

involvement of this group in relatively serious crime, it would be politically extremely difficult to draw them into the juvenile justice system with its inherently milder sanctions. It is nevertheless realistic to develop the specific sanctions which can be imposed on persons under the age of 21 by the juvenile criminal law (as is the case in Germany) and thus to reduce the application of custodial sentences. It is therefore not desirable to seek to abolish the classical juvenile justice system entirely. However, it is not acceptable anymore to impose custodial sentences on juveniles on grounds of special prevention and thus to detain them for (relatively) indeterminate periods. It is essential to return to the classical principle that the sentence should not be disproportionate to the crime. The fashionable view that all educational efforts are valueless, should, however, be rejected. Only the principle, 'education instead of punishment' (see *Pieplow* 1989; *Viehman* 1989, *Walter* 1989; *Kaiser* 1990; *Heinz* 1992), guarantees that the treatment of juveniles will not be too harsh and the episodic nature of juvenile delinquency will be recognised. Of course, this principle needs to be strictly limited by the application of the constitutional doctrine of proportionality in order to ensure that the educational measures do not result in exceptionally harsh sentences, but this does not undermine the principle. From the point of view of both special and general prevention it is justifiable to establish an independent system of social reactions which is characterised by sanctions which are relatively mild in comparison to the criminal law for adults. This is applicable even to the most serious crimes committed by juveniles and young adults. The multiplicity of developments in national systems of juvenile justice in Europe remains desirable as it offers diverse solutions to the many problems in this area.

10. Propositions for the Further Development of Juvenile Justice Systems in Europe

1. One cannot do without a juvenile law which is independent of criminal law for adults, which is characterised by educational instead of penal sanctions, and which places particular emphasis on the problems of development and integration faced by young people. It is not desirable to apply to juveniles the criminal law for adults with only a few special rules to mitigate the punishment of juveniles. Such an approach is contrary to recommendations of the Council of Europe and the United Nations (see the Standard Minimum Rules for the Administration of Juvenile Justice of 1985).

2. Juvenile (penal) law should be structured in such a way that the reaction to criminal offences committed by younger people is milder than that to offences committed by adults.

3. This requires a separate system of juvenile courts in which the officials involved (juvenile judges, juvenile prosecutors, social workers attached to

the juvenile courts) are specially trained in those aspects of education and criminology applicable to young people.

4. Independently of the adoption of a welfare or juvenile justice approach, the fundamental principles that the procedures should be fair and aimed at intervention of minimal intensity (the principle of subsidiarity) should be adopted.

5. Fundamental procedural safeguards must be guaranteed. These include the right to legal assistance, the possibility to appeal also against measures which have a primarily educational objective, and the requirement that standards of proof and standards for the evaluation of evidence be the same as those for adults.

6. Access to legal assistance must be guaranteed comprehensively from the investigatory stage onwards. In cases where there is a threat of pre-trial detention or of a sentence to juvenile detention the assignment of a legal adviser shall be compulsory. Furthermore, steps must be taken to secure the participation of the guardians (parents) and of social workers who can testify to the social circumstances and possibilities of integration of the juvenile.

7. In many countries, including Germany, the right of convicted juveniles to appeal is restricted on educational grounds. There is no justification for continuing to impose such restrictions. The educational ideal should not lead to juveniles being disadvantaged on the procedural level in comparison to adults.

8. In many countries pre-trial detention is imposed disproportionately often on juveniles and misused as a form of punishment. Young foreigners or members of ethnic minorities are most in danger of becoming 'victims' of such practices. It is accepted that the opening of borders in Europe has given rise to a particular type of crime problem because of 'travelling' offenders. There is concern that pre-trial detention is misused as a preventative strategy in both criminal policy and immigration policy. Pre-trial detention must remain a means of last resort ('ultima ratio') where it is the only way to guarantee that a trial can take place. This is especially true for young persons charged with a criminal offence in order to protect their human rights. This tendency to misuse pre-trial detention can be combated by statutory limits on when pre-trial detention may be ordered (limits on the ordering of detention on grounds that the accused will abscond or interfere with the investigation of the case) and by placing an increased burden on the courts to justify decisions to detain, as well as by a stricter limit, based on the doctrine of proportionality, on the duration of detention.

9. A promising development in the struggle to reduce pre-trial detention is, in addition to the compulsory assignment of legal counsel, the provision of assistance on detention decisions by social workers attached to the courts (e.g. probation officers), who attempt to find alternative accommodation for accused juveniles before a detention order is made. The development of alternatives to detention should include hostels and other forms of supervised accommodation. However, leaving aside its dubious efficacy in comparison to traditional forms of supervision by social workers, there are considerable reservations of a legal-ethical and constitutional nature about electronic monitoring, when it is used in combination with house arrest or other similar sanctions.

10. The juvenile justice system should apply to offenders up to at least the end of their eighteenth year. This is the practice in most European countries. The tendency to increase its scope to include young adults (from 18 to 21 years of age) is to be warmly welcomed, as also in this age group one often has to do with episodic misconduct which is linked to the stage of development of the offender. The special measures of the juvenile penal law can fruitfully be applied to such conduct (see the reforms proposals in Germany and Austria).

11. One cannot make a definite recommendation about the age of criminal responsibility. However, in most European countries punishment cannot be imposed before a juvenile reaches the age of fourteen or fifteen years. Punishment which involves detention in a juvenile institution should not be allowed before the juvenile is at least 16 years old. There should be no provision for placing juveniles in (closed) educational institutions against their will, or without the concurrence of their guardian or the social worker attached to their case (see the reforms to the juvenile welfare law, *Kinder-und-Jugendhilfegesetz*, in Germany in 1990).

12. Reactions to juvenile criminality should be bound to a system in which restitution and resolution of the conflict between offender and victim take priority at all stages of the proceedings.

13. The priority which should be attached to the reconciliation of offender and victim can best be expressed by providing that for specific offences, in particular property offences, criminal damage and petty assault, there should be a restriction on further proceedings where attempts at reconciliation have been successful. As is the case in Austrian juvenile penal law, it should not be possible to proceed with a prosecution in these cases. This means that the prosecuting authorities or the juvenile court should not have the discretion to decide whether or not to abandon the proceedings.

14. Where serious offences have been committed, or where the restitution only takes place in the course of the proceedings, the prosecutor or the juvenile court may abandon the proceedings if legal harmony has been restored by the actions of the offender. At the very least, the effort of the juvenile offender to make reparation should be seen as a mitigating factor which must be taken into account when choice and severity of punishment are considered.

15. A juvenile justice system can provide for the following seven levels of intervention:

Level 1 Extra-judicial reconciliation between offender and victim.

Level 2 Priority for informal, less interventionist, sanctions over formal sanctions (withdrawal by the prosecution combined with educational measures, limited restrictive conditions or a warning). Within this programme of diversion withdrawal without preconditions has priority over withdrawal subject to the fulfilment of conditions. The reconciliation of offender and victim is a specific ground for withdrawal.

Level 3 Measures adopted by the juvenile welfare authorities on application by, or with the consent of, the juveniles concerned (e.g. a training course or supervision order).

Level 4 Imposition of specific obligations (compensation, monetary penalty, community service, suspension of a driving licence).

Level 5 Suspension of sentence with probation (e.g. juvenile punishment of up to two years or without limit, linked to submission to supervision by the probation service).

Level 6 Suspension of sentence with probation providing intensive supervision and control (reduced case loads for probation officers in order to provide aid for specific needs of recidivist offenders with serious problems of reintegration into society).

Level 7 Juvenile punishment not suspended with probation on the grounds of the heinousness of the offence, as 'ultima ratio' (no incarceration on educational grounds any more!). Where juvenile punishment is unavoidable it must be kept as short as possible.

16. In the six level model sketched above the first level takes priority above the second, the second level above the third and so on. Only in the case of the third and fourth levels can an equivalence of value be assumed. The

juvenile court judge must decide whether it is appropriate to impose an educational measure or a punishment such as a fine or community service which will cause the offender to reflect .

17. The principle that the sanction must be proportionate to the offence must also be applied to educational measures and the imposition of specific obligations *(Auflegen)*. Thus, for example, temporal limits must be imposed. Training courses should run for a maximum of three to six months, whilst other forms of social work supervision should not exceed twelve months. For fines and community service there should also be absolute upper limits (e.g. a maximum of 60 hours community service as in Austria or 120 hours as in France).

18. There should be no compulsion to participate in educational programmes. If the juvenile avoids the supervision of the social worker, this should have no negative consequences, unless he commits a further offence. In the case of recidivism the juvenile court will, as a rule, seek another suitable sanction. A failure at one of the early sanctioning levels should not lead automatically to an escalation of the intensity of the sanction.

19. Only in the case of the specific obligations is there provision for substitute sanctions. As a last resort this could include short-term detention (for example, of up to four weeks). Before this happens the offender should be given the option of fulfilling his obligations in another way, e.g. by performing community service instead of paying a fine and vice versa. Reparation for damage can also be made by working directly for the victim.

20. In contrast to the forms of supervision at the third level, probation at the fifth level (suspension of sentence on probation) is linked with the threat of imprisonment if the suspended sentence is put into operation. (This also applies to the Anglo-American form of probation where a renewed inquiry into the appropriate sentence for the original offence leads in most cases to the imposition of a sentence of imprisonment).

21. In connection with intensive probation different forms of partially suspended sentences might be considered (as in the criminal law of Austria) or other forms of restrictions of liberty, e.g. house arrest. However, the danger of an (unjustified) extension and intensification of social control is obvious ('net-widening'). The idea of a 'short, sharp shock' preceding a probation sentence or parole (shock probation or shock incarceration) cannot be seen as a superior (or even an appropriate) means to integrate young offenders with serious problems. Taking the principle of proportionality seriously, shock incarceration, therefore, has to be rejected. There is no evidence that short term incarceration is more effective in comparison to traditional forms of probation and parole.

22. Electronic monitoring in combination with house arrest - as practised in the USA (and currently introduced in England and Sweden) - is neither necessary nor appropriate and creates serious doubts in terms of human rights because of the danger that persons who are exposed to such measures become mere objects of state control and intervention (see also above under point 9).

23. The heinousness of the offence committed, and not the perceived educational needs of the offender, shall be the precondition for the imposition of a sentence of imprisonment or for the referral of the juvenile to an educational institution. When the decision is made on whether, or for how long, the offender should be sentenced to imprisonment, previous conduct (previous convictions) shall not be considered, so that even when petty offences are committed repeatedly, imprisonment will continue to be regarded as a disproportionately heavy sanction. Proportionality of the sanction guarantees as limiting principle that the punishment will not be out of proportion to the specific offence.

24. There should be additional restrictions on the imposition of imprisonment on juveniles in respect of certain offences and age groups (e.g. the exclusion of 14 and 15-year-olds from juvenile punishments). Also in respect of temporal limits further differentiation is possible (see the draft bill of 1990 in France).

25. Sentences of imprisonment imposed on juveniles may not be longer than those imposed on adults in equivalent cases. On the contrary, specific provisions to mitigate punishment should ensure that juveniles are not only sentenced to imprisonment less often than adults but also that they are sentenced to terms which, on average, are significantly shorter. One way in which this can be achieved through legislation is by prescribing an absolute maximum for juvenile punishments (in Germany five years for juveniles: its reduction to two years except for offences of homicide is currently being discussed). In Austria the solution which has been adopted is to lay down that the appropriate punishment for juveniles is half that for adults.

26. An increased minimum juvenile sentence or term in an educational institution (for example, in order to guarantee that a particular training programme or educational course offered in prison can be completed) cannot be justified on empirical grounds.

27. As far as deprivation of liberty (especially in juvenile prisons) seems to be inevitable, the regime of the institution should be of an educative nature and a variety of rehabilitation programmes should be provided. In small units, concepts of living groups and of therapeutic communities could be

realised. As far as possible the institutions should be oriented to be open and to integrate the parents and the community into the rehabilitative efforts. School and vocational training is of special importance. The institution should try to motivate young offenders to participate in these programmes. Legal guarantees and the respect of human rights are particularly important in the situation of deprivation of liberty. The public and the politicians have to pay more attention to the problems of young people deprived of their liberty (see the United Nations Standard Minimum Rules for Young Offenders Deprived of their Liberty of 1990).

28. Harsher regimes of detention as practised in the so-called 'boot camps' in the USA should be rejected as the special preventive effects of such 'militaristic' programmes seem to be doubtful and legal guarantees of the inmates are widely neglected. Special concern should be given to closed institutions which are emerging in some countries for the institutionalisation of young foreigners, violent offenders, unemployed or homeless people (see e.g. the discussion about educational camps in The Netherlands). Juvenile (penal) law cannot solve the crime problem and counteract the shortcomings in other areas of policy like social welfare and the treatment of foreigners (the politics concerning asylum seekers, refugees, immigration etc.). Juvenile (penal) law and practice has to reject being 'instrumentalised' for repressive interests of criminal policy.

29. Juvenile justice systems in many countries (especially those countries which have the constitutional structure of a federal state) show considerable regional variations in the practice of diversion, juvenile court decisions and in the execution of custodial sanctions or other forms of deprivation of liberty. As in most cases the same (federal) laws are applicable, these differences must be seen as problematic especially with respect to the principle of equal and just sentencing. Although the power to impose individualised sentences is an integrative element of juvenile justice the differences e.g. of between 43% and 91% 'informal' reactions (diversion) shown above in a comparison of the German Federal states (for the same group of offenders) can hardly be justified. Similar variations can be observed concerning pre-trial detention, suspended sentences, parole, short term incarceration ('Jugendarrest', i.e. detention centre, in Germany) and the regimes of juvenile prisons (proportion of inmates in open facilities, number of prison furloughs, inmates in work release programmes etc.). The efforts of harmonising these divergent practices by circulars of ministries (in the case of diversion) sometimes (as the German example proves, see *Heinz* 1994) have no impact. Therefore legal rules are necessary which describe more precisely the preconditions of the different sanctions, especially of juvenile imprisonment.

30. The juvenile justice system has to be modest. It is clear that juvenile penal sanctions will not solve the juvenile crime problem. At the same time

longitudinal studies on the development of careers of juvenile offenders justify the hope that even repetitive and serious young offenders will be socially integrated on reaching adulthood (episodic nature of juvenile delinquency). The juvenile justice system should develop constructive measures for those juveniles who have serious problems and should avoid reactions which endanger the process of (re)integration, especially by imposing sentences or measures of deprivation of liberty (closed educative institutions of the welfare system, pre-trial detention, juvenile imprisonment).

Note: A comprehensive Bibliography prepared by Frieder Dünkel and relating directly to this part of *Section II* can be found at the end of the book.

Legal Frameworks and Interventions

Martine Mérigeau

The apparent diversity of legal systems should not overshadow the common historical origin of the establishment of juvenile criminal justice in Europe, nor that of its current evolution towards the harmonisation of these principles under the aegis of international instances, be it the General Assembly of the United Nations adopting the 'Beijing Rules' on 29 November 1985, concerning juvenile criminal justice, or the Committee of Ministers of the Council of Europe by the Recommendation (R(87)20) dated 17 September 1987 on Social Reactions to Juvenile Delinquency, or more recently the so-called Riyadh Directing Principles for the Prevention of Juvenile Delinquency (1990) or The Minima Rules of the United Nations for the Protection of Juveniles in Detention (so-called Havana Rules of 1990). Under the influence of the adoption of these international texts by individual states and with the support of the legislator by progressive adaptation of national law, legislation is on the way towards harmonisation, or at least an effort is being made to respect the minima principles concerning the treatment of minors. This orientation is particularly noticeable in Eastern European countries, now in a transitory period following political upheaval, which are in search of new legislative models. Be it Slovenia, the former Czechoslovakia or Poland, which are the three Eastern countries to respond to our inquiry, it is expedient to keep in mind an image of positive transitory law.

Legal Systems

Among the legal systems applicable to juvenile delinquents, it is necessary to distinguish, in a schematic fashion, two large groups of systems. The first system, called 'penal' or 'justice model' followed by most countries, is constructed on the foundation of criminal law but with a primarily educational perspective; therefore it is a question of 'educational criminal law' as in Germany and The Netherlands. This double route, founded on the recognition of the lack of criminal responsibility of minors and/or limited responsibility, implies a system of bipolar reactions, devoted to educational measures on one hand and penalties on the other. The second system, termed the 'protection model' or 'welfare model' is founded on a single concept of law, applicable without distinction to juvenile delinquents (who have committed an offence) and deviants (beggars, vagabonds) or minors in danger (including safety and moral danger). Juveniles benefit from a presumption that they cannot be sentenced. In these different cases, the same judge (juvenile court judge) will be involved, who will be competent to order protective measures only. Consequently, these systems envision measures oriented towards protection

75

and education, the aim being more one of socialisation and education than of castigation or punishment of a crime. Here it is supposed that the causes of delinquent behaviour are to be found in the social, economic or family background of the young person, considered more as a victim than a responsible guilty party. In accordance with this view, these systems have not maintained the traditional distinction between penalties and educational measures, as any intervention is educational by definition and does not correspond to the offence committed. Thus in Belgium, the 1965 law relative to the protection of youth had established a double system of protection, one legal, exercised by the juvenile court, the other social, where prevention was delegated to Committees for the Protection of Minors. Currently, four of the countries consulted have a single law with a double system of social and legal protection, which applies equally to juvenile delinquents and young people in danger: Scotland, Luxembourg, Poland and Portugal. Already it seems that this one-way system is being broken up (England and Wales, Northern Ireland and Belgium have already separated the areas of competence between institutions). This system is being replaced more and more by special arrangements which tend to separate the two categories of young people in difficulty and deviants or young delinquents, and apply two different systems to them.

In order to facilitate global knowledge and understanding, from the 17 countries consulted, three themes concerning the treatment of minors have commanded our attention:

- age thresholds (age of criminal responsibility);
- recognised rights of minors;
- reform projects.

Age Range for Jurisdiction of the Juvenile (or Youth) Court

The question of age brackets is fundamental, for on the answer depends the nature of applicable legislation (for example adult criminal law or juvenile criminal law), and the determination of the competence of jurisdictions or other institutions in the matter. To this question is added that of criminal responsibility, the conception of which varies from one country to another, according to the importance given to the moral element of the infraction committed by a minor. But the concept of moral responsibility applicable to minors is continually being detached from adult criminal law, being expressed either traditionally along the lines of the concept of discernment, or in terms of personality, closely linked to the ability to be criminally responsible for one's acts, that is, to use the expression of M. Merle et Vitu 'the aptitude to benefit from the penalty'. Sometimes the two criteria will even conflict, as in Germany.

In principle, there is no incrimination specific to juvenile delinquents; the general rules concerning the constitutive elements of the offence apply to them. In other words the scope for intervention of juvenile criminal law is determined by the commission of a criminal offence. Consequently, most countries at least have a law, if not a special system of criminal law specific to juvenile delinquents. Usually this legislation is drawn up separately (Germany, Austria) and is not therefore incorporated into adult criminal law. But a certain number of countries do not have special laws concerning minors. Often the measures concerning juvenile delinquents are subject to some special arrangement in the penal code. This is the case in Holland, Sweden, Switzerland, Slovenia and Greece. These countries (except Holland) also have neither special procedural rules nor legal texts for the treatment of minors in detention (except Greece since a 1989 law which came into force on 1 January 1990).

The law or special legislation applicable to minors governs essentially the legal effects, or the reactions and interventions of the state relative to offences committed by juvenile delinquents. In addition many arrangements depart from common law concerning the organisation of proceedings (in particular the existence of special juvenile courts) and the development of criminal proceedings in favour of minors. Sometimes strongly federal political structures of a given country profoundly change the laws applicable to minors regarding minors within the country. Thus in Switzerland, the organisation of the court system and legal procedures applicable to minors on a cantonal level are sometimes very different from one part of the country to another. This is also the case in Belgium which has turned towards a federal structure (law of 8 August 1988) and had installed a new division of competence, attributing to each of the three linguistic communities (Flemish, French and German) legislative competence in the matter of protection of minors and the carrying out of legal measures of protection concerning juveniles who have committed an offence. This implies the necessity to distinguish and clearly define which community legislation is involved when mentioning Belgium.

In bringing up the question of age limits, we are also raising the problem of the definition given to juvenile delinquency. However, in the light of results obtained, it is clear that this notion varies in practice from one country to another. In this respect it is necessary to distinguish the age of 'criminal minority' from 'criminal majority'. 'Criminal minority' generally refers to the age of criminal responsibility while 'criminal majority' can be defined as the age from which the young person will be subject to general law, that is, adult criminal law. The fixing of the age of 'criminal majority' at 18 is accepted by most countries. Only Austria has fixed it at 19 years. Northern Ireland and Poland have adopted the threshold of 17 years, while England and Wales have recently brought it to 18 years. In Portugal and in Scotland it has been set at 16 years. For these latter countries it should be stressed that the age of 17 or even 16 from which adult criminal law applies does not necessarily mean a reinforcement of punitive ideas regarding this category of minors. Most countries operate a period of transition where young adults may be given the benefits of the (less punitive) law designed for minors.

The age of 'criminal minority' - age of criminal responsibility - is the age from which special laws designed for minors apply. In other words this age serves as a demarcation point for the competence of the courts; below this age, children 'depart from the criminal system'. While most countries have effectively fixed a lower limit there is little agreement as to what this limit should be. For example, the threshold has been fixed at seven years by Switzerland and Greece, eight years in Scotland, ten years in Northern Ireland, 12 years in both Portugal and Holland. Poland has set the threshold at 13 years, Austria, Germany, Italy and Slovenia have set the threshold at 14 years while Sweden has fixed this threshold at 15 years. Neither France nor Belgium has fixed a minimum age. In the case of France, it is a judicial solution which prevails in this matter (*Laboube* judgement of 13 December 1956). This judgement stipulates that the lack of responsibility of the child does not exclude guilt, except for very young children who do not possess the faculty of discernment, for participation in a material act presupposes, even in the case of an unintentional infraction, that the perpetrator has acted with intelligence and will. Since that decision young children cannot be charged with an offence. As a general rule the judges fix the threshold at 13 years, according to circumstances, for the purpose of ordering measures of protection for irresponsible minors.

There are further uncertainties regarding the concepts of the age of criminal responsibility and 'criminal minority'. In most cases, the age of criminal responsibility coincides with that of criminal minority. Greek law operates a clear distinction. While criminal minority is fixed at seven years (the child cannot be subject to any measures and *a fortiori* criminal proceedings), that of criminal responsibility is fixed at 12 years. In England and Wales and in Northern Ireland the age of criminal responsibility is set at ten and children under that age cannot be found guilty of a criminal offence. However, children between ten and 13 are presumed in law to be *doli incapax* (incapable of criminal intent) and this presumption must be rebutted by the prosecution before they can be convicted. In order to rebut the presumption, the prosecution must show beyond a reasonable doubt that the child appreciated that what he or she did was 'seriously wrong' as opposed to merely naughty or mischievous.

In principle legislators have distinguished two categories of minors: on one hand, children who are regarded as having a complete lack of criminal responsibility (who cannot be punished) and are not subject in any way to juvenile criminal law (or arrangements designed for minors) or adult criminal law, and cannot be made subject to any measures as in Greece, in France praetorian situation, or Holland. The child can only be made subject to measures of protection, assistance and education, most often reserved for minors in danger and ordered by socio-educational, administrative or supervisory services, (Germany, Austria, Slovenia, Portugal) or by the juvenile criminal justice as in France and Holland. On the other hand we have children and young persons who can be made subject to the law dealing with juvenile delinquency, who usually benefit from reduced criminal responsibility.

Although minors aged 12 years are declared as lacking criminal responsibility in Holland, they can be subject to measures of investigation carried out in the framework of criminal proceedings (such as body searches and examinations and any act of confiscation or seizure). Interrogation will be carried out by the juvenile criminal justice who serves as an investigating judge. However these measures taken against the child are of a strictly civil nature. In this framework, the judge can order supervision of the child; this measure is close to the French institution of educational assistance. This supervision is entrusted to the Council for the Protection of Youth, the key (public) organisation in this matter, working in both criminal and civil matters in each court (corresponding to the judicial resort of the Court of Greater Instance in France). This Council nominates a responsible person, who can be either a member of the family or a probation officer, or, if the situation of the minor demands it, order removal from the family environment, or a placement.

The underlying idea of the criminal responsibility of minors places emphasis on criminal capacity, that is, the ability of the juvenile to benefit from the penalty imposed. It is only from the moment that minors can be responsible for their actions that they can be accused of the consequences. To evaluate responsibility, we can refer to two kinds of criteria: either that of discernment (ability to understand and desire) or that of the personality of the minor. These two criteria can be taken separately or together.

Therefore the age of criminal responsibility determines not only the question of ability to commit crime but also when special laws applicable to juvenile delinquents come into effect and the nature of applicable sanctions and measures.

In this respect there exist great disparity in the age threshold of criminal responsibility, as we have noted above, from seven years in Switzerland to 18 years in Belgium and Luxembourg. This disparity concerns both the age at which the minor becomes responsible and liable to criminal penalties in the eyes of the law, and the age of 'criminal majority', after which adult criminal law can be applied. In principle, it is the age at the time of the offence which is the determining factor.

Few legislations have a particular system applicable to young adult delinquents, or young people having reached majority in the eyes of civil and criminal law. There sometimes exist arrangements designed to prolong certain educational measures beyond the age of 'criminal majority'. It is in this way that, since 1975, a measure of judicial protection has been installed in France, permitting juvenile jurisdictions to prolong for five years and within the limit of 23 years, educational measures in an open environment or in a residence, set out in the order of 1945. If the measure is carried out in a residence, its continuation beyond the age of 18 requires the consent of the young adult. Germany, Holland and Slovenia have introduced a category of young people aged 18 to 21 (not past the twenty-first birthday), who can be judged according to rules applicable to minors. But in Slovenia and Holland, young adults are subject to adult courts and not juvenile courts as in Germany. In

Switzerland, young adults are aged from 18 to 25. The Portuguese system also distinguishes the category of 18 to 21-year-olds in setting out special measures, such as measures termed corrective (reprimand, a list of duties to fulfil, fines, or placement in a 'detention centre'). These measures are also applicable to the category of young people aged 16 to 18.

The German legal system, which distinguishes children, adolescents and young adults is a representative example of these legislations. It has installed a system of responsibility particular to minors, which refers both to the personality of the juvenile and the criterion of discernment. With regard to this last criterion, the Italian legal system presents the same peculiarity; the judge assesses the ability of the juvenile (aged 14 to 18) to understand and exercise free choice.

German law distinguishes in fact children aged under 14, for whom the law on juvenile jurisdiction does not apply (art.19 of the German penal code (StGB) due to immunity from criminal proceedings), juveniles, aged from 14 to 18 (not over 18) subject to the 'Jugendgerichtsgesetz' (JGG) and young adults aged 18 to 21. Juveniles from 14 to 18 benefit from reduced criminal responsibility according to personality defined by the subjective criterion of maturity. The young person is therefore evaluated according to moral and intellectual development. This rule is also to be found in Slovenia. In addition there is the criterion of discernment, for the ability to understand the illicit nature of the act is combined with the faculty to act according to this understanding. The judge verifies this correlation and will have experts intervene if necessary. In all cases where juveniles are considered responsible, they will be 'owing' for the offence committed and subject to the legal consequences set out in the juvenile jurisdiction laws. But when the court has removed this responsibility, the juvenile court will remain competent to order protection measures.

Finally, German law distinguishes an age bracket specific for young people aged 18 to 21 (not over 21), classed as young adults. They are subject either to the juvenile delinquent system or the adult system, according to the criteria defined by para. 105 of the law on juvenile jurisdiction, relative to the nature of the offence committed or maturity of the offender. They are judged by juvenile courts and not regular courts, except in exceptional cases enumerated in the law.

In Holland, there is a distinction between four groups of young people. Children under 12, who, as has already been seen, are not criminally responsible, minors aged from 12 to 16 who are judged exclusively according to juvenile criminal law, juveniles aged 16 to 18 who are in principle subject to juvenile criminal law, but exceptionally to adult criminal law, and finally young adults aged 18 to 21 who benefit from this option according to the legal system which applies. Thus in Holland the judge, with regard to the personality of the young person and the gravity of the offence committed, can apply either juvenile criminal law or adult criminal law for an offence committed by a young adult. But in contrast to German judicial practice, juvenile criminal law is seldom applied in these cases.

80

Belgium fixes at 18 the age of criminal and civil majority, but also the threshold of criminal responsibility. Consequently the law of 8 April 1965 applies to all delinquents under 18. However a law of 9 May 1972 takes away from the juvenile court and attributes jurisdictions competent in general law, the requisitions of the public ministry with regard to minors aged over 16 prosecuted in cases of motoring offences and in cases of violations of articles of articles 418, 419 and 420 of the penal code (homicides and intentional bodily harm), where they are connected with motoring offences. This dispensation is not valid in cases of connection with proceedings against the perpetrators of other infractions.

As for young people who have committed an offence after reaching the age of 17, measures can be co-ordinated by a judgement for a period of unlimited duration, which must not extend beyond the young person's twentieth birthday. Moreover, at the petition of the young person or at the requisition of the public ministry in the case of persistent bad conduct or dangerous behaviour of the young person, a prolongation of measures can be ordered for a period of undetermined duration which must not extend beyond the young person's twentieth birthday. These two provisions are the result of a recent legislative change (24 December 1992).

In Portugal, the age of criminal responsibility has been brought to 16 years. A single system of protection applies both to young people in danger and juvenile delinquents aged from 12 to 16 years. Beyond this age limit, the mode of protective, disciplinary or punitive intervention depends on the age of the offender at the time of the infraction. Portuguese law distinguishes two categories of young people: those aged 16 to 18 and those aged 18 to 21. The principle is the application of protective measures in the case of offences committed by a minor aged 16 to 18. However, corrective measures, (implying, as has already been mentioned, restriction or deprivation of liberty) and even penalties appear to be equally applicable to this category.

In Sweden, the age of criminal responsibility is fixed at 15; the applicable law concerns juvenile delinquents aged from 15 to 18 (not over 18).

If the definition of juvenile delinquency covers many different situations, it must be noted that only acts considered to be criminal offences according to adult criminal law are judged in court. There is no special incrimination for minors except to distinguish certain infractions which can only be committed by them, for example driving a motor vehicle without having reached the legal age of 17 or consuming alcohol under the age of 18 in the United Kingdom. Poland and Portugal recognise a state of pre-delinquency (minors in a 'state of demoralisation') for minors under 16 which includes certain violations of social rules, the consumption of drugs or alcohol, prostitution, vagrancy and gang membership. In Portugal the situation of pre-delinquency - including situations of idleness, begging and vagrancy - is taken into account to form a criterion for intervention on the part of judicial or social institutions.

Competent Jurisdictions and Institutions

Most legislations recognise jurisdictional privileges for juvenile delinquents and have installed special juvenile courts (or at least a courtroom specialised in the problems of young people, as in the former Czechoslovakia) or autonomous sections subject to the jurisdiction of general law, composed of judges and prosecutors. On the other hand, Sweden has no juvenile courts; only the social services are competent if the child is aged under 12. Until the age of 15, the inquiry is carried out by the police, but resolution of the litigation is subject to the public prosecution department, youth services or the courts. No juvenile courts exist in Sweden in the sense of specialised jurisdictions for juvenile delinquents. The latter are subject to the criminal jurisdiction of general law, composed of professional judges, assisted by assessors with experience in treatment and education.

In Eastern European countries, as in Poland, it is the family court (since 1978) which has a general competence in matters where juveniles are involved, whether they are delinquents or in danger. It replaces the juvenile court which was created in 1949. The family court is competent where a minor aged 13 to 17 has committed a criminal offence. This does not however exclude the intervention of public organisations.

In some countries, such as Portugal, there is an increase in the role of socio-administrative services (called Commissions of Protection) compared to judicial institutions. The reform of 1978 has set out the possibility of intervention by the 'Commission of Protection' for minors aged under 12 (an administrative organisation dependent on the Ministry of Justice) who are in a situation of delinquency and for whom the juvenile court cannot intervene. Parents however must not be opposed to this; in the latter case, the case is referred to the juvenile court. The new law of 1991 widens the domain of competence of this Commission to minors aged under 12 in a state of pre-delinquency.

A special place must be given to the Scottish system of children's hearings (according to the provisions of the Social Work (Scotland) Act 1968 (but see, now, *Appendix IV*) not only regarding their composition but also their area of competence. The children's hearings are closer to a social or administrative process than a judicial one. On the other hand it has wide jurisdictional powers, exercised by the 'Reporter'. Its area of intervention includes both juveniles in need of protection and minors aged eight to 16 years. The children's hearings have general competence, involving offences committed by minors, except those defined by the Lord Advocate, which are subject to the Sheriff's Court and the High Court. These are serious offences for which the notion of public order is paramount.

Vienna has its own juvenile criminal jurisdiction (*Jugendgerichtshof*) which besides has general competence including cases where care (protection) measures are necessary, where the juvenile is in danger.

The competence of specialised (juvenile) jurisdictions must be extended to young adults aged 18 to 21 in Germany (not over 21).

Jurisdiction is in general exclusive with regard to minors, with the exception of motoring offences as in Belgium or in the case of delegation to the Community Executive competent to take any necessary placement or supervision measures, or offences of the 'fourth category' (regulation) which come under police jurisdiction. This last rule concerning infractions also applies in France (except for offences of the fifth and most serious category) and in Slovenia.

In England and Wales, with the adoption of the Criminal Justice Act 1991, the name 'youth court' was substituted for that of 'juvenile court' to define the jurisdiction competent to judge young people aged 10 to 18.

One often notices the existence of an organisation of prosecution and preliminary investigation specialised in offences committed by minors as in Germany, consisting of the public ministry in Germany or the examining magistrate in France. In Italy there is a judge 'charged with the preliminary investigation', who is not an examining magistrate, but a juvenile criminal justice, different from the judge who will issue a decision. In Holland, the juvenile criminal justice also acts as an examining magistrate. An important institution is the Council for the Protection of Youth, a judicial organisation, charged with assuring the co-ordination of actions taken in favour of juvenile delinquents and minors in danger and measures concerning them. He or she is assisted in his or her daily task by private associations for the assistance of young people.

We often find, except in the case of Italy which sets out a general competence for juvenile courts for juvenile delinquents, the rule of competence of ordinary criminal jurisdictions in cases where both minors and adults are implicated (Greece).

The privilege of jurisdiction, combined with the principle of specialisation, has been introduced according to the educational objective assigned to legislation regarding juvenile delinquents. But the legislator has not completely excluded the legal possibilities of transfer between juvenile and adult jurisdictions and vice versa.

In fact this question concerns, in particular, systems of protection as in Belgium, Scotland, Luxembourg or Poland. It can be observed that systems of protection, not having actual penalties available, still envisage the possibility of setting this system aside in order to allow the possibility of resorting to other sanctions intended for adults. The problem of transfer from one system to the other is also present when minors and adults are implicated in the same case. There often ensues a joining of procedure where adults and minors are tried together.

It has been noticed that cases of abandonment of juvenile jurisdictions or other institutions in favour of ordinary jurisdictions are almost always included in systems of protection. In Belgium and Luxembourg (for minors aged over 16), this power of referral is founded on the desire to propose the most appropriate measure. Two kinds of referral are set out. The first concerns referral from juvenile to adult jurisdiction. 'When the minor is aged more than 16 at the time of the offence and the court considers inadequate an order of care, protection or education, it can, of its own motion, remove itself from the case and refer the matter to the public ministry for the purpose of proceedings before the competent jurisdiction.' This detachment can only take place after a social inquiry and a medical and psychological examination of the juvenile.

In matters of traffic offences, adult jurisdictions have general competence. However they can withdraw from the case and send the juvenile (aged over 16) before the public ministry for the purpose of proceedings in the juvenile criminal court, if discussion of the case makes it appear that a measure coming under juvenile law (care, protection or education) 'would be more adequate for the purpose'.

If the measure of protection taken by the court proves to be ineffective (a preliminary condition) due to persistent bad conduct or dangerous behaviour on the part of the juvenile, the court can decide that the juvenile should be subject to the Community Executive and will no longer benefit from juvenile protection laws. This disposition therefore implies the departure of the young person from the protection system and means that a placement in a penitentiary establishment can be imposed on minors over 16. However this last power involving imprisonment is no longer applied by a decision of community ministers.

In Scotland, there are also special arrangements for young people aged 16 to 20, which allows them to be judged according to adult criminal law.

Still on the subject of measures of protection, it is worth mentioning Portuguese law which has a legal mechanism of transfer between penal and supervisory jurisdictions. If a minor aged over 16 who has already been placed in a reformatory institution commits a crime, he or she will be judged by the juvenile court.

The Swedish penal code provides an original system of referral from ordinary penal jurisdictions to social organisations. In fact, referral to social organisations is intended as a measure which can be ordered by the judge after a crime committed by a young person between 15 and 20, a drug addict, an alcoholic or a person in need of care or psychiatric supervision, if it appears that measures taken in the social framework would be more appropriate. This referral (which in fact follows a declaration of incompetence) is preceded in all cases by an examination of personality (as well as social and family background). This mode of intervention is commonplace. It does not stop the court from subordinating the referral to the imposition of obligations to make good damage caused to the victim or imposing a fine on the juvenile.

In Germany, juvenile jurisdictions have general competence to judge crimes committed by minors and young adults; there is however an exception (para.103 of the law on juvenile jurisdiction: JGG) when adults (aged over 21) and minors are implicated in the same criminal case in financial crime as well a serious crimes (homicides). This detraction from the general competence of juvenile jurisdictions has only a limited practical importance.

Because there are two systems applicable to young adults (either juvenile criminal law or adult criminal law), the judge must decide which law is applicable in view of the criteria set out in para. 105 of the said law. Young adults will be subject to juvenile criminal law when the offences committed also belong to offences committed typically by adolescents and when their psychological and moral development is comparable to that of an adolescent. The arrangements for criminal proceedings designed for minors have only limited application to young adults.

In Holland adult criminal law is applicable to a minor aged 16 to 18 if the degree of seriousness of the offence committed and the personality of the perpetrator demand it (this possibility is essentially relied upon to impose prison sentences or prohibitions concerning driving). Conversely the judge can decide to apply juvenile criminal law to young adults aged 18 to 21, in view of the personal characteristics of the perpetrator.

The second question raised by transfer between jurisdictions is that of the competent jurisdiction when minors and adults are implicated in the same case. Generally in these cases we see an exception to the jurisdictional privilege introduced with regard to minors, who thus will be judged by ordinary criminal jurisdictions (such as in Northern Ireland), with the exception of Austria, which has a public order competence in juvenile criminal justice. The same is the case in the former Czechoslovakia. However, the legislator only intends transfer under certain conditions, often linked with the seriousness of the offence (Germany and Greece).

In Greece, but also in Slovenia, (where a similar situation exists), where minors and adults are involved in the same criminal case, they are judged separately in contraventional and criminal matters. On the other hand, the Parquet has the option of combining the cases into one procedure (before the adult courts) invoking legal imperatives, but only in matters of correction. The law requires a concrete motive for this decision but in practice this requirement is disregarded. In France, there also exists the splitting of proceedings into two when minors and adult accomplices are involved. They are judged by the juvenile criminal justice and the correctional court.

Recognised Rights of Minors

With regard to the defence of juvenile delinquents, it is paradoxical to discover that European legislations, while setting down the principle of exceptional jurisdictions, more protective of the interests of juvenile delinquents, and designing in principle the defence of minors or at least guaranteeing them the same rights as adults (Italy, France, Switzerland, Slovenia, Greece etc.), consider on the other hand that the rights of the child are already sufficiently protected in this way and do not organize in practice the right to defence by a lawyer. Often, it is the delegate (social worker) from a social service of the juvenile jurisdiction who will exercise the prerogatives of a lawyer (Germany, Portugal, Sweden). It is true that certain legislations, such as that of Holland, have extended the area of competence of these organisations, charged with representing the interests of the juvenile. Thus the Council for the Protection of Youth enjoys a legal status, largely that of protection of the juvenile, at all stages of the proceedings and in particular when restriction of liberty is involved. However the Dutch project of reform rejects this postulate according to which the protective nature assigned to all measures taken regarding juveniles is enough to guarantee their defence, and organises intervention by a lawyer at all stages of the proceedings. In refraining from organizing the defence of juvenile delinquents, European legislators have a tendency to sacrifice fundamental rights guaranteed to every individual, in the matter of the right to express oneself before a court and to be heard. Only Anglo-Saxon countries, due to the accusatory nature of their procedures, have given the lawyer a prime place in all criminal proceedings. Thus in Scotland, the rights to defence, such as the right to be present, to be heard, to be represented, to appeal decisions taken by the children's hearing or that of direct oral intervention with the Reporter are expressly recognised.

The most significant reform recently introduced in this area (22 August 1988) is indisputably that which has shaken the foundations of Italian procedural law. However not all new arrangements are applicable to minors. This is the case regarding the possibility given to the accused of personally intervening in debates between the prosecution and the defence as well as the cross-examination and the power to negotiate the sentence with the public ministry. But a certain number of legal guarantees have been enforced or newly introduced concerning minors. In this way efforts have been made to make minors more active and to awaken their understanding to enable them to understand the scope and significance of the legal proceedings. The interrogation of the minor can only be carried out by a judge, who henceforth has the obligation to explain the meaning of different actions in the process, as well as the substance and meaning of the decision taken. In addition, juveniles have the right to have present parents or another person close to them authorised by the judge. But in all cases, they have the right to assistance from educational services and a defence lawyer. Juveniles can also be removed from the courtroom when the discussions centre on their personality. Provisional detention of minors by the police can only take place when they have been caught red-handed committing a very serious offence. The juvenile will immediately be brought before the prosecutor. Parents and educational services are immediately informed.

However it can be seen that the problem of defence of minors, up to now neglected by legislators, is becoming a chief target for reform (Belgium, France, Holland) or has recently been subject to reform, as in Germany or Poland. There, a reform of civil law, has reinforced legal guarantees offered to the juvenile. Informing the minor (from the age of 13) who has committed an offence, explaining the operation of proceedings, as well as a right to information for the victim are now set out in law.

It is in this way that in Belgium a recent decree of the French-speaking Community (1991) lays down an extension of the rights of juveniles subject to a placement. In particular they have been granted :

- the right to communicate with any person of their choice, in the absence of a motivated decision to the contrary by the competent judge;

- the obligation to inform the juvenile, from the moment of being taken into care, of the right to communicate with his or her lawyer.

When young people are in the care of institutions which come under the French-speaking Community, the following obligations are imposed :

- the establishment of a medico-psychological report and a social study for every juvenile placed in an institution for a period exceeding 45 days, and communication with the placement authority;
- providing the young person's lawyer with both documents.

In addition the decree strictly regulates the conditions of putting the juvenile in isolation.

The considerable problem of defending juvenile delinquents is not only encountered on an institutional level, but also in the material sense of its organisation, with regard to the availability of lawyers and their remuneration, not to forget the question of their specialisation in this area. Thus in France local experiments in specialised defence are being carried out, with the support of particular training (legal and psychological/social/educational) of lawyers to improve the quality of defence of juvenile delinquents before the criminal courts. For while the defence of a juvenile is explicitly set out by the order of 2 February 1945, when the juvenile is subject to criminal proceedings, this practice is far from being general.

In Belgium, on the initiative of several Belgian Bars, services of voluntary lawyers are being organized in the courts, to enable a young person to come and consult them before the hearing. However, without a legal foundation, this practice is in danger of encountering opposition from judges.

In Germany, Austria and the former Czechoslovakia, the lawyer can intervene from the beginning of the proceedings. In France this is only possible from the moment the juvenile is charged. The planners of the draft of the 1990 reform have in this way set out that the minor will have the right to a lawyer at all stages of the proceedings; even during the initial investigation.

In Holland, a lawyer will be automatically appointed from the beginning of the proceedings or in the case of remand. For minors under 16, the lawyer is empowered to exercise all rights belonging to juveniles.

In Slovenia, a lawyer is expressly required by law during the preliminary stages (in contrast to the system applied to adults). With a reform in September 1989, anyone suspected of having committed a crime has the possibility of demanding the presence of a lawyer during police interrogation. This arrangement applies to both juveniles and adults.

Legislation has made intervention of the lawyer compulsory when the penalty incurred is greater than five years' imprisonment or when the judge deems this intervention to be necessary.

In Austria, Germany and Greece (where the lawyer intervenes during the investigative phase at the request of the accused), there are also cases of obligatory defence, where otherwise no proceedings can take place, for which the lawyer is chosen by the accused or appointed by the court. Thus, according to German law, in criminal matters, (i.e. when the offence incurs a prison sentence of more than one year) or in all cases if remand has lasted more than three months, and also if the accused is aged under 18 and is put on remand, a lawyer is automatically and immediately appointed. In criminal matters, Greek law stipulates obligatory defence during the hearings.

In Austria for example in cases of compulsory defence, lawyers are almost always automatically appointed for accused juveniles, for it is their own resources which are taken into consideration here and not those of their representatives. Otherwise all individual guarantees of procedural law apply to accused juveniles (presumption of innocence, the right to be heard, etc.).

In Poland, at the end of the preliminary inquiry, the family court judge transfers the case to the family court, before which two types of procedures can take place, civil or criminal. Proceedings will be criminal when the minor is aged 13 to 17 and the judge considers necessary a placement in a correctional facility, i.e. detention. In this case, the juvenile has the right to defence and can appeal. However, the right to consult files is determined by the judge.

As for appeal procedures, few precise details have been communicated on this subject. In Belgium, all decisions taken concerning the juvenile in the framework of application of juvenile law are subject to appeal by the public prosecutor or appeal and opposition by other parties concerned.

In Austria and Holland, appeal procedures are also extended to all decisions taken concerning a minor.

In Germany, after being taken in for questioning, the person arrested must be brought before a competent judge no later than the following day. The judge must inform a member of the family or a trusted person, carry out interrogation and decide on the continuation of custody.

In Greece appeal procedures are more limited than for adult offenders. In principle their extension depends on the penalty imposed. Educational or therapeutic measures are never subject to appeal; the court can change its decision at any moment. A prison sentence is only subject to appeal when it exceeds one year.

In France the juvenile can appeal (even without assistance) all measures (provisional or final), but in practice is rarely informed of this right.

Reform Projects

The examination of answers given to this question reveals a period of profound transformation of legal arrangements applicable to minors. The belief in the need for reforms to be brought to current law is almost universal, which gives an incomparable dynamism to the subject. Even countries which have recently reformed their legislation (for example Germany) admit that they are not entirely satisfied and envisage further modifications in the short term. This general movement which is driving juvenile criminal law reflects a considerable effort by practitioners, legislators and researchers to find better answers in the struggle against juvenile delinquency and to protect children in danger. In these reform projects we find guiding principles which appear unavoidable (supremacy of educational action, diminution of custodial sentences, emphasis on informal solutions accompanied with new forms of reactions (mediation, reparation, etc.) and, especially, development of the idea of making offenders responsible (particularly in France and Holland).

The common denominators of reform projects existing in practically all the countries studied (except Austria) have been elaborated under the pressure of international trends and the desire to harmonise legislation with new international rules (e.g. the Beijing Rules). In this respect the Slovenian project of March 1992, reforming the Penal Code, also sets out changes concerning juveniles and refers directly to these principles in introducing flexible educational measures and especially in emphasising the open environment. The reform law was passed by Parliament in 1994 and came into force at the beginning of 1995.

However, the reform movements noted also conform to national peculiarities.

In Greece it has been proposed to introduce new intermediate measures. In 1990 a commission of experts was called together to reform legislation and combat juvenile delinquency. This commission recommended the introduction of alternatives to remand in relation to adults and to combine procedures only in very exceptional cases. As for so-called therapeutic measures, the examining magistrate can send a young drug addict to a special centre for observation and/or therapy. Moreover, participation in therapeutic programs is encouraged, while at the same time parental obligations are transferred to suitable persons or services for the assistance of children. The juvenile can also be sent to a special section for observation and/or therapy. This reform comes under the international Beijing Rules.

Reforms in matters of legal protection have the aim of avoiding placement in an institution as a preventive measure and establishing open or partially open educational institutions. In this respect the three projects in preparation have been criticised with regard to a lack of determination of criteria of intervention. The domain of application of future legislation must be extended to young people aged seven to 21.

In France, the current project of reform of juvenile criminal law, made public on 10 July 1990, maintains the fundamental principles fixed by the order of 2 February 1945 (primacy of education over criminal sanctions, specialisation of jurisdictions and principle of continuity). It tends to restore the primacy of educational action and to favour the emergence of legal responses within a reasonable time-frame to delinquent acts committed by minors. The centre of gravity of the reform consisted of a redefinition of the system of applicable sanctions to juvenile delinquents and the proclamation of new principles. In this way, the imposition of a sentence should be the exception, and required the judge to justify his/her decision. In addition, only penalties intended for minors in the framework of the law were applicable to them. The imprisonment of minors was abolished as a correctional measure.

Today the project has practically been abandoned, but a ministerial circular of 15 October 1991 takes up certain points of the project in advocating the development of legal defence of minors, encourages the closing of cases with a caution or under the condition of making reparation and sets out a system of penalties specific to minors.

In Germany, the parliament, in adopting the reform of 20 June 1990, invited the government to make new changes concerning in particular the:

- penal system affecting young adults;
- relationship between educational and disciplinary measures;
- conditions for imposing prison sentences;
- reinforcement of the legal defence of minors;
- risk of the extension of supervision of the minor (concept of education and principle of proportionality);
- redefinition of the status of, and tasks delegated to, social services in juvenile jurisdictions;
- problems of investigative measures and channels of recourse;
- training of judges, prosecutors and defence lawyers;
- taking into account of the interests of females receiving sentences in the process of sentencing and the carrying out of legal sanction;
- re-evaluation of penal mediation.

A parallel discussion took place regarding the abolition of prison sentences due to 'dangerous tendencies' and the reduction of the minimum sentence. Some parties advocate the raising of the age of criminal responsibility to 16, extension of the field of application of suspended sentences and partial revocation. Also advocated were the abolition of the distinction between educational and disciplinary measures in favour of a single category of educational measures, improvement in the mechanisms of informal solutions and constitutional guarantees, changes concerning the obligation to record the disposition of cases in a criminal record, the limitation of remand and its exclusion for 14 to 15-year-olds. Finally it was strongly recommended that the system for young adults should be integrated into juvenile criminal law, and that the principle of proportionality as a maximum limit to all interventions should be precisely defined.

In Portugal current reform aims for a restructuring of supervisory services on the basis of a new educational model of intervention, intended to remove social stigma and to seek the active participation of the local community.

In Poland juvenile law is a neglected sector but current doctrine strongly encourages reform efforts.

In Sweden discussions on reform are at present dominated by the conservative view which advocated the reintroduction of indefinite deprivation of liberty for minors, abolished in 1980.

In the former Czechoslovakia a work group was established in January 1991, drawing essentially on foreign experiments such as the Cologne 'Waage' project and the Austrian model.

In this way penal mediation is a subject for experimentation and a departure point from which cases are transferred by the Public Prosecutor's Department to social workers for an extra-judicial solution.

In Switzerland the draft of a revision of juvenile criminal law by Professor M. Stettler in 1983 has been studied by a federal commission. The final report was published in 1993. Among the changes envisaged, it has been proposed to raise the age of criminal responsibility from seven to 12 years; therefor there would be a distinction between minors aged 12 to 16 (no longer 15) and adolescents aged 16 to 18. In civil law it has been planned to reduce the age of majority from 20 to 18. The draft of a bill emphasised the necessity of developing interventions in an open environment, introducing penal mediation, reinforcing community service as a measure of intermediate treatment as well as extending techniques of closing procedures. Moreover, a limitation of remand is envisaged with regard to minors aged over 15, as well as the extension of suspension of sentence with probation. It has also been proposed to reinforce legal guarantees for the juvenile, in particular regarding the assistance of an automatically appointed lawyer and the widening of channels of recourse.

In Austria, where the last reform dates from 1989, current efforts are to be found more on the practical level and aim to improve co-operation between legal and educational services and to develop intermediate measures.

In Belgium, the 'Wathelet' project proposes to modify the law of 8 April 1965 concerning the protection of youth. The Belgian report lists the essential points of the new reform:

- development of procedures necessary for the carrying out of legal protection for minors in danger organised by the decrees of the Communities, as well as the position of the rights of the minor before a juvenile court;
- modification of article 53 concerning the possibility of confining the juvenile to a detention centre;
- abolition of the measure of detention at the pleasure of the state.

In addition, a certain number of procedural guarantees will be reinforced with respect to minors:

- limitation of the duration of preliminary proceedings to six months (apart from cases where judicial inquiry is required);
- limitation to three months (renewable) of the duration of placement of a minor who has committed an offence, in a closed establishment within the community;
- the right of a minor, from the age of 12, to be heard personally by the juvenile court judge, before any provisional measure;
- the right to the assistance of a lawyer during any appearance before a juvenile court (including cases of provisional measures). If the juvenile does not have a lawyer, a lawyer must be automatically assigned. If

there is a conflict of interests, the minor must be assisted by a lawyer other than the one who would have been consulted by parents or other guardians;

- the right of the minor, parents or other guardians, to receive a copy of the order (therefore an obligation to inform the parties of facts concerning them and the factors justifying the order);
- in the case of appeal against a provisional measure, the decision must be taken within three months of the act of appeal;
- regulation of the possibility of appeal by a juvenile against an order of placement in a closed establishment;
- widening of the possibilities - for the lawyer and other parties - of accessing the dossier;
- the obligation to re-examine all measures taken with regard to a juvenile delinquent, before the expiration period of a year;
- the juvenile court must hear minors from the age of 12, in civil law litigations which concern their guardianship (parental authority, rights of supervision and visitation in the case of divorce, designation of a replacement guardian in the case of degeneration, the administration of the possessions of the minor, etc.).

It is important to note that a much more fundamental reform of Belgian juvenile law is undergoing study. According to the first options taken by the Commission charged with its preparation, the present 'protective' law could be replaced by a 'sanction-oriented' law, founded not on penalties but on 'educational sanctions' (reprimand, light fines, assistance, probation, placement with an educationally oriented person or institution). In this new system, which would apply the principle of the proportionality of social reaction to the act committed, legal intervention would have an educational and not a punitive aim.

The Dutch reform project, which was passed by Parliament in 1995 and came into force at the end of that year, deserves particular attention, in the sense that it corroborates exactly the signs of evolution of juvenile criminal law. This project, submitted in 1988, centres on two points: the improvement of the rights of juveniles during proceedings and the laying out of the system of sanctions applicable to minors. Regarding this first point, it is undeniable that the project departs from the idea according to which it is in the very (protective) nature of juvenile proceedings to assume the function of defence. In this project the right of the child to be defended by a lawyer has been proclaimed. If necessary the lawyer can be automatically appointed from the beginning of proceedings in the police station or even when the disposition of the case is being decided. The decision will b taken by the prosecutor with the participation of the judge and the Council for the Protection of Youth.

The second point of the reform concerns the system of sanctions. Among other things it is proposed to unify custodial sentences. Thus, in relation to, placement in a penitentiary institution these concern:

- the right of a minor, from the age of 12, to be heard personally by the juvenile court judge, before any provisional measure;
- the right to the assistance of a lawyer during any appearance before a juvenile court (including cases of provisional measures). If the juvenile does not have a lawyer, a lawyer must be automatically assigned. If there is a conflict of interests, the minor must be assisted by a lawyer other than the one who would have been consulted by parents or other guardians;
- the right of the minor, parents or other guardians, to receive a copy of the order (therefore an obligation to inform the parties of facts concerning them and the factors justifying the order);
- in the case of appeal against a provisional measure, the decision must be taken within three months of the act of appeal;
- regulation of the possibility of appeal by a juvenile against an order of placement in a closed establishment;
- widening of the possibilities - for the lawyer and other parties - of accessing the dossier;
- the obligation to re-examine all measures taken with regard to a juvenile delinquent, before the expiration period of a year;
- the juvenile court must hear minors from the age of 12, in civil law litigations which concern their guardianship (parental authority, rights of supervision and visitation in the case of divorce, designation of a replacement guardian in the case of degeneration, the administration of the possessions of the minor, etc.).

It is important to note that a much more fundamental reform of Belgian juvenile law is undergoing study. According to the first options taken by the Commission charged with its preparation, the present 'protective' law could be replaced by a 'sanction-oriented' law, founded not on penalties but on 'educational sanctions' (reprimand, light fines, assistance, probation, placement with an educationally oriented person or institution). In this new system, which would apply the principle of the proportionality of social reaction to the act committed, legal intervention would have an educational and not a punitive aim.

The Dutch reform project, which was passed by Parliament in 1995 and came into force at the end of that year, deserves particular attention, in the sense that it corroborates exactly the signs of evolution of juvenile criminal law. This project, submitted in 1988, centres on two points: the improvement of the rights of juveniles during proceedings and the laying out of the system of sanctions applicable to minors. Regarding this first point, it is undeniable that the project departs from the idea according to which it is in the very (protective) nature of juvenile proceedings to assume the function of defence. In this project the right of the child to be defended by a lawyer has been proclaimed. If necessary the lawyer can be automatically appointed from the beginning of proceedings in the police station or even when the disposition of the case is being decided. The decision will b taken by the prosecutor with the participation of the judge and the Council for the Protection of Youth.

The second point of the reform concerns the system of sanctions. Among other things it is proposed to unify custodial sentences. Thus placement in a penitentiary institution for minors and detention would be abolished in favour of a single penalty reserved for young people. In the same way, the current 'detention at the pleasure of the state' (which consists of placing the juvenile in an institution for an indefinite period) and placement in an establishment for special treatment (concerning difficult minors with psychological problems) would be replaced by a single custodial measure consisting of placement in an institution for young people. In the same pattern of moderation of penalties, it is proposed to introduce community service, reparation of damage by the perpetrator and participation in training programs, as alternatives to the most common penalties of fines and imprisonment.

In Slovenia, a general reform of the penal code, where arrangements concerning juvenile delinquents are included, was passed in 1994. Without overturning the foundations of criminal law, this project considerably widens the range of measures designed for juveniles, distinguishing measures in an open environment and those in a secure environment. Preference is indisputably given to measures in an open environment, for which two new modes are maintained: reprimand and supervision of the juvenile by the social service, while at the same time proposing to abolish present forms of supervision by parents or a designated family. Moreover, inspired by the German model, there is the wish to introduce a list of obligations to be fulfilled and restrictions to be observed, including compensation of the victim by material or non-material means (carrying out work for the victim) for the damage caused, or community service for a public institution or humanitarian organisation. In addition, there is also an intention to put into place courses of social education. The minor can be obliged to attend educational, professional or health centres or to take an examination on the Highway Code, or be banned from driving a vehicle.

Institutional measures have not undergone profound changes. Only the maximum duration of imprisonment for minors has been reduced from ten to five years. There is also the possibility of imposing a fine on a minor who has the necessary financial means.

Modes of Intervention

In almost all the legislations studied it is possible to distinguish measures of protection with an educational content and sanctions (of a penal nature) in accordance with the two-way system of sanctions (protective/punitive).

Only Belgium (and Scotland with the system of children's hearings, applicable until the age of 16), based on the absolute assumption of non-discernment and also lack of criminal responsibility of minors aged under 18, sets out measures of care, preservation or education, excluding the sentencing of minors. However measures of placement in a secure environment or measures of provisional placement in a detention centre for 15 days, do exist and can in fact have a punitive image in practice, even if the case is different in terms of the law. In other words, the punitive aspect is not excluded from a system of legal protection. In this respect, the Portuguese system, which has only measures of protection for children under 16 - whether they are delinquent or pre-delinquent - has not excluded penalties for young people aged over 16.

Beyond the traditional distinction of educational (protective) measures and penalties (sanctions with a punitive character) we must take into account the moment at which they are imposed. In other words, there is a distinction between pre-sentencing measures (before judgement) and measures imposed at the time of judgement (measures being taken here as a legal consequence of the offence).

In addition, Germany (as well as Slovenia) has measures intermediate between penalties and educational measures, termed disciplinary measures (with correctional content). In contrast with Germany, it appears that in Slovenia, these disciplinary measures, due to the flexibility of their modes of application, have received a great deal of approval from practitioners. But before considering these different formal modes of intervention, it is important to give a place to pre-sentencing measures (before judgement) which are being developed in all the countries consulted, independently of the legal system or opportunities governing public action.

Objectives

Legislation is imprecise, vague and sometimes silent concerning the aims assigned to interventions regarding minors. The concepts of education, assistance and protection recur as 'guiding principles' in most legislations (such as that of Holland), in accordance with the priority of the educational concept over that of retribution.

It appears that the educational concept is being neglected in favour of social insertion or reinsertion (France, Belgium, Ireland, Sweden in particular due to its social legislation). It is interesting to note the evolution of the educational concept in Germany. Criminal legislation applicable to minors had a clearly defined objective, at least in spirit. The educational concept has been put into operation as a limiting criterion in juvenile criminal law compared to adult criminal law, the latter being dominated by the principle of retribution. In fact education is no longer defined as an end but rather as a means to ensure the protection of society. The considerations of individual prevention are explicitly set out. The same is true of Austria, where the educational concept does not govern legislation on juvenile delinquents, or Slovenia, where aims linked to education, social reinsertion and the prevention of future offences are closely linked. Penal sanctions in Sweden are influenced by the same considerations.

In other words the greatest concern of legislators is to prevent the repetition of offences.

However, it is undeniable that the idea of making minors responsible, particularly in the area of sanctions, is growing in popularity (e.g. in Holland or in France).

In Greece the examination of personality plays a predominant role compared with the examination of the offence in the choice of sanctions (individualisation of treatment). This is linked to the predominance of individual prevention. What is sought is the sanction most suited to the personality of the juvenile; that which is sufficient and necessary to prevent repeat offending (danger prognosis).

Criteria

The criteria determining the choice of intervention (penalty/measure) are not clearly defined by explicit formulation in the law and appear to be greatly dependent on the type of legislation (penal/protective).

It seems however that the seriousness of the infraction has become the dominating factor in many legislations. This is the case in England, where the Criminal Justice Act 1991 made a decisive step in this direction, explicitly emphasising the seriousness of the infraction. Objective criteria, drawn from the principle of legality, like the proportionality of the sanction or the seriousness of the offence, are still present in penal systems (in particular those strongly influenced by the 'justice' model such as Italy or Germany), while in systems of protection, reference is made more often to the personality and 'needs of the minor' (Belgium, Scotland), to determine the most appropriate measure. In Poland on the other hand, where deprivation of liberty is concerned (in fact detention of a young delinquent) it is ensured that the measure is justified compared to the degree of 'moral degeneration' and also compared to the circumstances and nature of the infraction, especially if previous measures have been ineffective. The idea of 'moral degeneration' is the key concept of Polish legislation. It covers a certain number of circumstances on which the law is not exhaustive. This situation is established in the case of violation of social rules, the commission of a forbidden act, failure to meet school or work obligations, consumption of alcohol, debauchery or vagrancy. From the evaluation and confirmation of this state, all public intervention is legitimised, without referring to the criterion of the offence, as defined in terms of criminal law.

With regard to other measures of protection, emphasis is placed on the personality, age, health, degree of physical and mental development, peculiarities of character and behaviour, the degree of 'moral degeneration', the environment where the minor lives as well as legal precedents. It is however interesting to note that the Portuguese system subordinates the imposition of measures of protection concerning young people aged 16 to 18, to the personality of the minor, the circumstances of the offence and the penalty incurred, which must not exceed two years' imprisonment.

In most cases we encounter a combination of criteria: the seriousness of the offence, the circumstances of its commission, and legal precedents as well as the needs of the perpetrator, which determine the sanction.

In Switzerland, educational measures are expressly subject to 'particular educational needs'. In many countries such as France, Sweden and especially Holland, it appears that, above all, pragmatic solutions are preferred. The choice of sanction remains 'the affair of the juvenile court judge' or in Holland 'the affair of the prosecutor', who has incomparable leeway.

It is important to differentiate the system of educational measures and that of penalties. Often, in contrast to penalties, educational measures can be imposed, even in the absence of criminal offences, when the minor is considered to be in moral danger and liable to subsequently commit an offence. A preventive function is assigned to educational measures. In a system of legal protection, such as that of Poland (where the state of 'moral degeneration' of the minor is the question) all protective measures can be applied without the necessity to demonstrate the commission of an offence.

This rule can also be applied within a criminal system such as that of France, where the situation of moral danger of the juvenile is sufficient to justify the possibility of subjecting him or her to educational measures. In this sense, educational measures resemble security precautions.

The principle of proportionality, guaranteeing the moderation and sufficiency of the intervention according to the offence committed, does not appear in legislation, except in Germany, where intervention of whatever nature must be necessary and not disproportionate. It is in this way that the detention of minors is taken into consideration when, due to 'dangerous tendencies', educational or disciplinary measures are not sufficient or when the seriousness of the offence requires a penalty.

In France priority is given to the examination of the personality of the perpetrator, in the framework of investigative measures, which must make possible the imposition of the most appropriate measure. The examination of personality is carried out by a social inquiry and/or medical or medical/psychological examination, experts, consultation with an educational direction, or an educational report of orientation made by the educational service to the court. The examination of personality is mentioned in Portugal, Scotland (concerning children's hearings) and in Switzerland and Holland.

It seems that the seriousness of the offence or fault (as in Germany and Austria concerning prison sentences for minors, or Portugal and recently even England) is a determining criterion for the mode of intervention. This seems even to be confirmed in Belgium where, in principle, only the needs of the minor guide the choice of intervention. But, as the author of the Belgian report points out, 'it would be unrealistic to consider that elements such as repeat offending, failure of previous measures, or the security of society, do not interfere with the decision of the judge, even if these criteria do not appear in the law.'

With regard to Scotland, it has been established that measures of protection taken by children's hearings are not determined according to the seriousness of the offence, but according to the needs of the young person. However, in the case of infractions where the public interest is at stake (defined as already stated by the Lord Advocate), it is indeed criteria related to the infraction, such as seriousness of the offence, the circumstances, as well as the legal history of the juvenile, which are taken into consideration. Generally, the criterion of the seriousness of the offence is not used to impose heavier penalties on minors but to define the nature and severity of the penalty to be imposed for serious offences. In this area the principle of imprisonment as a 'last resort' is applied, and is limited to the most serious cases.

In Germany, the only reference to the seriousness of the offence, or guilt related to the offence committed, found in juvenile legislation concerns the imposition of prison sentences on minors. Here, the reference made to 'dangerous tendencies' as a condition of the imposition of prison sentences on minors is indeed a remnant of the idea of danger potential and has often been used to justify incarceration. In this respect it is important to emphasise that Italian legislation has purely and simply abolished the notion of danger potential and even that of educational needs of minors which justify the imposition of prison sentences. Thus the possibility of detaining a minor 'judged a danger to society' in a correctional institution (prison) has been replaced in the new Code by a placement in an educational institution.

It is important to stress that even countries termed 'legalistic' are moving towards diversions based on the educational idea, in lieu of punitive measures. German (adult) criminal law stipulates for each incrimination a legal framework within which the judge must determine the penalty to be imposed according to the degree of guilt (fault). This fixed limit cannot be exceeded. In juvenile criminal law this rule does not apply. Even though the law does not determine a precise limit concerning the applicable measure, it is indisputable that the measure imposed must not exceed the maximum limit, fixed according to the seriousness of the offence, i.e. the maximum penalty incurred according to general criminal law.

It has been empirically demonstrated that practice is oriented less towards the personality of the perpetrator than the seriousness of the offence to determine the measure or penalty to impose. The measure is often marked by a 'supplement' of duration for educational reasons. It is therefore probable that for comparable crimes and perpetrators, the sentence to be served is longer for juvenile delinquents than for adults.

Such vicissitudes of the educational idea seem still more important in one-way systems of protection, where it is clearly stated that measures can be more severe for minors than for adults, due to the notion of 'educational needs' which determines the choice of measure. In addition, indefinite duration of measures, such as in Belgium, which can be in the form of placement in a secure environment leads to an increase in the severity of sanctions compared to adults. It is common practice in Belgium, for example, for a custodial sentence of less than four months to be suspended or not even carried out in the case of adults. This legislation which has, as a corollary, a great deal of individualisation of measures, implies a possible inequality of treatment between delinquent minors and adults.

The same is the case in Northern Ireland where it is emphasised that certain penalties can be more severe for juveniles than for adults. This statement has been illustrated by a concrete example. A juvenile can be sentenced to a two-year 'training school order' for an offence for which an adult would never be sentenced to two years' imprisonment. This leads, at least from the point of view of duration, to more severe sanctions being imposed on minors. In Portugal some so-called protection measures can be more severe and carry a greater stigma than correctional penalties.

The inequality of treatment between juveniles and adults can have structural origins and may be founded on the 'danger potential' or 'educational needs' of the minor. In Holland there are two measures, which were related in their function, to security measures, the 'detention at the pleasure of the state' and placement in an institution for special treatment. The two, particularly the first, were custodial, had an undetermined duration, dealt with serious offences and had no equivalent in adult criminal law.

The first of these measures is placement in an institution, ordered by the Minister of Justice, with regard to minors who are seriously threatened in their physical and moral development. This measure ends at the age of 18. The second measure is applicable only to minors who are found to be partially or totally lacking in responsibility; it involves confinement in a special establishment. In practice, there was no longer any difference between these two types of establishment and the distinction has been abolished by the new Dutch Law of 1995.

In Greece, as sanctions are determined according to the personality of the offender, they can sometimes be out of proportion to the offence committed, which is why legal doctrine recommends respect for the principle of proportionality in the sentencing of minors. The possibilities of lightening the penalty, such as suspension of sentence, fines or community service as a substitute penalty do not exist for minors. This can lead to inequality of treatment. In addition the minimum duration of sentences is six months (or five years for minors, in certain cases) and is ten days for adults. Here too this rule is liable to be weighted unfavourably against young adults, who can be more severely penalised than adults for the same offence. Moreover, the duration of the sentence imposed is not determined by the court, (as it is with adults) but is fixed during its execution.

Pre-sentence Measures

Measures to provide background information
Measures intended to provide information to the court are distinguished by their number and variety. They can however be grouped together according to the aims they pursue. As juvenile law is essentially oriented towards understanding the personality of the person who has committed the offence, a certain number of measures are acts of investigation ranging from social or

medical/psychological investigations to placement under observation. The investigation of personality is almost universal in juvenile legislation; experts have a place of choice in this area.

The second category concerns measures which are intended to guarantee good practice in procedures concerning the infraction committed by a juvenile, that is, all forms of detention before judgement, be it remand or supervision or even an institutional placement. However, provisional placement in an institution, of which the duration is rarely specified, predominates, at least in a qualitative sense (the former Czechoslovakia, Belgium, Germany, France, Portugal, Switzerland, Slovenia). It is also noted that there are few procedural guarantees which accompany these measures except the case of placement in a residence in Germany.

Generally, two types of inquiry are to be found concerning minors: the first, with medical elements, is designed to probe the personality of the juvenile. The second is social, concerning knowledge of the environment in which the minor lives (Germany, England and Wales, Austria, Belgium, Scotland, France, Greece, Holland, Northern Ireland, Italy, Poland, Portugal, Slovenia, Sweden, Switzerland and the former Czechoslovakia). In these two cases, the intervention of experts is unavoidable in criminal proceedings against a juvenile. The term 'expert' of course includes all specialists from the educational, social and medical fields as well as psychologists and psychiatrists. Attention is often attracted by the frequent establishment of educational (social) services within the court system composed of social workers (Germany, Austria, France, Greece, Holland, Slovenia), usually charged not only with participating in investigations, in particular with regard to the social environment where the minor lives, but also having a consultative and advisory role regarding measures to be taken, while at the same time providing assistance to minors during the proceedings, except in Holland where their role is greater.

The role of the specialist is therefor to provide the judge with knowledge and evaluation of the juvenile by means of a medico-psychological examination. Some legal systems make intervention of the specialist systematic and obligatory (France, Holland, Switzerland), during the phase of investigation. Thus in France, the expert must be consulted as part of investigative proceedings regarding the personality of the minor. The judge can only make an exemption by means of a specially motivated order.

In Sweden, also, the examination of personality is compulsory if the penalty involved is a prison sentence exceeding six months, a supervision order or referral to a social organisation. This examination is carried out by the Probation committee. The examination of personality is compulsory in Holland for criminal offences. It is carried out before judgement, either by an expert, if the case is complicated, or by a social worker. These investigative measures include a medical or medico-psychological examination of behaviour which can be accompanied by observation in an open or closed environment (maximum one month in Switzerland, Portugal, and Slovenia, three months in Poland). In the latter case, the clinical observation, which is compulsory before the imposition of a custodial sentence (in a correctional institution), is accompanied by a placement of 14 days maximum.

In Germany and Austria, the judge calls on the specialist to determine the degree of maturity of the juvenile, which affects his or her criminal responsibility. In Germany, the specialist will also intervene at the request of the judge to evaluate the degree of maturity of young adult delinquents (aged 18-21), which determines the legal system to be applied (juvenile criminal law or adult criminal law).

The inquiry into the social environment where the minor lives is found in almost all the countries studied; it is carried out by social workers or through the intermediary of services attached to juvenile jurisdictions. In Scotland, the inquiry into the social environment is compulsory before the children's hearing makes a decision on the measure to be taken. It is possible in certain cases to ask for the intervention of psychologists and psychiatrists.

Beyond these measures ordered within the framework of investigation, and aiming to prepare an individualised response, there are measures with the aim of protecting the juvenile for the duration of the proceedings; these can only be ordered provisionally.

It is in Belgium that the greatest variety of provisional measures exists, as all final measures, apart from reprimand, can be taken provisionally (measures of care, placement or surveillance) and are not therefore subject to any conditions regarding duration. They are not subject to actual control, but the judge is charged with their execution. Considering the importance of these interventions, the rights of the juvenile are not well protected as the assistance of a lawyer is not required until the stage of judgement. The most serious measure is remand for a maximum of 15 days in a detention centre, which in terms of the law will only be taken when it is 'physically impossible to find an individual or institution able to receive the minor immediately so that the measures set out in article 52 (provisional measures) cannot be carried out.' This arrangement in Belgian law was censured by the European Court of Human Rights on 29 February 1988 in the *Bouamar* case. Its application has since then been considerably reduced. At present it is expected to be adjusted by the addition of extra guarantees as follows :

- placement in a detention centre for a maximum of 15 days is only applicable to juveniles who have committed a criminal offence and were aged at least 14 years at the time of the decision;
- this measure can only be ordered once in the course of proceedings;
- the rights of the juvenile (possibilities of appeal) are better guaranteed and the decision of appeal must be forthcoming within five working days.

As in Germany these measures are taken with the aim of protection to avoid more serious damage to the juvenile and to preserve him or her from committing further offences. (In Sweden they apply in particular in cases of abuse and family conflicts, etc.) In this respect some legislations set out provisional placement in an institution (residence). In Portugal, the judge can return the juvenile to the family during the process of investigation, but also order a placement in a care establishment and observation by a specialised service. The maximum duration is fixed at 20 days.

In addition, as an example of provisional measures designed to accompany the juvenile, there exists the French system of probation. The measures of probation, with nomination of a delegate, permit the continued education of juveniles in their natural environment. This measure can be ordered, provisionally, during the investigative stage by the juvenile court judge or by the examining magistrate. It translates into observation in an open environment. It can also be ordered as an experiment, before a final decision is made. Finally, probation can be ordered as a final measure.

A parallel system exists in Austria. However it is only possible if such a measure is expected at the stage of judgement. Otherwise all educational measures which come under the jurisdiction of guardianship can be ordered provisionally, for the duration of proceedings.

In Poland, the judge can order the supervision of a minor, delegated to a guardian or other responsible person.

In Germany, the judge can take all sorts of measures relative to the education of a minor, but they must be devoid of coercion. In this case, the juvenile will be received into a residence, a family or a community. In the case of placement in a residence, the procedure concerning the relevant rights and guarantees (informing the family, the social services connected with the juvenile jurisdiction and the lawyer, hearing the minor and legal representatives) are the same as for remand.

The final category of provisional measures are designed to ensure the effective carrying out of investigative procedures and to avoid any risk of repetition of the infraction, such as remand or police custody. These measures are above all preventative and both imply an infringement of individual liberty through deprivation of liberty prior to judgement.

Preventive Measures Involving Deprivation of Liberty

Police Custody
This is exceptional for juvenile delinquents. France, Holland, Portugal, Italy, Sweden and Poland have systems of police custody, such as provisional arrest by the police, but the modes of application differ from one country to another. Moreover, the duration of police custody, when possible, (in France and in Portugal in the case of young people aged 16 to 18), is also not subject to special conditions or arrangements regarding minors.

With the reform of the Code of Criminal Procedure by the law of 4 January 1993, French legislators set out measures of adjustment of police custody in favour of minors and formally excluded this measure for minors aged under 13. For minors over 13 placed under police custody, 'the legal police officer must inform the parents, guardian, the person or service who has charge of the minor of the measure taken concerning the minor'. In addition the law transforms the *possibility* for the minor to be assisted by a lawyer into an *obligation*.

If no lawyer is chosen by the minor or legal guardians, one will be appointed automatically. Besides these recent adjustments, the system of police custody comes under procedural regulations applicable to adults. It will be seen that only Holland has truly designed a specific procedure in favour of juvenile delinquents. Sweden and Italy only mention police custody in cases where the minor has been caught red-handed. The maximum duration of police custody in Poland is 48 hours. In exceptional cases it can be prolonged by 14 days.

Thus in Italy police custody is subject to strict conditions. It must involve the arrest of a minor who has been caught red-handed and the crime must be serious, i.e. subject to a minimum of nine years' imprisonment. The public prosecutor is immediately informed. The latter can order that the minor should be taken to a centre of 'initial reception' or placed in an establishment for minors, or sent home pending further measures. Within 48 hours of the offence, the public ministry must ask the judge responsible for preliminary inquiries at the juvenile court for confirmation of the arrest and when conditions are met, the application of a so-called preventive measure (imposition of rules of conduct, placement in a family or institution or in remand in a penitentiary centre for minors). The centre of initial reception is an innovation of the decree of 28 July 1989. This is a small structure directed by a person with special training (social assistant or educator), where the minor is detained until the decision of the judge, who must rule on the requests of the public ministry. The period of detention must not exceed three or four days. Where possible, this centre will be situated within the court.

In the case of a crime of medium seriousness (subject to a minimum penalty of five years' imprisonment) and for which remand is not permitted, the police can detain the minor in their headquarters, but only for the period necessary to return the minor to the parents. The public prosecutor is immediately informed. If the parents are not found by the police within 12 hours of the arrest or if it appears that they are not capable of assuring the supervision of their child, the public ministry orders that the minor should be brought to a centre of initial reception or an educational establishment. Decisions of the prosecutor must always be confirmed by the judge.

The Dutch system presents some very interesting peculiarities from a comparative point of view. Generally, all investigative procedures applicable to adults are valid concerning minors. Thus the first interrogation by the police will last a maximum of six hours. Police custody is subject to strict conditions. Its maximum duration is fixed at four times 24 hours. Founded on the principles of the European Convention on Human Rights, this period has been reduced (provisionally pending the vote on reform) to three times 24 hours. The Council for the Protection of Youth must be informed. Apart from its legal obligation of preliminary assistance, it establishes a preliminary report, makes propositions as to remand and, especially, possible alternatives. In this respect, the Council can already prepare a course in social training and contact with the family. The major difference between the juvenile system and that of adults is constituted by the possibility of supervision at the home of the parents of the juvenile or that of a guardian or any other appropriate residence. Whatever form it takes, police custody, like remand, can only be envisaged for serious offences (crimes) which incur at least four years' imprisonment or when these measures are specifically mentioned in the law, or in matters of procuring, (which comes under the category of contraventions). The last possibility concerns crimes considered serious by a jurisdiction, comparable in its legal competence to a French correctional court, when the accused has no fixed abode or has committed crimes against property, in customs or tax matters and is in a state of recidivism.

Remand custody

Most often the legal system of remand is not governed by conditions peculiar to minors, but is subject to adult criminal law. Provisional detention is found in almost all the legal systems studied, except Portugal. However when minors have committed crimes, they can be placed under police supervision or in a care establishment until they are brought before a judge.

The motives invoked for a placement in remand are practically identical from one system to another (danger of flight, preservation of evidence, protection of witnesses and public order - particularly in France - necessities for investigation, risk of recidivism and seriousness of the offence).

The principle of the subsidiary nature of remand compared to other less serious measures is sometimes strongly proclaimed in legal texts (Austria, Germany, France, the former Czechoslovakia, Slovenia and Greece).

Only Germany and Holland stipulate the principle of proportionality of remand to the importance of the case and the penalty expected.

In most cases it is the duration of remand which is subject to restrictions compared with adults. In addition it is fixed and limited according to age brackets, except in Belgium, for a placement in a detention centre for a maximum period of 15 days. Provisional detention in Holland is for a maximum of 39 days; then the judgement hearing must take place.

Provisional detention is sometimes used for minors under 15 in Sweden or 16 in France, but only in correctional matters. In Sweden it is permitted only 'in absolutely exceptional circumstances' for minors aged 15 to 18.

To fight against the imposition of remand, French legislators have established educational services within the courts in order to propose to magistrates alternatives to custody. The law has made this consultation compulsory when such a measure is envisaged. Educational services have been established within courts since 1987 to achieve this objective. The legislators have also eliminated remand for minors aged 13 to 16 in correctional matters, and have limited it to a renewable period of six months in criminal matters.

Between the ages of 16 and 18, remand in correctional matters is limited to a period of one month renewable once when the sentence incurred is not more than seven years and in other cases cannot be prolonged for more than a year. In criminal matters, adult arrangements are applicable to minors, but within the maximum limit of two years.

In Greece, the maximum duration of remand is one year in criminal matters (renewable for six months) and six months in matters of less serious offences (renewable for three months). In addition, minors can only be put on remand if the infraction is subject to a sentence of more than ten years according to the terms of criminal law.

In Slovenia, remand is limited to three months.

The system of remand is often subject to special strict conditions, however departures from this system in its application are also very frequent. In this respect, the new Italian regulations present a sad example of the possible misdirections of the progressive spirit of a law.

The initial text of 22 September 1988, had stipulated that remand could be applied to minors who had committed a serious offence subject to a minimum sentence of 12 years' imprisonment. The new text, dated 14 January 1991, extended it to serious infractions subject to a minimum sentence of nine years. In fact, this revision has contributed to the extension of its area of application to almost all crimes, which immediately translated into a considerable increase in remand statistics. Thus in 1991, according to a statistical study made on the application of the new Code of criminal procedure, remand represented 34% of provisional measures, assignment to the home 26.9%, placement in an establishment 18.6% and, finally, measures of judicial control 20.5%. Its duration is half of that envisaged for adults, for minors aged 16 to 18. It is reduced by two thirds for minors aged 15 or 14. The judge is never obliged to take such a measure, but must consider 'the necessity not to interrupt the educational process which is already under way'. The judge can substitute preventive measures. Responsibility for supervising remand lies with the Juvenile Service of the Administration of Justice.

In most cases it is envisaged that the remand will be to a penitentiary establishment specially equipped and separated from adults, or even, as in Holland, in police headquarters, if there is a lack of room in the appropriate establishments. In Greece, minors aged 12 to 15 are placed in an educational residence and in a penitentiary establishment from the age of 15. In France, there is the desire to guarantee the possibilities of educational support and socio-educational or scholastic activities.

The educational (social) services within juvenile courts play an important role here, as in France, Austria, Germany, Italy, Holland, Slovenia and Portugal. They have the mission of assisting and informing the young person throughout the procedure. They often have a consultative role and give advice to the court concerning alternative measures to all kinds of detention.

Alternatives to Remand

There are few alternatives to remand which do not involve deprivation of liberty in countries which have retained placements in a secure environment as an educational measure (Germany, Belgium, Switzerland).

However, in France and Holland for example, the institution of judicial control, consisting of imposing on the accused a series of obligations (whose origins lie in the French system) constitute an interesting alternative to remand. Similar techniques are found in Austria. If judicial control in France is not specific to minors, in Austria, the obligations have been adjusted and adapted to minors (such as checks on school attendance). The Dutch judicial control offers an effective alternative to remand in this respect. As the list of obligations which the judge can impose is not limiting, there results a large variety and especially an adaptation of obligations imposed on juvenile delinquents (community service or courses in social training, for example). The conditions for remand are the same as those for supervision, but special motives are present (such as the danger of flight) which are found in all countries.

In Greece there is also a similar mechanism to judicial control by which the juvenile is under certain obligations and directives (guarantees of representation, limitation of the right to remain).

Germany and Sweden also have similar sets of obligations to which persons accused can be subjected.

France and Austria have measures of probation which cannot carry any restriction of liberty but which are characterised by a strict educational process.

Italy, as we have already mentioned, has interesting alternative measures where remand is permissible. For the record, let us cite the imposition of rules of conduct (imposed in the framework of judicial control), placement in a family or educational establishment, with the creation in this case of so-called centres of 'initial reception' and, finally, confinement to the home.

Measures of Closing Cases

The mechanism of abandonment of proceedings appears to be the formula of preference concerning the responses to juvenile delinquency in almost all countries, without considering the nature of the principle governing public action (opportunity/legality). This movement implies an increase in the role of the public ministry in matters of treatment of juvenile delinquents.

Modes of Intervention

In systems governed by the principle of law, we note a great weakening of this principle (of due process) in favour of the appropriateness of proceedings (for example in Germany, Portugal, Austria, Sweden and Italy), except in the former Czechoslovakia where the principle of the legality of proceedings is applied in the strictest manner. It is in the most wide-ranging system of alternative measures, i.e. diversion from the (juvenile) court by avoidance of criminal proceedings that the mechanisms of informal solutions are developing.

The closing of cases is a common part of the arsenal of state reactions to juvenile delinquency, except for Greece.

It is becoming increasingly common in legislation to introduce the so-called 'conditional' closing of cases, accompanied by mediation or reparation of damage by the perpetrator of the offence, where the closing of cases without follow-up may not be deemed appropriate.

France provides a good example of change in this regard. In recent years, there has been an establishment of projects of mediation and reparation, on the level of the phase of investigation by the public ministry. The law of 4 January 1993, introducing reform of criminal procedure, has instituted new practices of mediation-reparation in criminal matters. This has, de facto, introduced the conditional closing of cases, accompanied by mediation as a particular mode of its power to evaluate the appropriateness of proceedings. In terms of the new article 41 of the Code of Criminal Procedure, 'The Public Prosecutor can, prior to deciding on public action and with the agreement of the parties involved, decide to resort to mediation if it appears that such a measure is liable to ensure the reparation of damage to the victim, to put an end to the discord resulting from the offence, and to contribute to the reform of the perpetrator of the infraction.'

The closing of cases accompanied by conditions is very much a pre-sentencing measure in the respect that judgement will not take place if the juvenile has met the conditions imposed.

Traditionally there is a distinction between countries governed by the principle of law (such as Germany, Austria, Italy, Portugal, Sweden, the former Czechoslovakia) and those countries which have the principle of the appropriateness of proceedings (such as Holland, Belgium and France). In fact, only the former Czechoslovakia categorically excludes the abandonment of proceedings. Portugal has also excluded the abandonment of proceedings in criminal jurisdictions. It is however possible in welfare jurisdictions.

Generally speaking, it has been noted that the erosion of the principle of law in favour of minors is becoming ever greater and receiving a firmer legal foundation, at least in countries where the legality of proceedings is the rule. In these cases, mechanisms of abandonment of proceedings are minutely regulated by the law itself, except in Greece. In Germany, Austria, Slovenia and Italy there exists, besides, the possibility of closing cases due to the insignificance of the offence. In Italy however, this technique was censured by the Constitutional Court in 1991. The public prosecutor closed the case when the offence was minor and casual. This option was very often used in matters of contraventions of the Highway Code and minor thefts. On the other hand, conditional closing of cases, combined with a period of probation, has been maintained.

In Greece, the closing of cases depends on the nature of the offence committed or the penalty incurred. It is only in matters of drug offences that the legislator has set out a mechanism similar to a treatment order which permits the elimination of state action. A second area where closing of cases has been envisaged concerns contraventions after establishment of the facts and hearing of the person accused by the police authorities. A final peculiarity of the Greek system concerns private crimes (abuse, light blows and injuries, trespassing) for which public action only takes place if the victim initiates proceedings. The court has the option of interrupting the judgement hearing for the purpose of conciliation (delinquent-victim). The withdrawal of legal action by the victim means that the perpetrator cannot be penalised.

The public ministry is sometimes obliged to close the case. In Austria for example the public prosecutor must close the case if the following conditions are met: the offence does not incur a prison sentence of more than ten years according to general criminal law, the offence has not caused a death, no other measure appears necessary and it can be supposed that the court would only impose a light sentence.

Countries which maintain the principle of appropriateness are adjusting more and more the options opened by this mechanism in imposing, for example, obligations, in particular that of reparation of damage by the perpetrator of the offence (France, Belgium). But in this last case it is a question of unregulated and unofficial measures, where the public ministry has discretionary power to evaluate how to react to the offence.

In those countries which stress the principle of the legality of proceedings, all mechanisms of abandonment of proceedings as well as the extension of the powers of discretion of the public prosecutor are strictly regulated. The closing of cases is only envisaged for insignificant offences, imposed more by economic constraints (overloading of the courts) than by a choice of criminal policy.

Sometimes the prosecutor can close the case alone, in other cases it is necessary to obtain the agreement of the judge. Sometimes the prosecutor will have simply the option of closing the case, sometimes the obligation. Thus in Germany, the prosecutor will close the case alone without follow-up if proceedings are not in the public interest and if the offence committed is small. The prosecutor will be obliged to close the case if an 'educational measure' of any kind has already taken place and when it is considered that the intervention of a judge or the initiation of proceedings would be of little value for the prevention of future offences.

In certain Anglo-Saxon countries, as in Northern Ireland, jurisdictions have no power to evaluate the appropriateness of proceedings. It is the police who have this option, but jurisdictions can nevertheless suggest it to the police.

It is often noted that in the absence of such powers granted to the police, the police in fact have a certain leeway in that they may decide not to submit to the Public Prosecutor's Department all the statements of certification that a crime has been committed (as in France or Belgium).

Sweden and Holland have made the closing of cases, taken in a wider sense, the principle mode of settling litigation as it constitutes more than 70% of interventions ordered concerning minors.

In Sweden, fines and closing of cases are considered the most appropriate reactions regarding minors from 15 to 17. This position is largely confirmed by figures produced in this area, as these two modes of intervention form 90% of judgements. Moreover, the closing of cases is written down not only in the Code of Criminal Proceedings but also in social law. Since 1988, the police have obtained the very controversial right, in certain cases, to directly instruct the perpetrator to make good the damage caused. In this respect it is worth noting the practices of the Dutch police services which are still unofficial (but legalised in the project of reform which even envisages the presence of a lawyer). In practice police officers are accorded a right to close the most simple cases which have little importance. They can either close the case under the condition that damage be repaired, for example, with a cautioning, or simply close the case.

Despite the principle of legality of proceedings, the mechanisms of abandonment in Sweden are largely open to the prosecutor in the case of offences committed by minors aged 15 to 18.

If measures have already been taken by social services, or if the crime was committed without thought under an impulsion, or if there has already been a placement in a residence, the prosecutor closes the case. In addition, for minor infractions, or if a probation order is expected from the court or if the perpetrator suffers from psychological problems, the prosecutor also closes the case.

The greatest variety of measures for closing of cases is to be found in Holland. The aim is to avoid the referral of minors to the courts, which are judged to be too stigmatising and, in most cases, of little value. For this reason there have been legally established several modes of informal disposition of cases concerning juvenile delinquents. Besides the closing of cases carried out by the police for small offences, as already mentioned, the Public Prosecutor's department has at its disposal penal transactions and other modes of closing cases. These two modes of disposition resemble each other as systems, but the difference is to be found at the level of their effects. While the transaction has a definitive effect and the force of a judgement, the closing of cases has only a temporary effect and can be subject to future proceedings. (However the legal establishment has censured this interpretation). The transaction (as set out in the bill) and the closing of cases can also be accompanied by socio-educational or punitive measures (see infra). The prosecutor also has the power to close the case without any follow-up. If the prosecutor opts for this approach the opinion of the judge must be sought. However, the judge's opinion is not binding on the prosecutor.

These procedures for closing cases are being integrated into programs of diversion from the (juvenile) court (alternative measures) intended to prevent proceedings or a judgement.

Some countries give the same possibility of closing the case to the court (Austria, Germany, Slovenia and Poland). This technique is related in its effects to the legal dismissal of cases which exists in France for example. The court can thus provisionally close the case while placing the individual concerned under probation for one or two years, accompanied by obligations to meet under the supervision of a probation officer or imposing a certain number of obligations which the minor is committed to satisfying. In these cases, if the facts are clearly established and the degree of guilt is not too great, the court can close the case; this is a case of judicial closing of proceedings.

In Poland, the same power is attributed to Family Jurisdictions (and to the examining magistrate).

Imposition of Socio-Educational Measures

By the imposition of socio-educational measures at the closing of proceedings, the aim is to generate awareness, in both the offender and in society, of the existence of criminal law and the consequences of its violation. This generation of awareness has an educational objective and the aim of putting the offender through a process of developing a sense of responsibility. For this reason, if the minor meets the obligation, the case will be closed.

In this respect, German legislation offers multiple techniques widely used in practice. The closing of cases can be carried out on the initiative of the prosecutor, but also that of the judge (the case can be closed up to the point where judgement is final).

Analogous legal arrangements exist in Austria. When the case is clarified, the juvenile has not committed a serious offence and a sanction for the purpose of individual prevention is not required, the court can either fix a period of probation of one or two years, combined with conditions to be met under the supervision of a probation officer nominated for this purpose, or determine a certain number of obligations which the juvenile is committed to fulfilling.

Beyond the traditional technique of closing of cases, which is often however subject to strict conditions of application relative to the offence committed - it cannot be a case of homicide, the offence cannot incur a penalty of more than ten years' imprisonment according to general criminal law and the penalty expected must be 'light' - an original mechanism has been introduced in line with extra judicial mediation and reparation. It consists, for the prosecutor, of closing the case when the minor appears prepared to recognise the facts (admission of guilt is not compulsory) and to adequately repair all the consequences of the offence. In the absence of damage or consent of the victim or when the latter has too high demands, the juvenile has the possibility of making a social contribution (to the community).

Likewise in Portugal, Italy, Sweden and France (newly introduced by the reform of 4 January 1993) the conditional abandonment of proceedings and the obligation to make reparation appears to be a privileged technique of flexible intervention intended to make the young person accept responsibility for his or her actions.

With regard to the mechanisms of informal resolution of conflicts, i.e. outside the traditional judicial framework, the Scottish system of children's hearings deserves attention. The Reporter, an official attached to the Children's Panels, can take informal decisions. The Children's Panels have only one decision to make: to establish whether or not the minor needs compulsory supervision measures. The procedure has no solemn aspect and is carried out under the form of a meeting at a round table. This model is widespread in The Netherlands, during negotiations between the Public Prosecutor's Department, the judge and the Council for the Protection of Youth.

In countries with a system of 'appropriateness of proceedings', a number of experiments are under development. In France, before the law of 4 January 1993 institutionalised conditional closing of cases, reparation of damage by the perpetrator of the offence had become a condition for the closing of proceedings. The very recent character of this law does not allow knowledge of its practical application, which authorises us to mention practices in place until then and which have been ratified by the new law.

From the stage of supervision, the juvenile was informed of this possibility. The conditions were fixed by the substitution of an act of reparation in accordance with abilities, based on a report by the educational service concerning the aptitude of the juvenile to make reparation. The family was closely linked to this process of reparation. Reparation could take the form either of a direct service rendered to the victim who gave consent (under the form of apologies, compensation or work for the victim), or an indirect service rendered to the community.

In Northern Ireland and, in general, in Anglo-Saxon countries, the same unofficial practices are under development, but at the discretion of the police.

In Germany, when the accused has pleaded guilty and the prosecutor considers the launch of proceedings to be inappropriate and the imposition of socio-educational measures necessary, he will appeal to the judge so that the latter will issue the order. In the framework of these measures, the judge can order the accomplishment of a service of work, mediation between the victim and the perpetrator, the attendance of courses on the Highway Code, reparation of damage caused by the offence, and can also order the offender to apologise to the victim in person or make a donation to an establishment in the public interest. It is noted that these preliminary conditions of the closing of proceedings stem directly from the register of educational and disciplinary measure within juvenile criminal law. These different possibilities are at the discretion of the judge and may be introduced any time between the initiation of proceedings and the final judgement (judicial closing of proceedings).

In the framework of adjustments to the principle of law in Italy, a conditional closing of cases has been introduced. Here however it is the judge who is competent to suspend educational and disciplinary measure within juvenile criminal law. These different possibilities are at the discretion of the judge and may be introduced any time between the initiation of proceedings and the final judgement (judicial closing of proceedings).

In the framework of adjustments to the principle of law in Italy, a conditional closing of cases has been introduced. Here however it is the judge who is competent to suspend proceedings for a maximum period of one year (three years for serious offences) and to hand over the juvenile to the Juvenile

Service of the Administration of Justice. During this period, a program of treatment can be carried out, including the obligation to repair damage to the victim or mediation between the perpetrator and the victim. If, at the end of this period of probation, the obligations imposed have been met, the judge will declare the proceedings closed.

However it is the Dutch system which presents the most elaborate model. Penal transaction can be applied to any offence punishable by a sentence less than or equal to six years, which constitutes almost the totality of offences (90-95%). In adult criminal law, the transaction is made between the Public Prosecutor's Department and the perpetrator of the offence. In juvenile criminal law the judge must intervene and the individual concerned must give consent. The transaction can be combined with conditions fixed by law. The Public Prosecutor's Department can thus order the payment of a fine up to 500 guilders (most often imposed), the return of objects seized, the voluntary return of objects or sums of money illegally obtained as well as reparation of damage by the perpetrator.

Conditional closing of cases does not have a set limit as to the penalty incurred. Moreover, the list of obligations which the Public Prosecutor's Department can impose with the consent of the judge is not exhaustive; the prosecutor is free to order an obligation which is not included in the list of conditions of probation which is generally used. The reparation of damage by the offender, community service, compensation of the victim, treatment for drug addiction, taking into care of the juvenile by the Service for the Assistance of Youth, courses in social education, training programmes, and all the variations which can accompany the closing of a case.

With regard to referral to judicial or non-judicial sectors *after* the closing of a case, this measure is rare. In Slovenia, when the public ministry is required to report the closing of the case to the socio-administrative service, in order that the latter may take adequate measures, the lack of application of this mode of intervention can be noted.

In Belgium, however, 'nothing prevents the Public Prosecutor's Department from closing a case after having reported the case of a juvenile to a specialised organisation of social assistance, such as the service of the Council for the Assistance of Youth or the Committee of Concern for Young People (in the Flemish community) or any other service of assistance to young people or to the family.' This practice is however not common. These referrals therefore take place informally, i.e. directly, without the opening of a file. In the Flemish community a decree has ended all collaboration between the social and judicial sectors.

German law stipulates the reporting of the opening and disposition of a case to school authorities as well as the judge responsible for guardianship in appropriate cases, but without specifying the contents.

In Austria also, the judge responsible for guardianship can be informed of the final closing of the case and can order educational measures which can under no circumstances involve deprivation of liberty.

In France the Public Prosecutor's Department can add to the closing of the case a motion of the juvenile court judge concerned with educational assistance, invoking the state of danger of the juvenile.

In Sweden, there exists a possibility of transfer, ordered by the judge or even by the Public Prosecutor's Department in the framework of closing the case, to social services if such measures appear more appropriate than criminal sanctions. However the judge retains the possibility of ordering the minor to contribute to the reparation of damage caused to the victim and can even impose a fine.

The Polish system gives the family court judge the possibility of transferring the case to school authorities or to a social organisation.

Measures of Sentencing

Educational (or protective) measures
These are present in all legislations concerning juvenile delinquents (except in the former Czechoslovakia) and minors in danger. They are sometimes integrated into social law as in Sweden where measures of protection reserved for minors in danger or minors declared not to be criminally responsible, as in Germany, are part of the list of protective measures. The greatest difference between countries is along the lines of the legal nature of the protective measure. Is it part of independent measures or is it in fact a criminal sanction? Austria has a very clear position in this respect: educational measures are not part of the criminal category. If the jurisdiction which made the judgement does not impose any criminal sanction or does not close proceedings with an informal solution, the Family Courts are competent as a jurisdiction of guardianship, to impose educational measures. In France or Holland, educational measures can be imposed in a civil context. But in France, these measures are always subject to an entry in the criminal record of the minor.

It is therefore difficult to systematically group these measures together, for measures considered purely educational in one country are considered criminal sanctions in another. The most meaningful illustration of this problem is the service of work, or to use the France term, *travail d'intérêt général* (community service) which can be used as a penal sanction or as reparation of damage by the perpetrator of the offence. The main consequence of this distinction is to be found on the level of legal effects and particular entries in a criminal record.

Under the term 'educational measures' we note an extreme variety of these modes of intervention, ranging from a simple reprimand to a placement of unlimited duration in a secure environment. It is for this reason that it is important to present these different measures and attempt to categorise them according to their intensity. Generally speaking, two large groups can be distinguished: actual educational measures (in an open environment) and corrective or disciplinary measures, which in most cases involve deprivation of liberty, under the form of an institutional placement.

Educational or protective measures are the type of intervention accorded first place in legislation concerning juvenile delinquents: they can however involve a certain restriction of liberty, such as the placement of the minor in a family, or indeed in an institution, which is part of many legislations. The purely protective character of this type of intervention towards the juvenile, exempted from any punitive connotations, does not permit its exclusion from the category of educational measures. On the other hand, placement in a secure establishment, since it involves actual deprivation of liberty, cannot be put into this category.

In France, as in Italy or Belgium, the aim is to keep the juvenile in his or her natural environment (turning the young person back over to parents or probation) or placement in foster families (or handing over the juvenile to a person of trust) or in small residential units or centres offering academic and professional training. Children under 13 are handed over to social services. Parallel measures are found in Portugal. As in almost all legislations (Germany, Austria, Greece, Poland, Portugal, France, Holland, Switzerland, Slovenia) reprimand and cautioning are to be found. However it is, above all, the placing of the juvenile under the supervision of a service of legal protection, or more generally any supervision measures connected with the Anglo-Saxon institution of probation which deserves particular attention. This measure has the advantage of being carried out in an open environment, as the minor remains at liberty, while at the same time supervision is ensured, or educational supervision by a person designated by the judge or juvenile court. These modes characterise for example the institution of probation, as in the order of 2 February 1945 (France). But in these cases, this measure can also serve as an educational accompaniment, as it can also be applied to juveniles who have received a custodial sentence.

Generally, it has been observed that placement under supervision is very widely retained by most legislations, under somewhat different forms (England and Wales, Northern Ireland, Belgium, France, Holland, Sweden, Slovenia, Poland).

In Belgium, it can be combined with conditions enumerated by the law, such as:

- regular attendance of an academic establishment of education;
- the accomplishment of an educational or philanthropic service in relation to the age and abilities of the juvenile (reparations, community service);
- subjecting the juvenile to educational and medical directives of a centre of educational orientation or mental health.

This placement under supervision, under somewhat different forms, is the most common measure in Dutch law. The minor is subject to the supervision of a trustee (or guardian), The criminal court judge will make the decision and fix the duration of this measure; the execution, the choice of guardian and the determination of the form it takes is the responsibility of the juvenile court judge. The latter has wide-ranging competence concerning the carrying out of this measure and can place the minor in a foster family and even in an educational establishment, revoke or prolong the measure of supervision.

In Anglo-Saxon countries this measure, known as a 'supervision order' consists of supervision of the juvenile allowed to remain free, by a probation officer who has the responsibility of counselling, helping and befriending the minor. The youth court can order a certain number of obligations to be met or respected (concerning place of residence, the occupation of free time, medical treatment, etc.). Since the Criminal Justice Act 1991, this measure can be applied to all juvenile delinquents who come under the jurisdiction of the youth court.

In this regard, Northern Ireland and England have a measure designed to control the use of free time, called an 'attendance centre order'; it was introduced in 1948. The juvenile is obliged to go during the weekend to an institution where he or she will learn how to use leisure time in a constructive manner (manual work, physical training, etc.). The minimum duration of this measure is 12 hours, the maximum is 24 hours for minors aged under 18 and 36 hours for others. Since 1983, this measure can be used in England as a substitute penalty in the case of non-payment of a fine.

Special mention must be made of the Swedish system which has a system of supervision combined with probation for a duration of three years. This measure can also be combined with a custodial sentence lasting between 14 days and three months.

German law provides a great variety of educational measures which are not ordered 'because of the offence' but 'on the occasion of the offence'. In accordance with criminal systems applicable to minors, the commission of a criminal offence is the only criteria for intervention taking place.

Educational measures are directives under the form of prohibitions or orders designed to act on the juvenile and her or his lifestyle (similar orders apply in Portugal). Among these directives are community service, measures accompanying the taking into care of the juvenile, attendance at a course in social education or on the Highway Code, or mediation (between the delinquent and the victim). In addition, protective measures reserved for minors in danger are also applicable, with the consent of the minor. In this category are to be found in particular educational assistance, placement in a residence, as well as all forms of accompanying measures. Besides these measures, there exist more specific measures such as treatment for drug addiction.

In Poland there is also a very wide range of measures, particularly those falling under the category of obligations imposed by the Family Court. Emphasis has been laid on the relationship with the victim, in giving a primary place to reparation of damage by the offender and an apology to the victim. The judge can also order the minor to take up a training course, forbid him or her from going into certain places or being in the company of certain people, driving vehicles, consuming alcohol; the judge can also order the confiscation of objects illegally obtained. The minor can also be placed under the supervision of parents or of a trusted person or even a youth association or a guardian, chosen by the court.

Parallel measures, designated by the expression 'protective measures' are to be found in Portugal. They are legally applicable to minors aged 16 to 18, but also by extension to minors aged under 16. They consist of the imposition of rules of conduct or attendance of an educational course or placement in a foster family, educational residence, or even in 're-educational care institutions'. This final measure is excluded for children aged under nine.

In Switzerland the choice of educational measures is guided by the need for particular 'educational care' measures in an open environment, in particular educational assistance, under the form of monitoring of education and assistance to parents in the administration of their duties. This approach is preferred for both children (aged 7 to 15) and adolescents (aged 15 to 18). However, in Switzerland, there is a distinction between two types of minors: children and adolescents. The nature and mode of intervention vary according to the category concerned. In terms of the law, 'educational assistance is oriented towards providing the care, education and instruction needed by the child' As for educational assistance designed for adolescents, it is intended to 'provide the care, education, instruction, and professional training needed by the adolescent, the same as ensuring regularity of work and the constructive use of leisure time and earnings'. This measure can be prolonged up to the age of 20 for children and 22 for adolescents. In addition, 'the adolescent can be made subject to rules of conduct, in particular concerning professional training, place of residence, abstinence from alcoholic drinks and reparation of damage within a determined period'. As in most legislations, placement may be in a family or in an institution (educational home).

Greece has solved the problem of the legal nature of measures termed educational by putting them into the category of administrative security measures: the judgement ordering this type of measure is not a penal judgement. Educational and therapeutic measures are categorised according to their seriousness: reprimand, placement under the educational responsibility of parents or legal representatives, placement under probation carried out by categorised according to their seriousness: reprimand, placement under the educational responsibility of parents or legal representatives, placement under probation carried out by the educational service attached to the court, placement in an educational residence - there is also the possibility of placement in a therapeutic or other establishment if the state of the minor necessitates particular treatment. The application of these last measures, termed therapeutic, is extremely rare.

A special place should be given to the Swedish system which, in the framework of measures which can be taken following referral by ordinary criminal jurisdictions to social organisations, sets out voluntary measures, reserved in other countries for minors in danger, the carrying out of which depends on the consent of the juvenile and the family. This is an original step in which the juvenile contributes (by giving the consent necessary) to his or her own 'sanction' in a wide sense. In addition, the contents of measures which can be taken in this way are not part of any legal category, but entirely left to the discretion of social organisations. Moreover, the minor can be subject to measures termed 'semi-voluntary' under the form of the assistance of a 'person of contact' or insertion into an educational project.

Institutional placements
Placement in an institution is a constant in legislation concerning juvenile delinquents (Germany, England, Belgium, Greece, Northern Ireland, Poland, Portugal, Sweden, Switzerland, France), but in the last mentioned country, closed centres no longer exist since 1978. Such a placement is considered as an educational measure. However many reports have underlined the paradoxical character of this concept of education which is so restricting, its serious nature (especially if the duration is unlimited) and the stigmatising character of such a measure. Generally speaking, recourse to this measure of placement appears to be on the decline (Slovenia, Switzerland, Belgium).

It is worth giving a particular place to the Belgian system of institutional placements. In this system of protection, prison sentences are not intended as a sanction applicable to juvenile delinquents. Nonetheless, there exist many measures which restrict the liberty of minors. The judge can:

- place the juvenile under the supervision of the service of legal protection with a trusted person or any establishment deemed appropriate from the point of view of accommodation, treatment, education, instruction or professional training; or
- entrust the juvenile to the group of public institutions which come under the communities.

Placements do not have the same intensity, particularly since throughout Belgian territory a tendency to make regimes of placement more flexible have been observed in practice. The introduction of alternative measures and the reinforcement of the rights of juveniles has also been noted. Thus 'a measure of placement in a private establishment, or in a community institution, can cover a measure of granting autonomy'. This measure has been in use for several years. It consists of giving the minor independence regarding life in a place of residence, while at the same time maintaining the benefits of an educational framework. The second category of placement is that which involves actual provisional deprivation of liberty in a detention centre (for 15 days) or in a closed community establishment. In practice, adjustments to the carrying out of this measure have been observed concerning its undetermined duration. Thus the decree of the French Community (4 March 1991) stipulates that 'any juvenile placed in the care of public institutions for a period of more than 45 days, will be subject to a medico-psychological report and a social study communicated within 75 days to the judicial authority, the results of which will be communicated to the lawyer of the juvenile.' In addition, this same decree stipulates periodical systematic revision of measures taken and their cancellation after a period of one year, unless the measure is renewed, by a cancellation of funding ensured by the community. Most recently (law of 24 December 1992) this movement aiming to introduce guarantees concerning placement had been further reinforced by a modification of the law of 8 April 1965: from now on the judicial decision to place the minor in an institution must specify the duration of the measure and whether it will be in a closed educational establishment.

In Switzerland there exist several kinds of institutional placements which involve a graduation of severity. Institutional placement takes place in an 'educational home', intended to accommodate minors who are very difficult, abandoned or in serious danger'. This measure can take place in an 'institution of education at work' when the minor has reached the age of 17. Juveniles who turn out to be 'extraordinarily difficult' can be transferred to a 'centre of therapy', or to a 'centre of re-education' if they are 'intolerable'.

Institutional placement in Slovenia takes two forms: in an 'educational' institution for a duration of six months to three years and in a 're-educational institution' for a period of one to three years. This placement is made based on the needs of the juvenile (for help, re-education and supervision) or where removal from his or her natural environment appears necessary.

In Sweden, too, there is the possibility of placing the juvenile in an institution, secure or open, until the age of 18. These restrictive measures are only envisaged as a last resort, 'when the health and development of the juvenile are seriously compromised by criminal behaviour'. These conditions are verified by an administrative tribunal, at the request of social organisations (law of 1980), and used either by the prosecutor (in the context of abandonment of proceedings) or by the penal jurisdiction. It is the social organisation which is charged with the carrying out, planning and choice of the establishment or foster family. The placement ends at the age of 20 at the latest. These measures of placement (also placement in a foster family) must be monitored after six months at the latest. The juvenile can appeal these measures.

As a measure involving deprivation of liberty, Greek law has placement in a residence which is the most serious educational measure. Like any measure or custodial sentence, its duration is undetermined. A ministerial circular has fixed a minimum duration of six months. In practice it is in fact two or three months as it is accompanied by an educational follow-up which can extend beyond the age of legal majority, until the age of 21 years.

In the framework of placements, it is important to note certain measures of a therapeutic nature (treatment for drug addiction or treatment of psychological or neuro-psychological illnesses), implying also a placement in specialised institutions. Germany, Belgium, Holland, Greece, Slovenia and Poland have this type of measure.

Corrective measures

A mode of intervention which is found in the German, Swiss, Dutch, Portuguese and Slovenian systems is provided by measures termed disciplinary or corrective. Poland has similar corrective measures but they are closer to penalties in their forms and functions.

The most varied palette of disciplinary measures is offered by German law. Of unequal intensity, these range from simple reprimand (as in Switzerland) to the imposition of obligations to make reparation or apologise to the victim, or to pay a sum of money to a public establishment, to a short detention which can be up to four weeks' incarceration in a special centre. This final measure has three forms: it can take place during leisure time i.e. during weekends (a maximum of two weekends), for a short period (at most four days) or a longer period (minimum of one week, maximum of four weeks). In addition, this detention becomes a sanction concerning incidents in the carrying out of a directive or an obligation. However these disciplinary measures do not have the legal status of a penalty and are not entered in a criminal record. The introduction of detention in Germany in 1940 under National Socialism was influenced by the theory of 'short sharp shock', according to which a short detention could be useful for preventing the juvenile from committing fresh offences. In the very formulation of the objective assigned to disciplinary measures, there appears a punitive connotation: 'if the penalty of imprisonment is not required, the judge punished the offence committed by the juvenile by disciplinary measures, which must lead the juvenile to a profound recognition of the wrongness of the act, which must be answered for.

In Slovenia, there existed, until 1995, two types of disciplinary measures: reprimand and placement in a 'disciplinary centre' similar in its nature and methods (the maximum duration is 30 days) to detention in German law. This placement can take place for several hours in the day, without affecting the studies or work of the juvenile, or during weekends. The 'disciplinary centre' has been conceived on the German model but has been used as an educational measure and not as a form of discipline. Consequently this measure has been abandoned today in favour of more flexible measures of short duration. The new law of 1995 abolished the term 'disciplinary measures' and kept only the (now 'educational') sanction of reprimand.

Measures of correction set out by Portuguese law are normally reserved for young adults aged 18 to 21. However the courts have decided to apply them also to minors aged 16 to 18, when they are felt to be appropriate. Beyond reprimand and the imposition of certain rules of conduct, there exist fines and placement in a 'centre of arrest or detention'. In this case, the minimum duration is three years and the maximum is six years.

Switzerland has available 'disciplinary punishments' for children (aged seven to 15) which consist of:

- reprimand;
- community service; or
- one to six half-days of school detention (this formula has today been more or less abandoned by the majority of cantons).

119

If the infraction is not serious, the judgement authority can abandon disciplinary penalties and 'hand over the task of punishment to paternal authority'.

In Holland, until 1995, an institution existed which was comparable to this form of detention, in its duration (ranging from four hours to 14 days), in its function as a form of cautioning, in its methods of implementation (during leisure time and weekends), and in the term used. As mentioned above, the new Law of 1995 abolished this form of detention and introduced a single sanction of juvenile imprisonment.

The penalty of imprisonment
The criminal sanction which every system (except for Belgium, Scotland, Portugal and Poland which have excluded this penalty from their legislation regarding delinquent minors) has maintained is the penalty of imprisonment. However, it has been observed that countries which have adopted a one-way system of protection of youth, while officially rejecting incarceration, have not excluded all forms of detention with regard to minors.

In the case of Belgium, the legal situation is not so simple as there does indeed exist a measure involving deprivation of liberty, consisting of a provisional placement for 15 days in a detention centre or an educational placement in a secure environment. The same is true of Poland which has a 'placement in a correctional institution' which in fact corresponds to a prison sentence of undetermined duration, of which the minimum period is six months.

The single law for the protection of youth in Poland, which applies to juvenile delinquents aged 13 to 17, envisages a dispensation permitting the judgement of those aged 16 or more who have committed a serious offence (homicide, bodily harm, aggravated robbery or rape) to be judged according to criminal regulations applicable to minors, if the circumstances of the offence and the personality of the minor require it. In this case, custodial and financial sanctions are applicable to minors. A second dispensation concerns the young person aged 18 at the time of judgement who committed an infraction incurring placement in a reformatory while aged under 17. The judge must then alter this sentence to a sentence of imprisonment, if the corrective measure is deemed insufficient. Such a commutation also takes place if the young person is aged 18 and the running of the corrective measure has not yet begun.

Modes and duration
A simple comparative glance shows that legislative arrangements, however different they may be, assign the function of a last resort to the imprisonment of minors; this sanction, when it is possible, is reserved for serious offences.

The differences between the imprisonment of adults the imprisonment of juveniles are most often connected with arrangements both at the level of conditions of application of the penalty, which in principle are more strict, and at the level of special modes of implementation (Germany, Northern Ireland,

Portugal, Switzerland, France and Greece). Sometimes there exists specific terminology reserved for this penalty, *Jugendstrafe* as in Germany, Austria or Switzerland, to distinguish it from the penalty of imprisonment for adults. The implementation takes place in a special penitentiary establishment reserved for minors.

If imprisonment as a penal sanction is a constant of different legislations, the modes of implementation, in particular the duration and conditions of application, vary from one country to the other. Imprisonment seems to be becoming more and more the exception for anyone under the age of 16.

This is in part related to the raising of the age of criminal responsibility, under which no criminal penalty can be imposed, but also to the establishment of categories of minors who, due to their age, have a reduced criminal responsibility. It appears that incarceration is reserved for the older individuals in this category.

Legislatures do not operate a distinction as to sex (England has abolished the penalty of detention of four months intended for male juveniles). As for the duration of sentences, legislation in most cases sets out special minimum sanctions for minors while making distinctions according to the age of the minor, with the exception of French, Italian and Austrian law. However, according to the French system of law, a minor aged 13 to 18 cannot receive as heavy a sentence as an adult: the penalties set out in common law cannot apply and a maximum is stipulated in the law (art. 66 of the Penal Code).

In 1980, Sweden was in the process of abolishing the only special sanction designed for minors. It consisted of a custodial sentence of undetermined duration, initially intended for young adults (aged 18 to 21) and extended through judicial practice to minors aged 15 to 18 and subsequently to young adults aged 21 to 23. Today in Sweden, there is only one custodial sentence of undetermined duration, between 14 days and ten years and for life. This penalty, in its conditions of application and modes of implementation, (penitentiary system) carries no distinction for adults, minors and young adults. But in order to avoid more severe treatment of minors and young adults, Swedish legislation has at the same time made certain adjustments. This custodial sentence is only applicable to adults over 21. The legislator has explicitly excluded imprisonment for minors under 18, except in absolutely exceptional cases, and authorised it only as an exceptional measure for 18 to 21-year-olds. As a result, in practice and with reference to statistics from 1980 to 1989, there are no longer any prison sentences imposed on juveniles under 18.

In Slovenia and in Portugal only minors aged 16 to 18 can be sentenced to prison.

The conditions of application of prison sentences are very restrictive with regard to minors. The juvenile delinquent must be aged over 16, the offence must be a serious one incurring a sentence of more than five years according to adult criminal law and the juvenile must be considered responsible for the act due to maturity. Finally, imprisonment has a secondary status and will only be applied if other measures turn out to be insufficient. The minimum duration has been brought to one year and the maximum is ten years.

In Greece a special type of prison sentence exists for minors, but in certain cases it is possible to resort to adult prison sentences regarding minors aged over 17. In this case the mitigating circumstance of minority must be applied to reduce the sentence.

In fact, only Greece still retains sentences of undetermined duration with regard to minors. The judge fixes a minimum and a maximum within legal limits. The actual duration is determined during the sentence. Imprisonment for minors lasts from six months to ten years, while for adults the duration (which is determined at the moment of judgement) is for a minimum of ten days and a maximum of five years.

With regard to minors, the minimum is brought to five years and the maximum to 20 years if the crime committed is subject to a sentence of more than ten years or to the death penalty. Sentences of less than six months, i.e. short prison sentences, can be imposed on a minor when the court imposes a penalty which comes under adult criminal law.

In England, imprisonment is reserved for young people aged under 21 who have committed particularly serious crimes (e.g. murder), for which a prison sentence would invariably be imposed for adults. As to the reforms of the Criminal Justice and Public Order Act 1994 see the report of Dünkel above in this volume. ('Current Directions in Criminal Policy').

The same is the case in Italy, where prison sentences are reserved for minors who have committed particularly serious and violent crimes.

In France, the order of 2 February 1945 gave an exceptional character to the imprisonment of minors. In terms of the law, a minor aged more than 13 can be subject to a criminal penalty, 'if due to the circumstances and personality of the delinquent such a penalty should be imposed'. If punitive jurisdictions can impose criminal penalties applicable to adults, they are required to follow the special rules intended to reduce the severity of sentences and in particular the mitigating circumstance of being under age, which can only be disregarded concerning a minor aged over 16 and where the decision can be justified. There are now practically no more prison sentences imposed on minors aged under 16. If a prison sentence for life is incurred, in this case it can be commuted to a sentence of at most ten or 20 years. If a minor incurs a prison sentence of ten to 20 years, or five to ten years, the sentence imposed will be for a maximum of half that period. More and more, there are efforts to avoid any form of detention regarding minors. Thus, all arrangements which permit a measure of probation or placement of a minor in a detention centre for failing to comply with an educational measure were abolished in 1989.

In Austria, life sentences are commuted to sentences of a maximum of ten years for a minor aged under 16 and 15 years for a young person aged 16 to 19. In addition, there is no longer any minimum duration of sentence for minors.

In Germany short prison sentences of less than six months have been removed from the system of sanctions applicable to juvenile delinquents and the duration of sentences has been limited to five years for minors aged 14 to 18, unless they incur, through a given offence, a sentence of more than ten years according to general criminal law, or if the case involves a young adult delinquent aged 18 to 21; in these cases the maximum sentence is raised to ten years. However, even if Germany does not have short prison sentences, it has nevertheless an original institution (which also exists in Slovenia) of detention 'Jugendarrest'. This measure is not a penalty in the legal sense of the term, but a disciplinary measure which does not carry any consequences of penalties (in particular entry in a criminal record). By the mode of implementation and its content (it entails a short deprivation of liberty up to four weeks) it is intended to give a serious warning to the juvenile.

There existed a parallel but much shorter measure (from four hours to two weeks) in The Netherlands until this was replaced by a single form of juvenile imprisonment in 1995.

Portugal has also progressed along the same lines, regarding the abolition of short prison sentences for young adults. The minimum has been brought to one month and the maximum to 20 years, except for the centres of detention where the minimum duration is three years and the maximum six years.

In the former Czechoslovakia, life sentences have been reduced to five or ten years. As for imprisonment for definite periods, there is no minimum - as in France or Austria - and the maximum has been brought to five years (exceptionally to ten years).

A common feature intended to reduce the duration of imprisonment compared to adults is 'mitigating circumstance' granted on the grounds of being under age (Germany, France, Italy, Austria, Switzerland, Scotland, Poland and the former Czechoslovakia, but in the latter country the maximum penalty incurred cannot be more than five years and the minimum cannot be more than a year). In France, the juvenile court can rescind the benefit of mitigating circumstances for a minor aged over 16 in the case of a criminal offence. In Poland, the technique of reduction of the penalty allows the imposition of a sentence of less than the legal minimum set out for the offence.

In England, the Criminal Justice Act 1991 has abolished the differences in treatment which existed between male and female minors aged 14, by standardising the minimum age at 15 and raising the minimum duration of detention in a 'young offender institution' to two months for all young people aged under 18. The maximum duration has been fixed at two years for minors aged 15 to 17 by the Criminal Justice and Public Order Act 1994.

In Sweden, the minimum has been brought to 14 days and the maximum to ten years (exceptionally to 18 years).

Sentences are shortest in Holland with a minimum of one month and a maximum of one year for 12-15-year-old offenders, and two years for 16 and 17-year-old offenders, and can only be imposed in the case of a criminal offence. The extremely short duration shows that it is more a matter of

123

punishing the juvenile than of using the period of incarceration as a method of re-education.

In Scotland there exist special arrangements in criminal law for young people aged 16 to 21. These prohibit the imposition of prison sentences for this category of persons. The sentence of undetermined duration called 'Borstal' no longer exists. If the duration, now determined by court, is between 28 days and 4 months, the implementation will take place in a special 'detention centre', otherwise in a penitentiary centre for young people where the person sentenced can serve the sentence until the age of 21, exceptionally until 23.

Alternative Measures

Most of the alternative measures and penalties which have been mentioned here are part of the list of criminal measures applicable to adults, and are therefore not specific to minors, with the exception of certain obligations imposed in the framework of probation, as in Holland.

In addition, the systems for the protection of youth, like that of Belgium or Poland, which have only protective measures, have no alternatives as, by definition, there exist no penalties or custodial sentences in these systems. But in practice certain measures are being developed as alternatives to a placement which implied deprivation of liberty. Thus in Belgium, certain judges instruct the juvenile to carry out an altruistic or educational action or propose mediation between the victim and the offender. In this framework, the young person is asked to complete either 'an action of reparation or a journey (project of change of environment), which tests the will of the juvenile and his or her capacity to overcome difficulties and live in a small group'.

In Flanders 'day centres' are being developed, which are drawn from the inspiration of the 'Bodaert Centra' of The Netherlands, and are characterised by being situated between a measure in an open environment and deprivation of liberty. It is in fact a semi-open measure. This day treatment is founded on several principles:

- ordering educational assistance to parents by the daily reception of the juvenile at the centre when school finishes (4 p.m.) and until 7 p.m.;
- ensuring intermediate treatment of the family in weekly and fortnightly sessions;
- ensuring systematic accompaniment of the minor regarding homework and academic obligations;
- ensuring individual treatment of the minor in case of need.

Regarding the choice and implementation of these alternatives in various countries, we note the existence of a socio-educational service attached to the court, which is a public judicial institution, charged in most cases with making social inquiries, assisting the juvenile during proceedings and making proposals as to measures to take concerning the juvenile (Germany, Austria,

Northern Ireland, France, Holland, Belgium, the former Czechoslovakia and Portugal). In the absence of such a service, these functions are ensured by the probation service (Sweden).

In most cases, the lawyer, the social or probation services, the legal representatives of the juvenile and the Public Prosecutor's Department are invited to participate in the decision-making process. However a great deal of freedom of assessment on the part of the juvenile judge, who is guided by the principles of appropriateness of the measure, has been observed.

The victim is almost always absent from this decision-making process except in Austria and in Holland in cases of extra judicial reparation during mediation which is a condition of the closing of the case by the prosecutor or by the police. In Holland, the law stipulates, during the decision-making process on the measure to be taken, the compulsory deliberation of three principal parties: the juvenile court judge, the Public Prosecutor's Department and the Council for the Protection of Youth; this is known as 'triangular consultation'.

As a penal sanction, fines are present in almost all legislations (Germany, England, Austria, Greece, France, Holland, Italy, Switzerland and Portugal). In the former Czechoslovakia this penalty is however reserved for young people who are earning money. Generally, the amount of the fine is limited (from five to 500 guilders in Holland) and fixed according to the ability of the minor to pay or the system of paying fines by instalment. Its implementation can be partially or totally suspended (Austria, Holland, France).

In England and Wales the Criminal Justice Act 1991 introduced a new measure of enforcing the penal responsibility of parents or persons with children aged under 16 in their charge. An obligation on parents to supervise the child (binding over) ordered by the court for a period of up to three years, under pain of being fined, has been retained as a sanction.

The mechanisms of probation with, at the head of the list, suspension of sentence with probation are an integral part of interventions intended for minors. In most cases it is a question of the suspension of the carrying out of a sentence of imprisonment (Austria, the former Czechoslovakia, Germany, France, Switzerland) and the implementation of a fine (Austria, Holland). Partial suspension exists in France, Holland and Austria. In these last two countries partial suspension can be applied to the suspension of fines and imprisonment, and even to detention, as in Dutch law. The judge is free to choose the obligations which are to accompany the suspension of sentence. Unlike French judges, who are obliged to choose the obligations from a fixed list arising out of legal texts, the Dutch judge can even create new ones. In the list of obligations are to be found community service, reparation of damage, compensation of the victim, courses in social training (Holland, Germany) and educational projects (Holland),

Suspension of sentence in France is divided into two main categories. It can be straightforward, affecting only the imposition of the sentence. It can be revoked in the case of a fresh imposition of a criminal or correctional penalty. On the other hand, suspension of sentence with probation entails a socio-educational follow-up of the person sentenced, placed under the control of the juvenile court judge, acting as the judge of the implementation of sentences. The juvenile is required to respect the obligations fixed by the judge. With regard to minors aged 16 to 18, suspension of sentence with probation can be combined with community service.

Suspension of sentence does not exist in Greece for minors. In Sweden there exists a short custodial sentence ranging from 14 days to three months, combined with probation lasting from one to three years.

In the framework of sanctions involving probation, i.e. a trial period accompanied by a certain number of obligations imposed by the judge, the deferment of the sentence, or measures of supervision such as monitored liberty in France, are being applied more and more to juvenile delinquents. Monitored liberty, in France, has the peculiarity of being applicable as an accessory measure both to penalties and educational measures, and even as a pre-judgement measure before any final decision.

Measures of supervision are generally included in probation techniques as they are taken on in most cases by probation services or by social services. In addition, they are part of the list of criminal sanctions. However the measure of supervision as a protective measure, as it is envisaged in systems of protection of youth (Belgium or Poland, for example), is technically related to the probationary guidance which exists as a penalty in other countries.

In Italy, the measure called 'monitored liberty' is a system of carrying out a sentence in an open environment. It can be applied to any prison sentence of less than six months. In these modes of implementation, it can be compared to a kind of 'trial placement with the social service'.

The deferment of sentence is a sanction available in France, Switzerland, Germany and Austria. In France it can be straightforward, i.e. without the addition of obligations or can be accompanied by probation and in particular on condition that reparation be made to the victim.

In Austria, exemption from sentencing is applied when the offence committed is subject only to a light penalty. In addition, Austrian law contains a system parallel to the French system of deferment of sentencing with probation *Schuldspruch unter Vorbehalt der Strafe;* the conditions of application are however strongly influenced by considerations of individual prevention. Thus, the court, after having found the minor guilty, can defer sentencing in subjecting the juvenile to a period of probation combined with obligations to meet if this measure is designed to prevent the commission of fresh offences. In the case of violation of these obligations imposed the court enjoys a great deal of freedom of assessment as to the decision to be taken; it is in no way required to impose a penalty.

In terms of Swiss law, the judge can defer the decision 'when it is impossible to establish with certainty if the adolescent should be subjected to a measure or a penalty'. A period of time is then fixed (from six months to three years) and rules of conduct are imposed. If the adolescent does not conform to the conditions, the judge imposes a fine, detention or one of the available measures, but otherwise can refrain from imposing any penalty.

This exemption from sentencing is a legal resource left to the discretion of Dutch, French, Austrian, Swiss and Swedish judges. Since 1983, this exemption from sentencing with a verdict of guilt has become an alternative (therefore with the status of a main penalty and in the place of a prison sentence) in Holland. Exemption from sentencing in Switzerland can be made to depend on sincere atonement on the part of the juvenile (e.g. reparation of damage) or the passing of a year since the offence or the accomplishment of an adequate measure or a punishment.

Deferment of sentencing as set out in German law can be applied when it is not possible to establish with certainty the existence of 'dangerous tendencies' in the act committed by the juvenile. The judge can, while at the same time recognising the young person's guilt, defer sentencing, subject to probation.

Swedish criminal law has a similar technique. The criminal court judge imposes a sentence, combined with the obligation to lead an 'honest life', to meet his or her own maintenance costs, and to make good damage caused. The trial period is two years.

Related to the technique of deferment of, and exemption from, sentencing, the Italian system of 'legal pardon' deserves attention. In cases of a first sentencing for an offence which does not incur more than two years' imprisonment, and when the judge thinks that the juvenile will not commit further offences, the judge pronounces a legal pardon which entails the straightforward cancellation of the offence. From a statistical point of view it is clear that this method of disposal is very important in Italy and currently fulfils a function of 'non-intervention'. In fact, if we refer to statistics resulting from research done on the application of the new Code of criminal procedure (1 January 1990 to 30 June 1990) in a total of 66,118 cases, 53,424 were maintained, of which only 3,103 were sent before the juvenile court and 842 for an immediate appearance. This adds up to a total of 3,945 prosecutions, i.e. 7.4%. On the other hand, 49,479 or 92.6 % were terminated with a legal pardon.

In this respect, it is also worth mentioning the institution set out in Austrian law permitting immunity from sentencing for juvenile delinquents aged under 16. As for the conditions of its application, two types of cases exist. In the first case, the offence committed cannot carry a maximum sentence of more than three years, the fault behind the offence must not be serious, and finally juvenile criminal law does not apply in this situation. In the second case, reference is made to the stipulations for immunity from sentencing set out in the penal code: when the fault behind the offence is not serious, when there is no damage or when reparation has been made. Obviously, immunity from sentencing becomes a possibility when the juvenile is judged as lacking criminal responsibility due to immaturity at the time of the offence.

While probation techniques are widespread in criminal systems applicable to minors and used extensively they are not devoid of all danger to minors, given their function as a substitute penalty for imprisonment. Thus,

127

the French report rightly underlined that suspension of sentence with probation, frequently applied to juveniles can turn out to be particularly severe as failure to meet an obligation imposed by the judge can entail incarceration of the juvenile.

In Greece no sanction in an open environment is available except in cases where a penalty which comes under adult criminal law is applied. In a complementary fashion, the court has the power to order certain extra obligations (such as compensation of the victim according to the means of the offender). This practice is still very rare according to our correspondent.

The alternative to incarceration which has become the most widespread in recent years is community service. Although in Germany and Switzerland 'services of work' have been present in legislation for a long time (since 1974 in Switzerland) their imposition has become more frequent in recent years. The 'community service order' in Anglo-Saxon countries is now included in legislation in many countries (England, Austria, France, Greece, Ireland, Italy, Portugal, Slovenia, but not in Poland) as a sanction applicable to juveniles. In Scotland, Children's Hearings are not empowered to impose this penalty, but the Sheriff Courts and the High Court are. Community service was introduced in 1988 in Northern Ireland for juveniles from the age of 16.

In France, community service is an alternative to prison sentences, applies to minors aged 16 to 18 and lasts from 20 to 120 hours (i.e. half the duration applicable to adults). The follow-up and implementation of community service are ensured by services for legal protection of youth, under the control of the juvenile court judge. In France, it can be imposed either as a main penalty or a particular condition of suspension of sentence with probation (as in Holland).

In France, community service is accompanied by an educational follow-up by a specialised educator. It must be with the consent of the individual concerned (likewise in Portugal).

It has been noted that community service, if it has not already been set down in the text of laws, as in France (duration from 20 to 120 hours) and in Portugal (duration from nine to 180 hours), is a feature of many experimental projects (as in Sweden).

In England, the duration of community service has been brought by the Criminal Justice Act 1991 to 240 hours for young people aged over 16 (which corresponds to the duration envisaged for adults). A new measure (called a 'combination order'), which combines the 'probation order' and the 'community service order' is applicable to young people aged 16 and over. The young person is monitored by a probation officer during a period lasting from 12 months to three years and must perform community service of from 40 to 100 hours.

Among legal innovations, the Swedish report mentions the introduction of 'contact treatment' for drug addicts, by which the person concerned makes a declaration of readiness to observe an individualised program of treatment, the duration of which is determined by the judge, during the process of judgement.

Numerous experiments along the lines of mediation and reparation of damage by the offender are under development in France and Belgium. In France, this final measure has been given legal foundation by the law of 4 January 1993, which reformed criminal procedure. Measures of reparation, but also of assistance, can be imposed either by the Public Prosecutor's Department, in the form of a disposition of the case, or by the judge in the form of a judgement. The introduction of measures of assistance and reparation by juveniles, through a new law, is not only a legislative novelty but also a consecration of efforts of professionals who had, outside the legal framework, established these experiments. Article 12(1) has been inserted into the law of 4 January 1993, which permits magistrates of the Siege and the Public Prosecutor's Department to order a measure of assistance or reparation with regard to minors, subject to the consent of the juveniles and the parties with parental authority, when it is ordered before judgement, and after having gathered their observations when it is imposed by judgement.

With regard to its implementation, it is worth referring to former practices. Associated specialised services reported on the implementation to the magistrate. The measure necessitated the agreement of the juvenile, the parents or of the victim, when reparation was carried out directly (apology, compensation of the victim). The French report also mentions another aspect of reparation provided by experiences of indirect reparation in the form of services to the community (services rendered to transport organisations, the town hall, etc.).

Through these new measures, the educational objective, perceived more as an effort to make the juvenile more responsible, acquires all its meaning. It is a question of 'making the minor aware of the existence of criminal law and of the consequences of its violation'.

In Germany penal mediation was established by the law of 1990 as an educational measure. The agreement of the person concerned is sought before such measures are carried out. In this domain, the Austrian institution of extra judicial mediation and reparation plays an important role. After the completion of reparation by the offender, the public ministry and the court must close the case (in the latter case it is a matter of closing the matter from a legal point of view).

The reform of the Code of criminal procedure in Italy has made possible among other things the regulation of practices of penal mediation and reparation of damage by the offender, as obligations accompanying suspension of sentence with probation.

Finally, in the framework of alternatives to imprisonment, comes the new English measure termed 'curfew order', now set down in the law (but not yet in force). This measure, while it does not involve deprivation of liberty in the strict sense of the term, leaves a bitter taste regarding technologies which can be used to restrict the liberty of the person concerned. This confinement to home with electronic surveillance is applicable to minors aged 16 to 17. England is the only country to have introduced this measure for minors.

However there is discussion in many countries as to its implementation (for example in Holland). House arrest exists in Italy as an alternative to remand.

Treatment in an Open Environment

The importance of treatment in an open environment
Despite the enormous variety of texts dealing with juvenile delinquents, it is impossible not to recognise the unanimity regarding the priority given to modes of observation in an open environment and in particular the maintenance, as far as possible, of the minor in his or her natural environment (France, Belgium, Scotland, Northern Ireland, Holland, Italy, Switzerland, Sweden, Poland and Portugal). Concerning juvenile delinquents, treatment in an open environment is defined in comparison to all forms of deprivation of liberty, whether in the form of a placement, remand, measures involving arrest and detention or imprisonment. The open environment, which involves treatment of juvenile delinquents, refers to a very wide conception of measures or sanctions which do not involve deprivation of liberty and, *a fortiori*, all alternatives to imprisonment.

Incarceration in the form of a placement in a secure environment or in detention remains, according to the reports, a last resort, reserved for the most serious cases. At the risk of oversimplifying, it is nonetheless necessary to stress a fundamental role of criminal policy towards juvenile delinquents, which gives priority to prevention, assistance or supervision of juvenile delinquents. Punishment becomes a secondary task, made necessary by the failure of other measures. All evolution of juvenile criminal law could be summarised by the efforts undertaken, especially since the Second World War, to reduce the incarceration of minors to the smallest share of measures taken.

In this respect it is interesting to note what was at the origin of the German reform of 1990. Here the contribution of social sciences and especially criminology has been a determining factor in the same way as many practical experiments. New arrangements resulting from this reform are inspired by knowledge provided by research made on the meaning of offending behaviour in adolescents. Juvenile delinquency is now considered as a passing phenomenon. Offending does not necessarily indicate educational shortcomings, but much more a marginalisation linked to the process of development and corresponding to the attainment of adult age. This transitory phase does not repeat itself. For this reason a formal sentence is not essential. In addition, the advantages of informal disposition of cases in matters of minor and middle range offences, at the level of criminal policy, has been demonstrated. This means a reduction in costs, rapidity in disposition of the case and even effectiveness regarding prevention and recidivism, while at the same time offering solutions more suited to juvenile delinquency. Thus it has been shown that the new arsenal of measures in an open environment (intermediate measures) can be a perfect substitute for traditional sanctions (fines, detention, prison sentences) without increasing the risk of recidivism.

This concept takes on its full significance in countries which make informal disposition, i.e. without recourse to formal criminal judgement, the normal method of dealing with juvenile delinquency, in the quest to avoid any formal sentencing.

The best illustration of such an informal policy is given by Holland and Sweden. For this reason, these two countries do not have the same innovations on the level of sanctions such as community service, probation, intermediate treatment, mediation/reparation and in particular the increased importance of the open environment as just such measures have been applied to juveniles for years, but without the support of a judgement and before the legal machinery is set in motion. In this respect, it is certainly advisable to initiate more developments on the Italian model and reflect on the meaning of the results of the legal pardon. But whatever the explanation, one can only be amazed at the information provided, as 92.6% of cases are concluded in this manner.

For this reason, one can also reflect on the relationship between the development of new alternatives and their significance compared to traditional sanctions. In fact, knowing to what extent formulae of treatment in an open environment are replacing custodial measures for juvenile delinquents could provide an evaluation which is in fact indispensable for new practices observed in most countries. But it is not possible to provide an answer at present, due to the absence of empirical research in this field and especially methodological difficulties in undertaking such work. However, at a more modest level of observation, it is indisputable that the reduction in the number of custodial measures correlates with the number of measures in an open environment. Thus the drastic reduction in the number of remands in France (1,322 remands ordered in 1984 compared to 601 in 1988) is mainly due, on reading the report, to the intervention of educational services in the juvenile courts, which present an evaluation of the situation and a personalised educational project which allows the avoidance of incarceration.

The evolution of the last ten years concerning community service, probation, intermediate treatment as well as mediation and reparation show a true enthusiasm for these modes of intervention concerning minors. However, many doubts have emerged regarding the adequacy of the stated principles of these practices, which necessarily create a wide disparity between the minor qualitative importance of treatment in an open environment (particularly under the form of new alternatives to imprisonment) and its quantitative meaning. In addition, the evolution which has been observed in criminal matters, concerning the increase in measures in an open environment, in the majority of countries except in Greece, as well as the search for solutions less restrictive than incarceration or placement are to be found both in the sphere of criminal law and that of legal protection of youth. Through this reflection on treatment of juveniles in an open environment and its evolution in recent years appears the whole problem of juvenile justice; it is a question of finding, between educational measures and imprisonment, which is disappearing, new formulae which are at the same time restricting, rehabilitative and contribute to social reinsertion.

131

Generally speaking, we note in various countries many innovations connected with treatment in an open environment. This evolution is accompanied by an increase in their implementation by professionals in the last ten years (in France, Germany and Switzerland) and a decrease in all forms of deprivation of liberty.

The absence of statistics on this subject, due to the novel and therefore experimental character of certain legal measures (Austria, Germany), or their neglect or lack of reliability due to their imprecision, obviously make a summary or the presentation of the main trends, somewhat difficult if not hazardous.

For this reason the figures reproduced in this report can only have an indicative value.

Only Sweden is moving against the flow, for the movement relative to new care measures had begun in the 1970s. It appears that after having been stable in the 1980s, statistics show a certain reduction in these modes of intervention, with more and more recourse to deprivation of liberty. In 1985, 35 prison sentences were imposed, while in 1990 the figure was 77.

From new measures of treatment emerges penal mediation (delinquent-victim) in France, Germany, Austria and Holland, as well as reparation of damage by the offender, either by a direct service rendered to the victim (apology, compensation), or an indirect service to the community (Holland, France).

As for Belgium, besides the difference in its legal system, it is in a unique situation due to the existence of the French and Flemish Communities. In the French Community, there has been a decreasing tendency in placements (which make up 42% of measures taken concerning minors), accompanied by a search for methods of placement closer to treatment in an open environment. In this respect, 'placement in autonomy' of the juvenile by the services charged with finding a place for the juvenile in a residence has become more and more frequent in both the French and Flemish Communities. This is an intermediate measure between residential placement of a minor and maintenance in his or her usual environment (with or without conditions). This measure assumes an educational accompaniment of the minor, placed in a situation closer to an open environment. Placement in a foster family is also on the increase. Measures of supervision regarding minors constituted, in 1987, 24% of measures taken in the French Community and 36% for the Flemish Community.

In the Flemish Community, the number of residential placements is in continual decline. This trend will probably continue, given that 'residential assistance is being more and more reorganised into assistance in an open environment, and new guidance and family services were created in July 1991'.

In the French Community especially, the conditions of article 37 of the law on the protection of youth concerning 'a measure of supervision with the obligation to fulfil an educational or altruistic goal' (allowing community service) or measures of supervision with the obligation to observe the educational directives of a consultation related to education of mental health, is being rediscovered in the framework of the search for alternatives to residential placements. These measures can be imposed provisionally as a condition of a closing of the case without follow-up, or as a final measure in the form of an alternative to a residential placement.

In Germany, these new measures are being integrated into the movement of diversion from the (juvenile) court (alternative measures) made possible by the substitution of the principle of appropriateness for the principle of law concerning proceedings against minors or young adult delinquents.

A strong increase in the closing of cases combined with obligations, which are only new alternative measures, has been observed.

From 1981 to 1991, the percentage of so-called informal sentences (as they do not arise from a judgement) has risen from 44% to 62%. This percentage is even higher for first time offenders. This means that in principle there is no formal sentencing for the first offence. In addition, in Germany there is still a decrease in custodial sentences in favour of new modes of treatment (directives affecting the conduct of the young person and assistance in an open environment) as well as more traditional measures such as reprimand, various obligations and suspension of sentence with probation. In 1993, 7% of all sanctions of the juvenile court involved deprivation of liberty, furthermore 17% of all convictions were detention, i.e. a short period of detention (either on week-ends or up to four weeks) without the stigmatising effects of a real penalty.

In the framework of this type of intermediate measure, suspension of sentence with probation and directives are in a high position in a quantitative sense. The increase in this mode of intervention, the institutionalisation of new so-called flexible measures, including community service, care supervision orders, courses in social education, mediation and reparation of damage, arises directly from trial and error and experimentation.

At present, there are no statistics available which would permit the quantification of the use of these measures, but drawing on the results obtained by opinion poll, more and more frequent use can be established. Thus, supervision by probation officers follow the increase in suspension of sentence with probation. In 1955, only 32% of all prison sentences for minors are suspended, today (1993) the figure is 63%. It is clear that courts are becoming more prepared to suspend sentences of between one and two years. (see the chapter by *Dünkel* above).

In parallel, there has been a decrease in remand.

In France there has been a large increase in suspension of sentence, straightforward or with probation (with intervention of educators as probation officers). In this case the young person is subject to a certain number of obligations chosen by the judge, acting as a sentencing judge. In addition, mediation/reparation is under development, initiated by members of the public ministry. This practice has had great success in the context of abandonment of proceedings governed by the principle of appropriateness and has been given a legal foundation by the law of 4 January 1993, reforming the Code of

Criminal Procedure. The prosecutor, in the exercise of the power to assess proceedings, can now close the case without imposing the condition of reparation of damage.

There has also been a considerable decrease in sentencing in Austria (in 1989, only 15.3% of delinquent acts, or 2,808 juveniles). The same is the case in Germany and in Holland due to the increase in informal disposition of cases. Not only has the number of people taken in for questioning decreased in Austria, (17,493 in 1985, 12,006 in 1989), but also the number of sentences (7,083 juveniles aged 14-17 in 1985, 2,808 juveniles ages 14-18 in 1989). On 28 February 1991, 179 young people were in prison, of whom 119 were in remand.

Sanctions in Austria imposed in the context of judgement are divided up as follows; 9.2% were exempted from penalties, 26.3% of penalties were deferred, 34.5% were suspended fines or prison sentences, 5.3% were partially suspended prison sentences or fines and 24.7% were fines or prison sentences. In 1989, only 3.8% of minors suspected of having committed an offence were given firm sentences.

The purpose of criminal procedure in The Netherlands is to avoid formal judgement. In this respect, we have already mentioned the techniques for closing cases (by the police and the Public Prosecutor's Department). In the absence of statistics on closing of cases by the police, it is difficult to provide an exact figure on the number of cases which are closed in that phase of investigation. But out of 38,000 reported offences (committed by minors under 18), around 17,000 serious offences (crimes) were listed, of which 12,850 were resolved by closing the case (around 76%). These informal solutions lead to a considerable reduction in the number of minors judged, which was 5,479 in 1989, of whom 2,177 were sentenced to prison, 1,031 to detention, and 69 were 'detained at the pleasure of the state.' In addition, the duration of sentences served is extremely short, as two thirds of juveniles who are incarcerated serve sentences of under three months, and one third sentences of three to six months. Among new measures, reparation of damage, imposed as an educational measure on the offender, is becoming more and more common in Poland. This obligation can also be imposed on parents.

Fines are given a primary place in Sweden, essentially under the form of *jours-amendes*. In 1989, deprivation of liberty concerned only 0.3% of minors aged 15-18 who received sentences (around 16,000 per year) in Sweden. Fifty per cent were fined, 43% of the cases were closed, in 6% of cases probation was ordered, and sanctions with probation in 1% of cases.

When measures have already been taken by the social services, when the offence was committed impulsively or when there has been a placement in a residence, the case is closed. The case is also closed for minor infractions and when a probation order is expected from the court or when the juvenile suffers from psychological problems. As for 18 to 20-year-olds, (around 20,500 young people per year), 67% were fined, 10% received a penalty combined with probation, 9% of the cases were closed, 8% were placed under supervision and 6%, or around 1,200 young people were deprived of liberty.

134

It is noticeable that the prosecutor has a great deal of room to manoeuvre due to the power to assess the proceedings. For young people aged 15 to 18, the prosecutor decides the fate of the juvenile delinquent in 74% of cases (in 1991). The decision was referred to the courts in 54% of cases in 1989 for 18 to 21-year-olds.

Closing of cases appears to be the typical response concerning young people aged 15 or 16 (in 49-55% of cases), while fines predominate (in 52%-67% of cases) for young people aged 18 to 21.

Fines also predominate in Switzerland and make up 40.1% of sentences, while reprimand constitutes only 16.1%, work services 27.1% and detention 16.7%.

In French-speaking Belgium, the trend is characterised by the development of measures of supervision combined with services rendered to the community (accomplishment of educational or altruistic actions) or attendance at a centre of educational orientation.

For the French community there has been a decrease in two other custodial measures: detention at the pleasure of the 'Community Executive' and provisional placement of 15 days in a detention centre. Since 1989, minors detained at the pleasure of the Community Executive are no longer detained in a penitentiary establishment or confined to a secure community institution. These juveniles are oriented since 1989 towards a section of initial reception in an open system and are then placed in the charge of an educational team in the context of an individualised action in an open environment. Provisional placement for a maximum of 15 days in a detention centre has declined particularly since February 1989, as a result of the *Bouamar* order issued by the European Court of Strasbourg, which found Belgium guilty of violating article 5(1) of the European Convention on Human Rights. As the Belgian law had not ruled out the renewal of the measure, the juvenile had been subjected to nine placements in prison, i.e. 119 days of detention.

In Greece, among the 6,794 minors who received sentences in 1990, there were 80 children and 6,714 adolescents. For 75% of the children (60 in number) educational measures in an open environment were imposed. However, there has been a drop in the number of these measures (in 1980, 94.2% (226), in 1985, 98.8% (166) and in 1989, 86.2% (94)). Likewise regarding young adolescents, educational measures in an open environment represented 79.4% in 1980 (4,156) and in 1990 73.8% (4,953) of the total number of sanctions imposed on them. Only the Greek report raised the question of correlation between the nature of the offences committed by minors and the type of sanction. Juvenile delinquency is characterised (at least in Greece) by the 'over-representation' of violations of traffic laws, which are most often met with sanctions in an open environment (reprimand, placement under parental supervision or educational monitoring by delegates of educational services within jurisdictions). Thus in 1986 4,560 or 67.6% of young people who were dealt with using such measures had committed traffic

135

offences. After road offences comes crimes against property, which concerned 989 cases or 14.7% of juveniles made subject to these measures.

In Slovenia, juvenile delinquency is characterised by its small extent. Accordingly, social reaction has little in common with the other countries studied. Relatively restrictive criteria which determine the competence of the courts must also be taken into account in this matter.

In 1990 the courts imposed 581 admonitions out of 997 measures, 65 placements in a disciplinary centre (comparable to the German institution of detention). They ordered 'educational supervision' (probation) by the parents themselves for 71 cases and by the socio-administrative services in 216 cases. Institutional measures are only a small proportion of the total number of sanctions imposed. Thus the penalty of imprisonment was only imposed in three cases. Other institutional measures were divided up as follows: 38 placements in educational institutions and 23 in re-educational centres.

Implementation

The carrying out of measures in an open environment calls for a number of partners working together in an interdisciplinary way.

Because of decentralisation and the transfer of new powers to a local level in France, there has been a redistribution of power and a diversity of actions. The general councils and local authorities have become privileged consultative bodies, in particular in the implementation of community service and new measures of taking charge of young people. This has also led to the participation and extension of the whole associated sector. This tendency has been given a theme in France under the term 'participating criminal policy', to the extent that society is directly addressed in matters of delinquency. In other words, the open environment is an invitation for the social group and in particular the associated sector to actively participate in the implementation of these measures.

A change of this magnitude is not visible in other countries. However in Belgium it has been observed that the development of new modes of intervention in an open environment has favoured referral to the associative sector and engendered new co-operation. Thus new structures and services have been organised in the private sector for the implementation of educational and philanthropic services (which imply the collaboration of the organisations and resources of the local community), such as placements in autonomy, individual or family guidance and educational orientation. These structures - approved and subsidised by the Communities - are often organised into federations or associations who are partners in the elaboration of political orientations and implementations concerning the protection of youth. Also worth mentioning is the active co-operation of certain young lawyers/barristers moved by the concern of campaigning against measures of institutional placements and favouring treatment in an open environment.

It is significant to observe that the implementation of measures in an open environment does not give an increased role to so-called 'societal' instances in the majority of countries, which nevertheless extol the virtues of the open environment. This means that despite the opening of juvenile justice towards society, the legal system is still not prepared to confer or delegate certain powers of decision. Juvenile justice remains above all a judicial affair. Indeed we remain in the context of judicial or penal logic.

The control of the judicial authorities on the implementation of measures in an open environment well illustrates this caution. Thus in Germany, as in Austria, new measures are established thanks to public organisations (such as the 'Youth Office' or the probation services, social workers or private or public organisations dependent on social assistance to young people in Germany). Concerning the roles of the community, the family or the school, these organisations are only led to participate on the request of other organisations. In Germany, the monitoring of measures ordered is ensured by the jurisdiction which must be informed of any incident. The sanction depends on its nature (formal or informal). Thus if the measure has been ordered as a condition of closing the case failure to carry it out will lead in principle the initiation of public action. However, if it is a matter of measures ordered in the course of a judgement, they can be modified and can entail detention for wrongful failure to observe them.

In the Belgian and French reports, stress has been placed on the interventions of the associative sector.

In France, this sector deals with approximately two thirds of measures of legal protection, in the framework of educational assistance as well as measures of custody which take place in the criminal system. The authorisation for these establishments is delivered by the Ministry of Justice after the investigation of Services for the Protection of Youth, which represent the prefecture. Monitoring of the institutions and services of the associative sector is carried out jointly by the Ministry of Justice, general committees and magistrates.

In Belgium there exists a somewhat similar system. In both communities, legal texts fix the limits and conditions for intervention of the social sector. Subsidies are approved and granted for individuals and services which assure the protection of young people. Monitoring occurs both in educational and accounting matters.

In Austria there exists a strict separation between the ordering of measures within the legal system, and their execution which is the responsibility of social workers, probation and educational services.

The French report reminds us of the new role granted to these community initiatives by the various recommendations of international organisations (UN, Council of Europe) as well as the International Convention of the Rights of the Child (in force in France since 6 September 1990) concerning ways of dealing with juvenile delinquency. The role of the family is becoming more and more important. The decree of 22 July 1987 introduces procedural provisions to reinforce the participation of families in the system of legal protection of the child, and particularly in procedures of educational assistance (information, hearing, defence and information on channels of appeal, respect of religious and philosophical convictions). According to article 375-1 of the Civil code, the judge must seek the co-operation of the family with measures ordered. In criminal matters it is necessary to associate families with measures of mediation and reparation.

The new role attributed to the community in the framework of city politics must be underlined. Various services of legal advice associated with the local community have been established. Members of the community and departmental councils for the prevention of delinquency which bring together elected officials, associations and various representatives of different ministerial departments concerned co-operate in this role. The school is a privileged partner for the legal system regarding protection of young people.

In Belgium, the most recent provisions deliberately call on the co-operation and participation of the family in a wide sense. Thus in Flanders, 'family guidance is one of the special forms of assistance which the Committee of Concern can ensure and one of the thirteen distinct measures which the juvenile court can impose'. The day centres in Flanders are specifically intended to work together with the family. Thus, new decrees explicitly recognise a new social responsibility on the part of the family, the school and the local community in the development of young people.

While the associative sector is being developed in France for the protection of youth, it is astonishing that voluntary services are in decline in the judicial sector. In France it has practically fallen into disuse (e.g. probation volunteers originally introduced by the decree of 2 February 1945).

On the other hand, in Belgium there is a certain resurgence of interest in this form of participation which 'favours the opening up of the legal system to the public' with the introduction of new measures of a socio-educational nature (mediation and reparation). The training of these voluntary workers is encouraged by the Belgian government. However in Belgium as in France it appears that the number of voluntary workers in this sector is difficult to quantify due to a lack of reliable statistics.

Sometimes the voluntary sector is an integral part of a long tradition as in Slovenia or Sweden where training is practically institutionalised.

In Germany and Austria the voluntary services and the training of volunteers working in the sector of assistance to young people is regulated.

In Austria there are also voluntary probation officers. They receive training within the framework of this service but cannot deal with more than five cases (the number is fixed by law). They are therefore placed under the authority of professional probation officers.

On the other hand in Greece, as specialised training of voluntary workers is explicitly set out in law, the conditions of eligibility for such work are regulated and subject to proof of theoretical knowledge acquired at university or two years' professional experience in social work, as well as practical knowledge based on a study period of six months in the juvenile court.

After this survey of current forms of treatment of juvenile delinquents in an open environment, one can never stress enough the vital role played by the juvenile court judge, reinforced by the actions of the legislator who draws widely on the wisdom, good faith and experience in the matter of judges, giving them an almost discretionary power. Juvenile justice is pragmatic, justified by the principle of appropriateness of the sanction, taken in a wide sense. Around this affirmation centre new trends which can be seen in each country, particularly in the development of the idea of the secondary role of criminal proceedings (diversion from the (juvenile) court). Paradoxically, the aim of proceedings against a minor is to avoid this or at least to abandon it as soon as possible. It is with this view that all mechanisms of closing cases are being developed, from recording of offences by police and especially during the pre-trial investigation stage by the public ministry. The closing of cases, in its different forms, (without follow-up, conditional or penal transaction) is now, according to statistics received, the favoured form of intervention regarding juvenile delinquents, with few exceptions (the former Czechoslovakia). This diversification of modes of treatment and particularly the considerable increase in extra-judicial measures implies a re-centring of social reaction, but also, due to the increase in the powers of the public ministry which replaces judicial authority, a readjustment or reinforcement of guarantees and rights of minors, during this preparatory phase of the process.

As for the substance of social reaction to juvenile delinquency, we note a series of new elements which illustrate the opening up of juvenile justice.

The taking into account of the victim during the criminal process, as well as the defence of his or her interests, has led to a new redistribution of roles between intervening parties (victim-delinquent-society) in bringing together all sectors to participate in the reinsertion of the offender. The reparation by the perpetrator of damage caused by the infraction, as a direct service to be rendered to the victim or an indirect service to the community (for example community service), presupposes a true step of making the juvenile more responsible and aware of the offence committed. In this respect, mediation, which consists of confronting the two antagonists of the criminal trial (victim and delinquent) and making them participate actively in the process of reconciliation can be perfectly integrated in this process. The effort of reparation constitutes one of the keys to the vault of new social reactions.

The intertwining and combination of these elements in addition to their credibility in implementation have certainly contributed to the decrease in sanctions involving deprivation of liberty.

SECTION III YOUNG PEOPLE IN DANGER

This chapter is devoted to the approach to young people before the courts who are not delinquents. This category is much more heterogeneous and more difficult to define - often termed 'young people in difficulty', 'children in danger', or 'at risk' to use the most frequent expressions.

Our aim is not to elaborate here on the different legal systems applicable to these young people, but rather to bring out a number of reflections centred on two points:

- general orientations of the legislations concerned;
- interventions envisaged for young people in danger.

The countries or regions taken into consideration are the same as those dealt with in Chapter 2 on *Juvenile Delinquents:* Germany, Austria, England and Wales, Belgium (with its two principal Communities), Scotland, France, the Grand Duchy of Luxembourg, Greece, Northern Ireland, Italy, Poland, Portugal, Slovenia, Sweden, Switzerland and Czechoslovakia. For The Netherlands, the questionnaire (see *Appendix I*) did not lead to information concerning young people in danger.

The Legal Framework
Annina Lahalle Alenka Selih Colette Somerhausen

Description

Without wishing to describe in minute detail the approaches to young people in danger, as set out by legislation in the various regions studied, we feel nevertheless entitled to deal with general elements and specific traits which permit an appropriate representation.

General trends

The sector of aid to young people in difficulty or danger has undergone notable changes in many countries. The relevant legislation has recently undergone reforms, some of which have barely come into force, or only partially; rare are the countries or regions where no change is planned.

For example, Belgium, England and Wales as well as Northern Ireland have introduced new legislation, while in Scotland the relevant legislation in force since 1971 is being examined in order to identify and define desirable changes. The same changes can be observed in countries with German law systems: Germany itself adopted a new law on assistance to children and young people (in force since 1 January 1991), the principal idea of which is to provide young people with 'assistance in education' in ensuring social services. Austria has introduced a new law on juvenile courts (1988), where the rules of procedure are also applicable to young people in danger.

Greece, a country of the German tradition in matters of criminal law, has retained legal provisions for young people in danger which date from the 1940s. It concerns the law (much criticised) on the organisation and functioning of educational institutions and the law on the family: it is generally admitted that these provisions must be reformed.

A third situation is seen in former socialist countries (Czechoslovakia, Poland, Slovenia). In these three countries, it is either the Family Code or social welfare law which applies to the problems of young people in danger. This legislation is now in the process of being renewed, and it is almost certain that the position of young people in danger and especially the methods of dealing with this group will be changed. For (the former) Czechoslovakia, the correspondent underlines that since 1991, a procedure has been introduced to prepare new legislation; in Slovenia minor corrections were made in 1989, but new legislation is also expected, both for juvenile delinquents and young people in danger. In Poland, children in danger (termed 'morally deficient' by the law) are also subject to the law on minors (1982) which concentrates mostly on juvenile delinquents. A unique case seems to be that of Sweden: the two laws which govern the matter of interest to us - the law on the treatment of young people and the social law - are taken as laws of orientation of assistance to minors guaranteed by the state; however, it seems that the possible tendencies of changes envisaged are taking a rather 'non-progressive' direction.

The changes being introduced are more than a simple update. They appear to us to translate a new current of thought in the interpretation of problems posed by and for the young people concerned, as in the method of resolving them. We are in fact observing a new way of conceiving relationships between young people, the family and the State, in which the latter is much more a necessary provider of adequate services to families in difficulty than a substitute for failing parents.

Without being able to generalise - considering the range and variety of countries included in this study, marked by different histories, cultures and practices - several main patterns can be extracted, which we will gladly summarise (perhaps too schematically) in the following manner:

- the notion of protection giving way to that of specialised assistance;
- greater relegation of assistance provided by the State, in relation to first of all responsibilities and initiatives of the family, then aid from services and resources available in the community;
- re-centring of interventions concerning the young person in difficulty, viewed more than formerly as determining his or her own development and social insertion (obviously taking into account age, abilities and possibilities), along with what that implies concerning recognised rights of young people, the taking into consideration of their needs, desires and personal convictions and the seeking of their consent for proposed interventions of assistance;
- greater gradation between the fields of global social assistance where the offer of services is general, from specialised assistance where specific offers are negotiated and accepted on a voluntary basis, to imposed legal intervention. A tendency towards diverting assistance to young people in danger from the (juvenile) court, to the greatest extent possible, and towards minimising legal intervention to the extent strictly necessary, has been observed in several countries, in cases where recourse to imposed measures is unavoidable;
- a quest for measures of educational, social and psychological support to families, while keeping children within the family, but for exceptional cases;
- a primary role is therefore given to assistance in the environment of the young person, put with an increased participation of new partners in society and also classical institutional collaborators who usually, according to conceptions which are today being questioned, leave treatment of young people in danger or difficulty entirely to specialised services (national education, for example).

New situations and new categories of young people are being dealt with in most legislations. There is also however a new role given to the 'community' which appears in most legislations: the community where the child lives and the local community. The various laws of decentralisation have in certain countries transferred duties and responsibilities of treatment of minors in danger to local authorities (which is not always the case for juvenile delinquents). The term 'community' can be used differently according to the legislative texts examined, but the idea which emerges is that found in the international rules of the United Nations, in particular in the Convention on the Rights of the Child. 'Community' can have the widest meaning, from the associative sector to a group of volunteers working in an area of a city.

In this sense, the French report indicates that 'current educational trends have the aim of permitting the young person to return as soon as possible to structures of treatment in common law (school, professional training, medical provisions), favouring a true social insertion or reinsertion of the young people concerned.'

In several countries, the grouping together formerly operated between juvenile delinquents and young people in danger is becoming blurred. During previous decades, certain countries had likened one category to the other or at least considered young offenders as a category, among others, of young people in danger. As a result a single legislation could partially or wholly apply to both categories of young people (as in Poland, Luxembourg, Belgium, England and Wales, Northern Ireland, Portugal, Spain and, as for more distant legislations, most Latin American countries), or the same decision-making institutions were competent for both types of case (as in Belgium and Scotland), or juvenile delinquents could benefit from legislation designed for young people in danger (as in Germany and France, where educational assistance is often used for young offenders), or finally treatment of delinquents could be entrusted by the court system to organisations of social assistance designed for families and young people in danger (e.g. Germany, France, England and Wales, Scotland).

A reverse movement has recently made itself felt in certain countries, linked to a tendency on the one hand to 'decriminalise' juvenile justice and on the other hand to 'divert from the court' the situations of young people confronted with educational or social problems threatening their development, except in cases of urgency or where the social route has failed. It must be recognised that although the court system has, in certain countries, been the promoter and the instigator of assistance to children and adolescents in danger, at present social institutions are more in a position to take over and assume their role and now defend it with at times a certain amount of aggression towards legal institutions.

Thus in Belgium, recent legislative reforms introduce different systems for intervention according to whether juvenile delinquents or young people in danger are involved. In the same way, the reforms introduced in England and Wales, as in Northern Ireland, lead to a distinction from now on between legal instances competent to deal with delinquents and young people in danger. In these regions, the provisions relative to the legal protection of young people in danger are much closer to civil law, as is the case in Switzerland, than laws relevant to juvenile delinquents. For Scotland, where children's hearings deal

143

with both young people in need of protection and juvenile delinquents, one can consider that, conversely, since the Social Work (Scotland) Act of 1968, it is delinquents who have been taken away (at least to a considerable extent) from the legal system.

We must not overlook the impact which political transformations in certain countries have had on legislative change. In Belgium it is clear that the institutional transformations which have been taking place in the country for two decades are not unrelated to the division between laws related to juvenile delinquents and those concerning young people in danger. Originally a unified state, Belgium has progressively moved in the direction of a federal state, by the creation of regions and communities. Although the State has remained competent in matters of justice and delinquency, the Communities (with a linguistic basis) have as areas of competence above all social aid and legal and social protection of young people in danger, such as the implementation of legal measures aimed at juvenile delinquents. On these new foundations, the Communities have legislated in matters which concern them and have, in particular, each drawn up new systems of assistance to young people in difficulty.

It is evident that independent legislation is not the only feasible solution: in Switzerland, the legal framework concerning young people in danger is defined for the whole country by articles 307-317 of the Swiss Civil Code, but the competent care authority is different from canton to canton.

The range of situations envisaged by the legislations of different countries is extremely wide, as reality indeed demands. Explicitly and generally involved are young victims and potential victims of ill-treatment, neglect, irresponsible behaviour or delinquency on the part of their parents, young people exposed to physical or moral dangers, suffering from family relationship conflicts, brought up in living conditions or educational backgrounds dangerous for their development.

The law enumerates the types of situations or categories of young people in mind; it often does this in terms sufficiently vague to cover cases of a very varied nature. A shorter formulation is sometimes chosen, designed to adapt to the innumerable facets of the problem. Thus Swiss legislation, always remarkable for its clarity and conciseness, refers to the necessity to 'protect the child if his or her development is threatened'. The French Community of Belgium uses the generic term of 'young people in difficulty' and the Flemish Community uses the expression of young people in 'problematic educational situations' to replace the former expression of young people 'whose health, safety or moral welfare is in danger'. But the text of the Flemish decree stipulates that, by this new expression, must be understood 'a situation where the physical security, the possibilities of emotional, moral, intellectual or social development of minors are put at risk by exceptional events, relationship conflicts or living conditions.' The notion of 'young people in danger' has in fact provoked strong criticism in Belgium under the pretext that, by its imprecision, it has led to exaggerated and arbitrary interventions in families, which the original benevolent intention to protect minors cannot

144

justify. It appears however that this expression has not totally disappeared and that in any case there has not been success in substituting another formulation devoid of risk of misinterpretation.

The German and Austrian systems evoke situations in which physical, psychological or moral development is at risk, or educational difficulties. To generalise, we can say that it is a matter of situations where the welfare of the child is in danger.

The Greek law of 1940 uses the term 'bad habits', which demonstrates precisely the spirit of the time in which the law was devised.

As for the (former) Czechoslovakian system, State action is justified by 'endangerment of regular education' or 'maladjusted' behaviour on the part of the child. A similar terminology is found in Slovenian statutes, which speak of 'behavioural or personality troubles' of the child, which includes delinquent behaviour or behaviour that is not delinquent, but 'deviant'. Polish legislation, finally, mentions minors 'in a state of moral deficiency'. Several systems (the former Czechoslovakia, Austria, Sweden, Belgium) include, in categories of situations of danger, different forms of ill-treatment inflicted on children.

The origins of this danger are sometimes made evident: in Germany, this danger is considered the consequence of various types of behaviour which range from the abuse of parental power or neglect of the child, to the behaviour of third parties or the unwillingness or inability of the parents to remove the danger. An identical idea is found at the basis of (the former) Czechoslovakian provisions which often refer to cases where parents have been guilty of neglect or abused their power towards their children. In Belgium also, national legislation mentions ill-treatment, abuse of authority, widely known irresponsible behaviour or serious negligence on the part of parents; the legislation of the French Community decree widens the perspectives in taking into account the behaviour of the family or 'family unit', meaning the individuals who make up the family environment of the life of the young person, including foster parents. In France the notion of danger can be used for other guardians (even temporary) of the child, such as foster families, or again in the face of certain situations of institutional violence.

In fact, the young people who are to be protected are those whose physical, intellectual, emotional and social development or social insertion are at risk, if parents or guardians fail to take or are unable to take the necessary measures.

In comparing recent texts to earlier ones, it has been observed that moralistic connotations are on the decline; thus the concept of 'moral danger' of the young person has disappeared from Belgian Community legislation (however this terminology is still present in French legislation, as in Polish law, where the child in a state of 'moral deficiency' is mentioned). In a related sense, the lack of family discipline of the young person, begging or vagrancy are no longer explicitly retained in the same legislation: these situations are based on the sum of 'problematic educational situations' or are only means among others for the young person to express his or her 'difficulties'.

The definitions are therefore different from one country to another, even if it is necessary to admit that, in certain legislative systems, there is still the idea of State intervention to replace absent or failing parents.

In this way, one of the main ideas which emerges from many legislations is that of 'rights and duties' of parents towards their children. These duties are described in Civil Codes (France, Italy, Portugal), often in general terms, for example 'security, morality, health and education' for France, 'protection, education, development of personality' for Italy and 'security, health, moral upbringing and education' for Portugal.

A second idea which we will retain is the role of the State as an element of parental control in many European countries (limitation, subrogation). The foundation of State intervention is the 'protection' and interests of the child and adolescent. 'Protection tends, in all legislations, to invite institutional responses suitable for adaptation, in time and place, to the diversity of the situations and parties involved.'

If changes often distinguish delinquents from young people in difficulty, it remains nevertheless that the commission of an offence can be interpreted as a symptom of difficulties experienced by the young person, and consequently systems of aid to juveniles can be seen along the lines of alternatives to custody; this was clearly stated during preparation of the English Criminal Justice Act 1991. On the contrary, we observe that Portuguese law mentions 'action to prevent delinquent behaviour' as part of the protection of young people in difficulty. Although the principal objective of laws is to assist the young person threatened, whose development is at risk, they nevertheless often specifically address parents or even other people responsible for the education of the juvenile. Thus the decree of the French Community of Belgium applies primarily to young people in difficulty, as well as to individuals who are encountering great difficulty in the exercise of their parental obligations.

The diversity of the situations and individuals needing to be taken into account, whether aiming for prevention or correction has led some countries to legislate with determined dangers or distinct parties in mind. Thus the protection of children who are victims of sexual abuse or ill-treatment is subject to specific legal texts (France, Portugal and both Belgian communities for example), as is the decline in the rights of the parental authority.

This evolution in legislations in relation to situations traditionally dealt with, but also in the face of new situations arising out of social change, or in relation to the coming to light of new methods, also gives rise to new definitions, such as that of 'mistreatment'.

This is the case in France concerning the law of 10 July 1989 on 'the prevention of ill-treatment'. Although the law has, for more than a century, given to judges the classical means of protection of the abused child, the notion of 'mistreatment' introduces a wider definition than the repression of criminal acts. New collaborators are called upon, in particular at a local level. Information, training and social protection are added to the problem already established by juvenile law. New instruments such as a 'toll-free telephone hotline' are made available by the public sector to individuals concerned by the phenomenon, children and adults.

This is also the case for the Portuguese law of 1991 which creates the Commission for the Protection of Minors (social, administrative or community service), which focuses especially on the problem of mistreatment (this term also appears in the Portuguese response): 'mistreatment requires, above all, interdisciplinary and inter-institutional intervention, and the participation and total devotion of the local community'.

In matters of specialised social assistance organised on a voluntary basis, it is observed that the young person takes on a central role in most recent legislation, according to the movement which wishes to make this an issue of rights.

With regard to the objectives of these legislations, not surprisingly, no lower age threshold limits interventions of assistance and protection which, generally speaking, take into consideration minors from birth to the age of legal majority. In Scotland, however, the provisions of the Social Work (Scotland) Act 1968 apply only up to the age of 16 (but see now *Appendix IV*). In Belgium on the other hand there now exists the possibility of granting assistance, on a voluntary basis, beyond the age of majority, provided that this assistance was sought before the age of 18 (French Community), or of prolonging assistance beyond the age of legal majority (Flemish Community) until the age of 18 years and six months, 20 and 21 years, according to individual cases. Parallel possibilities also exist elsewhere, such as in England and Wales. Likewise, the French law of 18 February 1975, regarding the legal protection of young adults, contains possibilities of prolonging measures taken while the young person was still a minor up to the age of 21.

It is necessary to note that legislations (e.g. Germany and Slovenia) make a distinction between 'children' (usually aged 0 to 13 or 14) and young persons (from 13 or 14 to 18 or 19). The highest age for obtaining educational assistance appears in the German system, which includes young adults up to 27.

Instances of Intervention

Beyond the divergences which exist between countries concerning their institutional set-up, a distinguishing characteristic can be noted for numerous countries: a disparity exists between instances charged with providing assistance on a voluntary basis and those which forcibly intervene. This division is however not apparent in certain former socialist countries. Poland recognises a wide competence of the Family Courts, which deal in principle with all family problems, including children in danger, but of which a part also comes under the competence of juvenile courts (for delinquents). On the contrary, Slovenia has specialised instances of the legal system which are competent to deal with minors (aged 14 to 18) who have committed criminal offences; but also all other forms of behaviour termed 'deviant', and, whatever their behaviour, all minors under 14 who come under socio-

147

administrative instances which are not asked by the law to seek the consent of the child (or the adolescent): these instances provide assistance if and when they consider it necessary for the welfare of the child. On the other hand, the system of a country where socio-administrative services also play an important role, Sweden, is also based on the consent of the child. A mixed solution emerges in Greece, where decisions affecting institutional measures are taken by the ministry and based on the assessment prepared by the juvenile court magistrate.

In most countries, therefore, assistance which is sought or at least accepted is provided by socio-administrative services, and compulsory aid is decided by a judicial organisation. In this case, it is a question either of a juvenile jurisdiction (competent also for juvenile delinquents) as in Belgium and Northern Ireland, or a juvenile jurisdiction with civil legislation, such as in France, or a civil jurisdiction as in Switzerland, Poland, the former Czechoslovakia, England and Wales, where recent reforms have reorganised the legal structure with a competence closer to that of a family jurisdiction. Still other countries (such as Austria and Germany) resort in these cases to tribunals of guardianship or even an administrative court (in Sweden). Without a doubt it is necessary to give a special place to the Scottish children's hearings, which, by their particular composition, have the characteristics of a social organization with jurisdictional powers. Some of these jurisdictions appeal to lay personnel, as well as to magistrates, no doubt to facilitate the socio-educational orientation of measures imposed.

In France, the protection of young people in difficulty is entrusted to administrative and judicial authorities according to a double-sided provision. Legal protection of children is entrusted mainly to the juvenile court judge. The judge can impose measures concerning 'minors whose health, security and moral welfare are in danger or whose conditions of education are greatly deficient' (art. 375 of the Civil Code). Administrative protection of children is part of the system of common law. The parents can request aid from the administrative authority, subject to their consent and to guarantees fixed by law. Since decentralisation, the essential part of the administrative protection of children is the responsibility of the President of the General Council, elected at a departmental level, whose mission is to provide 'aid to children who are confronted with social difficulties likely to seriously undermine their well-being' (law of 6 January 1986). The law of 6 June 1984 (inserted into the Family Code) defines the conditions under which services of social assistance are applied concerning minors: compulsory written consent of parents after being informed beforehand of the nature, consequences and duration of the measure (limited to one year), modes of intervention taken with the agreement of the family. The law on the prevention of mistreatment (dated 1989) sets out communication between the services of social protection and legal protection in particular situations, 'when a minor is or is assumed to be a victim of bad treatment and it is impossible to evaluate the situation, or if the family manifestly refuses to accept the intervention of the service of social aid to children, the President of the General Council immediately informs the legal authority and reports on action already taken.' The measures imposed by the legal authority are supported by classical procedural guarantees: hearings, summonses, notifications, the right to defence for the child and parents, and appeal channels. In addition the judge must seek the unity of the family and take into account the philosophical and religious convictions of the family. Temporary measures are limited to six months and final measures to two years. The minor can refer directly to the juvenile court judge, without any assistance from legal guardians, and independently of age or sex.

In Italy, with regard to young people in difficulty, the juvenile court judge has a double competence: 'civil competence' (acting on parental authority) when the child is in danger because of parents, and 'administrative or re-educational competence' when the minor is showing behavioural problems ('irregularity in conduct or character'). The articles of the Civil Code ('civil competence') concern, in general, interventions which limit parental authority. They therefore apply in all cases where there is abuse by parents of their authority or when they conduct themselves in a manner harmful to their children. These articles can also be applied by the juvenile court in cases of irregular conduct of the minor when this conduct is accompanied by serious negligence or educational incapability on the part of the parents. In the case of minors who 'show manifest proof of irregularity in their conduct or character', the applicable text is the law of 1934, which organises the administrative or re-educational competence of the juvenile court. The only measure of this text which can still be applied is that which consists of entrusting a minor to social services. The principal objective of 'civil measures' is the protection of the minor. 'Administrative or re-educational' measures envisage, besides protection, an aim of education or social reinsertion. The application and control of measures ordered by the juvenile court judge are the responsibility exclusively of local social services.

Both in France and Italy, treatment of a juvenile delinquent (criminal procedure) can be accompanied by a procedure of civil protection, if the magistrate judges that the delinquency stems from serious maladjustment and a situation of danger for the minor. The two procedures are disassociated and follow their course in parallel, in accordance with the laws peculiar to delinquency and the protection of minors in danger. In countries without a law peculiar to delinquency, such as Portugal, this difference and judicial separation do not operate.

In Portugal, the protection of minors in danger is primarily administrative and entrusted, in accordance with the law of 1991, to the Commission for the Protection of Minors. Only in serious cases (refusal of the family to co-operate with the measure envisaged or necessity to remove the child from the family) will the case be brought before the juvenile court (or normal courts in cities where there are no juvenile courts).

In the Portuguese law of 27 October 1978 (Law of Organization of the Protection of Minors - *organisação tutelar de menores*) we find a description of motives of intervention and the age brackets concerned: from 0 to 18 for all minors who are victims of ill-treatment or abandonment, or whose health,

149

security, education and moral welfare are in danger; from 12 to 16, the juvenile court judge can take steps of protection, assistance or education concerning any minor who shows serious difficulties in adapting to a normal social life or is drawn to begging, vagrancy, prostitution, licentiousness, alcohol abuse or drug use; from 14 to 18 for minors who refuse the 'discipline' of the family, place of work or institutions where they are placed; for minors aged 16 to 18 (who have reached the age of criminal majority) who become involved in begging, vagrancy, prostitution, licentiousness, alcohol abuse or drug use, when these activities do not constitute (or are not related to) a criminal offence; finally, the juvenile court judge is empowered to assess the requests of minors under 18 for protection against misuse of family authority or that of the institutions where they are placed.

It is observed that the range of competence of juvenile court judges varies from country to country. For example, competence in matters of adoption belongs to juvenile justice in some countries (Italy, for example) and comes under civil jurisdiction in others (France, Portugal), and the Italian juvenile court judge is competent for the authorisation of marriages of minors aged over 16 and late recognition of natural children.

In Western European systems, where the divide between voluntary and compulsory assistance exists, the socio-administrative services charged with providing social aid which has been accepted, see their intervention made subject to the agreement and consent of the family and of juveniles if they have reached a certain age. Thus the decree of the French Community of Belgium stipulates that 'no decision on individual aid can be taken by the counsellor without the agreement of the young person if aged over 14, or otherwise the agreement of the de facto guardians of the young person'. If removal from the family environment is envisaged, 'the agreement of those who have guardianship of the child is required'. The requirement of written consent and certain formalities are intended to prove free consent to the aid concerned; they can also contribute to invite active participation of the different actors concerned. No doubt the free nature of consent given can sometimes be questioned: the disarray of the individuals concerned, their dependence on the social services, the apparent 'power' - sometimes experienced as such - of the professionals, the underlying threat of a legal measure in the case of refusal, can weigh, consciously or not, on the decision of the young person and the family. One can hope however that informing the population, the expansion of the idea of 'the right to social assistance', the professional training and conscience of social workers will limit more and more the risk of social assistance functioning without real participation of the clients.

The situation in countries where consent is not required by law appears to be the reverse: the competent service makes an effort to obtain it, in the knowledge that, without consent, the work is almost impossible to carry out. This ambiguous situation also causes ethical problems for the specialised service (especially the social service) as its professional role along the lines of social aid is confined to social control.

Assistance which is voluntarily requested or accepted is generally organised on as local a level as possible, in such a way as to bring together the offer and request for services, facilitate spontaneous requests and make the local community more conscious of its responsibilities and obligations towards its members in difficulty. This conception does not lead to uniformity in the organisation of services of specialised assistance, seen here as a specific organisation (e.g. Belgium, Switzerland, Germany, Austria, Sweden), there as an element inserted into the structure of local services of social assistance (e.g. England, Scotland, the former Czechoslovakia, Slovenia). A particular case is that of Greece where aid is ensured by Organisations for the Protection of Youth, situated in the headquarters of the regional courts, which are under the control of the Minister of Justice.

The anxiety to adapt the organisation of these services to local social, cultural and political peculiarities leads in some countries to the conception of different structures from one region to another. Thus structures differ in Switzerland, according to the cantons, in Belgium, according to the linguistic communities, in France, according to the *départements*, in Germany and Austria according to the *Länder*, and in Poland according to the *wojewodstwa*.

Whatever the form given to these services (cantonal services in Switzerland, social aid to children in France, services inserted into the local department of social services in England and Northern Ireland, Counsellor for Assistance to Young People in French-speaking Belgium, Committee of Concern in Flemish-speaking Belgium, the communes in Sweden and the Youth Office in Germany and Austria), they show a marked professional character. In Belgium, where, under the previous legislation, the exercise of social protection was the responsibility of a committee of citizens assisted by a service of social workers, the change has, on the contrary, placed emphasis on the professionalism of interventions in entrusting them to a Service of Assistance to Young People, directed by a professional counsellor in the French Community and in the Flemish Community to an Office of Special Assistance to Youth, a specialised element of the Committee of Concern, which organises assistance in the intervention of the social service of the committee.

This professionalism is very marked in countries which have a long tradition of specialised services for children, such as Germany, Austria and Sweden. The same observation is valid for Poland (at a different social level) which has also had specialised services for the protection of children for a long time. The situation in Slovenia is marked, it appears, by the fact that the previous system of 'self-management' has used the community (citizens) in the wide sense of a 'hypertrophic' manner; the current reaction since then is that more and more competence is given to State authorities.

Again, generally speaking, especially in countries which are undergoing significant social development, the action of the social and administrative services is considered auxiliary. It comes into play when general services of aid to individuals and families, envisaged as the first services to turn to, have not been able to provide adequate assistance. This principle is clearly stated in

German law which expressly defines public aid to young people as being auxiliary. As another example, in French-speaking Belgium the Counsellor for Aid to Young People is obliged, when asked to intervene, to first of all direct the parties concerned towards the appropriate individual or service, then to follow the implementation of these steps and to engender co-operation between the different services which may be called upon to intervene, and can also, on the request of the young person or a member of the family, call on any public or private service to request information on its action or refusal to intervene. It is only after having established that no service or person is in a position to provide appropriate assistance to the young person that the counsellor can 'exceptionally and provisionally' entrust to his or her own services the task of providing the assistance desired for the necessary period of time.

However, this does not appear to be the case in former socialist countries. In these countries, as the network of voluntary non-governmental agencies has developed very little and the network of social assistance agencies are organised in a general manner, it is very possible that the socio-administrative service takes action before any other form of aid and protection is used much earlier than in systems where the involvement of specialised services is really 'the last resort'.

The specific nature of these services justifies the entrusting to them of either tasks of general prevention, or the implementation of legal measures. The provision by the same service of social measures and legal measures does not appear to pose any problems in Anglo-Saxon countries. The same seems to be the case in Germany and Austria, while in Sweden the socio-administrative service is still more engaged in the two areas of activity. The situation is identical, or similar, in Poland, the former Czechoslovakia and Slovenia. Here, however, it has been noted, during a study carried out during the 1980s, that a malaise exists among social workers under the jurisdiction concerning juvenile delinquents: a conflict between social work and social control has become apparent. This situation is even more pronounced in Belgium where the services responsible for voluntary aid and those which work under court orders are now totally separate.

In many countries, the ill-treatment of children has been increasingly seen in recent years as a field of action requiring particular training and competence of those intervening; consequently services have been created whose specialisation and independent organisation do not exclude a certain amount of collaboration with the specialised services of aid to young people in danger.

As we have previously mentioned, a strong movement of diversion from the court has marked the sector of aid to young people in difficulty. It has been accentuated in the most recent legal provisions.

The will to limit recourse to judicial authorities only to cases where social assistance turns out to be impossible or ineffective, where coercion is essential to protect the young person or provide necessary assistance, is evident in many of the countries considered here. Of course, judicial institutions have competence when it is a question of penalising the behaviour of adults which is harmful to children to the point where it is considered a criminal offence. The judicial system is confined to a secondary and specific field of intervention, defined by the needs of the young people, the urgency of the situation, the impossibility or failure of action undertaken on a voluntary basis (as far as intervention has manifestly taken place), and more rarely by the necessity to arbitrate conflicts between the organisations which offer voluntary aid and their clients.

In France, according to the double protection already mentioned, the choice between the administrative and judicial routes is based on the notion of 'real and present danger'; presumed danger does not justify the action of the juvenile court judge (except in cases of ill-treatment reported by the President of the General Council according to the law of 1989).

It would be inaccurate, in our opinion, to consider that the restriction of judicial competence means simply a shunning of the legal system. Rather it can be held that the development of social services now allows them to take on tasks which are appropriate for them, without any requirement that the judicial system should, as previously, substitute for their inadequacies.

Recent German legislation is moving in the same direction. The guardianship court can only take action if 'the physical, psychological or mental welfare of the child is in danger' and then only if this danger has been demonstrated by behaviour enumerated in the law (abuse of parental power, neglect of care due to the child; behaviour of the parents or a third party; the fact that the parents did not wish to remove the danger or are not in a position to do so). Austrian and Swedish legislation stresses the absence of consent, which is necessary for the court to be able to act.

In the former Czechoslovakia, Poland and Slovenia, the law does not mention this point. The last reform (1989) in Slovenia has however brought limits on the duration of institutional measures intended for children in danger, a solution considered more respectful of the rights of the child than the previous solution.

One realises that the objectives pursued by social and judicial instances are very similar:

- putting an end to the dangerous situations and problems of the young person;
- favouring the general development and social reinsertion of the juvenile.

It must be stated that the most recent legislation, the German law on assistance to children and juveniles, is the only law which states as the basis of educational assistance the right of the juvenile to development and education in order to become a responsible person capable of adapting to the community; this is without doubt the consequence of new trends in the area of rights of the child.

153

Some jurisdictions have the welfare of young people in mind and seek their best interests. However the methods of attaining this objective differ somewhat, to the extent that social instances wish to assist young people and their families, to stand by them, to guide them along this route, to help them exercise their roles and responsibilities, while judicial instances, intervening as a last resort, protect by means of coercion. This imposed protection however translates less into separations or prohibitions than by the offer of educational support, by techniques of social work where an effort is also made to engender the co-operation and participation of the parties concerned. Recourse to 'judicial protection' is therefore justified by the lack of ability of families and juveniles to act, their refusal to do so or the actual urgency of a situation of danger. But, as soon as possible, imposed protection gives place to voluntarily accepted assistance.

Transfer

The priority of intervention given to socio-administrative authorities, or according to the case, services specialised in dealing with ill-treatment, does not exclude the hypothesis of a transfer from the social sector to the judicial sector. Such a transfer is justified by the failure of a social measure, refusal to co-operate or the urgency of an intervention.

In some systems a particular importance is given to the consent of the legal representatives or, as expressed in German law, 'persons required to take care of the minor'. This is the case in Germany, Austria and Sweden. However, the following question can be asked: What is the importance given to the consent of the child? It is not difficult to imagine cases where the interests of the parents on the one hand and those of the child on the other are not identical, or worse still, in opposition.

If the failure of social measures strongly justifies transfer from the social to the judicial sector, some systems set out compulsory transfer in cases where the child commits a fresh offence during the implementation of the measure. This is the case in Greece, for example.

Let us state again that some systems do not make a very clear distinction between the socio-administrative sector and the judicial sector. In the former Czechoslovakia, measures of social aid in an open environment can be imposed by the socio-administrative service or by the court. In Slovenia, similar measures, which differ only by legal definition, (socio-administrative measures or educational measures, a category of criminal sanctions), can be imposed by both authorities. The first is justified by forms of 'deviant' behaviour, the second by criminal offences. Let us note finally that the transfer from the socio-administrative sector to the judicial system can also be seen as a kind of guarantee of a fair trial. One can theorise that any administrative decision which affects individual rights must be subject to judicial control after all means of appeal or recourse have been exhausted. In this way, in Slovenia, the decision to place the minor in an institution can be made subject to monitoring by the Supreme Court. Let us add, nevertheless, that this is a possibility which has never in fact materialised.

We must again remember, as an obstacle to this transfer, the existence of filtering mechanisms or functions, such as the Reporter in Scotland or the Commission of Mediation in the Flemish Community of Belgium. Let us add that when this Commission of Mediation decides to refer the case to the juvenile justice system, the public ministry must have discretionary power of decision as to the disposition of the case: the prosecutor can therefore close the case without follow-up.

In France, assistance to parents in the framework of administrative protection is the rule and judicial intervention the exception, as we have emphasised earlier. When an administrative follow-up turns out to be inadequate and the minor is considered to be in danger, it is the administrative authority which must report the case to the juvenile jurisdiction. The 1989 law concerning the protection of abused minors has set out the procedure of referral to judicial authority. General provisions for dealing with situations of children who are ill-treated or in danger are established in each département by the president of the general council, according to the modes established in common with the judicial authority and the total number of private and public services competent in matters of protection of children for the département. The public prosecutor therefore examines the opportunity of requiring the opening of a dossier of educational assistance. As a result of the judicial intervention, when the juvenile court judge envisages the ending of the measure ordered, the services of protection are normally informed, in order to be able to ensure a continuity of monitoring of the family.

Transfer from the judicial to the social sector is particularly favoured in French-speaking Belgium:

- as we stated earlier, a judicial measure can be replaced by a measure of social assistance which will be applied by the counsellor after its authorisation by the juvenile court;
- in case of urgent necessity to be able to ensure the placement of a child in serious danger, and if the consent of the parents (or of the child if aged over 14) is lacking, the counsellor reports the case to the juvenile court so that the latter may impose a provisional measure of assistance or authorise it. But from the moment that the counsellor has received notification that the measure has been authorised, the possibility of implementing a voluntarily accepted measure must be examined with the child and the family. In the case of agreement, the court authorises this new measure which will be applied by the counsellor: social assistance regains priority in this way.

In many other systems the transfer from the judicial to the social sector is carried out through various forms of diversion from the court. The powers to close the case without follow-up, sometimes given to the police and more often the Public Prosecutor's Department, or the juvenile court, are often

155

accompanied by the obligation to transfer the case to another instance; often it is transferred to the social sector.

Rights of the Child

The recognition of the rights of young people and the imposition of guarantees for the implementation of these rights are the principal traits of the evolution which has marked the protection of minors in danger and young delinquents as assistance to youth in recent decades. This is true above all for the most progressive countries.

This movement appears clearly evident in the case of young offenders, less so perhaps with regard to young people in danger. In fact it is now the case that a young delinquent before the judicial system must enjoy all the rights connected with the case of an adult and many international directives encourage revision of national legislation in this direction. However, things are more blurred in the case of young people in danger as the very foundation of judicial intervention is the protection of juveniles while acting in their interests. However, and this may at first appear contradictory, in several countries, particularly in Belgium, criticism has been levelled in recent years against legal systems which intervene too much, however worthy the intentions. These criticisms also find support in the fact that the legal systems intervene on the grounds of perceived dangers which are the possible result of the behaviour of juveniles themselves, and in this way the system exercises social control over young people.

In matters of social assistance young people in difficulty have benefited from the general movement towards the recognition of the rights of clients of social services as well as from the world-wide attention recently given to the rights of the child as set out in the International Convention on the Rights of the Child.

In this way, young people in danger appear as true subjects of law and the social and judicial approach to their problems is the subject of guarantees related to the respect of these rights. Without either wanting or being able to enumerate all the recognised rights of the child, let us mention some which are particularly in evidence in recent legislation.

In matters of social assistance to young people in danger:

- the right of the young person to specialised assistance, and the obligation on the part of intervening authorities to provide this assistance to young people and families to best serve the interests of the minor;
- the right of the young people to be heard, listened to, and see their needs and wishes taken into consideration;
- the right to personally consult the service concerned, to be informed of rights and obligations and to be accompanied by an adult of their own choice;

- the right to be consulted on every measure concerning them and the obligation for the services, on some occasions and in some cases, to obtain the written consent of the young person;
- the right to ask for a measure to be modified or revoked;
- the right to appeal or to ask for arbitration when assistance has been refused or in case of conflict as to the aid to be provided.

It is interesting to note that one of the most recent and progressive legislations, the German law on assistance to children and juveniles, does not contain an independent right of children to ask for educational assistance. This right however emerges from the particular provisions of the law which specify the legal status of the child. Thus the young people must 'participate' in the decisions which affect them; they can consult the youth office regarding every educational matter which concerns them; in the case of application of a measure of assistance the office is required to take into consideration the abilities and needs of the child, who must be counselled; in the case of separation from the family, the child must be 'included in the process of choice'. The provisions of this new law represent a profound change in the key ideas on which the previous law (the law on the welfare of young people) was founded: while the former law attempted to restore order and prevent possible damage, the new law attempts to 'ensure the well-being of the child'. To reach this aim, German legislators have introduced in the new law *measures of support* in place of *measures of intervention* as with the previous law. These different aims have, of course, the consequence of providing opposing solutions concerning the position and rights of the child. The lack of consent can also lead to transfer from social sector to the judicial system (Austria): a solution based on the principle according to which only the magistrate can impose coercive measures.

Let us note finally that, in Sweden, the principle of the voluntary nature of assistance to children governs all the activity of the service and consequently the right of the child to consent is the most important right, as all the activity of the service depends on it.

An interesting situation has come about in Poland where the Code of Civil Procedure governs the procedures of the Family Court. However, this code is not clear concerning the legal position of the child. Two opinions have therefore developed, one which recognises the child as a party to the procedure and the other which denies this legal status.

We also note in many legislations a guarantee linked to the obligation to place a time limit on interventions.

The application of these rights, obviously affected by the consideration of the age of the minor, makes the young people subjects of law and puts into effect the principle that they also have the right to participate in decision-making concerning solutions to apply to the problems they are experiencing. We also observe the insistence with which some recent legislation depends chiefly on the primary responsibility of parents who themselves must find support from the social services.

The new importance attached to the rights of young people is illustrated in particular by the institution, in 1991, of a new function in the French Community of Belgium: the General Delegate Concerning the Rights of the Child and Aid to Young People. This role consists of ensuring respect for the fundamental rights of all young people and defending their interests. To do this, the Delegate may, for example:

- inform the public of the rights of young people and in particular make recommendations to the appropriate authorities;
- ensure the correct application of statutes concerning juveniles;
- propose new regulations;
- receive complaints concerning juvenile law, examine them, make the necessary investigations and inform the Public Prosecutor's Department if there is reason to do so.

In matters of legal protection of young people in danger, we note as examples:

- the rights of young people to be heard when their age permits it, the right to be present and advised, the right to have parents or legal guardians present;
- the right to be defended, possibly by a person other than the individual representing the interests of the parents. One then thinks of the English *guardian ad litem,* an institution which is found in Austrian, German, Czechoslovakian (as was) and Slovenian law;
- the right to benefit from expertise. The reports of specialists are generally carried out by educational and social services of the juvenile court; in certain specific cases, the magistrate can call on other experts;
- the right of young people to ask for modification of a measure concerning them and to appeal a decision;
- limitation of the duration of provisional and final judicial measures.

In Italy, the juvenile court judge must hear the minor in administrative or re-educational procedures and the juvenile has the right to the assistance of defence council. On the other hand, in civil procedures, the judge must hear minors aged over 12 only in the case of pre-adoption placements; in other civil procedures, hearing the minor is optional.

In France, minors must be heard by the juvenile court judge when their age and state permits it. They can benefit from the appointment of a lawyer chosen by parents, by themselves, or automatically. The system of judgement is explained to them from the age of 16. They have in all cases the right to appeal and use channels of legal recourse. Provisional measures are limited to six months; final measures imposed cannot exceed two years if they are the responsibility of an establishment or service. Provisional placement, whether in foster families or in institutions, is an educational measure which can be accompanied by certain conditions which limit the exercise of parental authority (rights to visits, accommodation and to receive mail), in accordance with the interests of the child. Certain rights such as the right to consent to marriage, emancipation, adoption, abortion and certain surgical interventions, belong only to parents in all cases.

In Portugal, the legal defender of minors is always the 'Prosecutor/Guardian of Minors', who in France or Italy would be the Deputy Public Prosecutor of Minors. This representative of the public ministry does not have a role of accuser, but only that of defender of the rights of the juvenile. We found a 'guardian of minors' representing the interests of the child also in procedures of family law (separation, custody conflicts, etc.). There are private institutions which have the role of assistance and defence of children in difficulty, such as the Institute of Aid to Children or the Portuguese Association for Juvenile and Family Rights.

Certain legislations contain extra guarantees regarding respect of the rights of young people outside the family. Thus the decree of the French Community of Belgium contains many rights of young people who have been placed outside the family, such as:

- the right of juveniles to communicate with any person of their choice;
- the obligation to inform juveniles, placed under a court order, of their rights to communicate with their lawyers and the obligation to facilitate the actual exercise of this right;
- the obligation to obtain the agreement of the young people aged over 14 to transfer them from one residential service to another (except for medical or security reasons) and the obligation to inform young people of the motives of the transfer and the characteristics of the new environment.

We observe, both on a social and a judicial level, that young people in difficulty take the role of chief protagonist, provided with rights, the application of which is guaranteed. The attention given to their co-operation and personal participation in measures which concern them is extremely remarkable.

We must however qualify these matters. In the most progressive countries the recognition of the rights of the child and the imposition of guarantees for their implementation have been the basis of reforms brought to systems of protection. However, the situation is not the same in all countries. While the right of children to be heard, to be consulted and other rights of a similar nature are recognised, even in countries where their welfare is seen more in the perspective of the State than of children themselves (Greece, Slovenia) there are also countries where children do not have the right to make independent proposals (the former Czechoslovakia) and others where their right to consent to interventions is ignored by the law (Greece, Slovenia), although - according to the information provided - the social services seek nevertheless the co-operation of the child.

One can say that there is a movement (towards recognition of the rights of the child) in progress, generally speaking. But the important thing from now on is that these rights are effectively planted in the mentality of intervening parties, at all levels of the system, and are reflected in professional practices.

Reforms Envisaged

Many of the countries included in this study have just, or are about to, carry out what is in many cases a fundamental change in legislation: England and Wales, Northern Ireland, Belgium, Germany, Austria, Slovenia, the former Czechoslovakia and Greece.

Where reforms are still incomplete, other changes must be expected in the near future. Thus in Belgium new community legislation implies that the national legislator should introduce procedural rules necessary to carry out judicial protection of young people in danger, as it is now conceived in each of the linguistic communities. Apart from provisions relative to juvenile delinquents, the bill which has been prepared, but whose passage was interrupted by the early dissolution of Parliament in 1991, also sets out that the juvenile court must hear minors from the age of 12 involved in civil litigation which concern the governing of their person, particularly in matters of parental authority and the designation of a substitute guardian where one is lacking.

In Scotland current legislation is being analysed and evaluated in view of identifying the changes which could be imposed, for example concerning emergency measures or the duration of certain interventions. The Scottish Office is also re-examining the function of the Reporter, one of the pillars of the system introduced in 1968.

As for France, it must be noted that the law on 'legal aid' which will favour quality defence of minors, and within the management of judicial protection of youth, the introduction of departmental schemes intended to make the most of existing means, département by département, and to co-ordinate their use for the best interests of minors under judicial protection.

In Portugal a reform of the organization of various establishments is expected. The aim of these reforms is to establish a new model for intervention which would make it possible to avoid stigmatisation and to find substitute measures to counteract the absence of the family. With this objective, it is necessary to look for the active participation of the community of origin and/or of the local community. A new law on adoption is also under study. It will facilitate, among other things, the adoption of children whose biological families are considered unsuitable for their upbringing (guilty conduct). This will also regulate international adoption.

In Italy a bill on sexual violence against minors within the family is now under discussion.

In Switzerland the lowering of the age of civil majority from 20 to 18 would inevitably have repercussions on the system of legal protection of young people in danger.

In Germany the new law on assistance to children and young people has, it seems, indicated that the area of juvenile delinquency must also be reconsidered. From that point certain changes have been envisaged concerning young adults, the system and choice of sanctions, the problems of young girls and women, etc.

In Sweden there is no discussion of legislative reform but public discussion in Sweden is rather 'non-progressive'.

In Greece, where a reform seems necessary, preparatory work is under way. Changes in the form of assistance to children (semi-open and open institutions) are expected, the purpose of which is prevention and rehabilitation. However it is reported that legislative reform could be hampered in practice by limited material and manpower resources.

In former socialist countries the routes to reform appear to be more complicated. Their legal systems need to be transformed in most areas and consequently priorities must be chosen. However, legislation on the family, which deals with the problems of children in danger, is not a top priority. In this perspective, one can understand the Czechoslovakian report (in March 1991), which placed emphasis on changes in juvenile criminal law and not family law. In Slovenia, with regard to children in danger (in June 1992), there were no formal reform proposals; in literature it is suggested however that the framework in which the status of this group is located should be reconsidered. It is proposed to extend the competence of the court in such a way as to create a kind of family court which would have decision-making power in cases of conflict of interests and when it is a matter of imposing coercive measures.

The Interventions
Annina Lahalle Alenka Selih Colette Somerhausen

In legislations which deal with young offenders measures for juvenile delinquents are precisely stated and generally have limited duration. For children in danger on the other hand, the application of measures is widely left to the evaluation of each situation by the authority responsible.

Besides, measures available vary according to the 'means' at the disposal of the institutions charged with treatment; differences can be seen from country to country and from region to region. Thus, for example, in Portugal, there exist at present juvenile courts in only eight cities (Lisbon, Oporto, Faro, Coimbra, Setubal, Aveiro, Funchal and Ponta Delgado), while France has a juvenile court in every jurisdiction of a court of appeal (or 125 juvenile courts in mainland France alone). The demographic importance of the youth population also has an influence on the resources of the State and the range of possibilities for dealing with them. Finally, some countries place more emphasis on control of juvenile delinquency than on solving problems encountered by young people in difficulty.

Types of Intervention

It would be tedious to list all types of intervention as set out in the legislations studied in this research. In fact, under various names, many measures present characteristics which are sufficiently similar to one another to enable us to carry out some classifications.

Interventions with *freely accepted assistance* are often conceived in a very wide sense, which makes it possible to offer to young people in difficulty, and to their families, opinions, advice, support and all kinds of assistance, including financial. Besides, one of the primary tasks of specialised socio-administrative services often consists of redirecting individuals concerned towards any appropriate service and assisting them to obtain the aid requested. Intervention tends therefore to facilitate for individuals concerned access to resources intended for the general population. When the service intervenes in residential matters, it draws up a programme of aid adapted to the type of case, and the assistance can take any form required by the situation of the young person, including, but only in exceptional cases, a form of temporary removal from the family.

Two traits however characterise these interventions:

- the concern that parents continue to exercise their family roles, the wish to help them to take on these roles and to integrate them in the programme of assistance;
- the wish to favour assistance given in the natural environment of the young person, to deal with maladjustment with and within the family;

162

removal of the young person should only be envisaged in exceptional cases.

The young person and the family are being approached more and more systematically.

In the judicial framework, interventions are perhaps more precisely defined and the targets sometimes more diverse. Some measures primarily concern parents, others young people, or all the juveniles of the family, even if the protective aim is always the same.

We will cite, only as a reminder, the possibility of criminal proceedings against parents who have committed offences against the person or at the expense of their children.

But to remain in the area of non-punitive measures with a protective aim, parents can have imposed on them instructions or directives relative to the care and education of their children. Italian law permits the imposition on parents of 'conditions apt to guarantee the moral assistance, maintenance, education and upbringing of minors'. The English Children Act 1989 provides that parents may be prohibited from making certain decisions without the consent of the court. Generally, parents can have imposed on them an educational obligation. The management of family and social funds, which exists in Belgium as in France, is a measure which also has an educational aspect, but in which is involved the financial management of contributions paid for the benefit of children in danger.

The most severe measures which can be taken concerning parents (or one parent) consists of removing or diminishing all or part of the rights which come under parental authority. Everywhere this measure is considered as the ultimate measure of protection.

One must however ask questions regarding measures which limit or suspend parental authority. Are we in the category of 'protection' or is there also an element of 'punishing' the deficient parent?

The removal of parental authority does not come under the competence of the juvenile judge in all countries. In France for example this extreme measure is the responsibility of the civil court, except in cases where the measure is accompanied by criminal sentencing. In the same way in Portugal, in cases where parents, considered guilty of not having exercised their parental duties, are to be deprived of their authority, the competent jurisdiction is the Family Court.

Swiss civil law (art. 310) has an interesting measure which prohibits parents from taking back children who have lived with foster parents for a long time, if there exists a serious threat that their development would be compromised in this way.

For young people judicial measures are varied and encompass, under different denominations: the imposition of supervision, directives or insertion into an educational project, the guidance of educational or orientation services, placement under observation, measures of accommodation outside the family, with an individual, a foster family or a residential institution. Removal from

163

the natural environment is generally conceived in terms of education, treatment or professional training of the young person. More rarely is it conceived as protecting young people from their own behaviour. Consequently, in this latter case, removal is only allowed under strictly defined conditions.

The duration of measures is almost always limited (and is sometimes very brief), especially when young people are removed from their family environment. In addition, in some countries, the court can authorise young people, from a certain age (16 to 17) to live in an autonomous or supervised residence.

German law can provide an example of modern trends. In principle, the law abandons coercive measures in favour of measures of 'educational assistance' which are offered by services primarily private, but also public. This assistance is founded on the theory that children are not receiving education which ensures their well-being. This assistance calls into play educational services, and, in co-operation with them, therapeutic services. In the general framework, the legislator has set out a palette of measures: educational consultation, group social work, educational assistance (under two forms), family socio-educational aid, education in a day group, upbringing in another family, placement in an institution or other form of shelter. It is interesting to note that only parents have the right, according to the principle that it is voluntary assistance. The law also contains provisional measures: temporary placement with an individual or in an institution, under very restrictive conditions, and, in cases where guardians do not consent, a decision of the guardianship court is required. This legislation, a very detailed model of regulation, is in contrast to the Slovenian solution, which - with regard to the powers of the socio-administrative service concerning measures in an open environment - finds sufficient a very terse provision: 'The service is required to take any necessary measure required by the education and protection of the child or the protection of his or her inheritance rights or other rights and interests'. The underlying philosophy is linked to the idea that the modes of implementation of these measures are governed by the professional rules of the specialised disciplines concerned. An analogous approach is to be found in the Polish system which entrusts this competence to the Family Court.

On the level of judicial aid, as for offered assistance, the recognised principle is that of maintaining juveniles in their natural environment and only removing them in the case of immediate danger (as an emergency measure), if the circumstances of their upbringing impose this necessity, or, in some countries, if the minor shirks other forms of intervention or eludes parental control.

The most recent legislation unequivocally calls for prioritisation of aid provided or imposed in the natural environment of the young person. The general trend which seeks to limit the number of measures of placement of juveniles is often supported by elements such as limits on the duration of the measures or the possibility of applying at any time a measure of individual aid, in particular at the request of the young person.

The Role of Experts

In matters as blurred and complex as assistance and protection for young people in danger, it would be presumptuous for magistrates, civil servants or social workers, no matter how specialised, to consider themselves as *deus ex machina* capable of understanding and evaluating a situation alone, and of proposing or imposing the most appropriate solution. The answers obtained are unanimous on this point. The Swiss report puts it perfectly: 'At all stages of the procedure, the role of experts (social workers and others) is simply decisive; without them, the juvenile court judge would be unable to function'.

Whether suggested or ordered by a children's hearing, a juvenile jurisdiction or a socio-administrative service, the preliminary analysis of the family, the social and psychological situation of the young person and the choice of appropriate intervention require the collaboration of specialists in social sciences in the widest sense of the term. The decision(s) taken must be justified by adequate social, psychological and educational knowledge. The support of these specialists is also necessary in order to know what resources exist in the community on which intervening parties can base their action.

In France experts play a prominent role in informing the magistrates during the period of investigation of the personality of the juvenile. The Public Prosecutor's Department, during the phase of orientation of the proceedings or at any other time, can call upon the 'educational service within the court' in each juvenile jurisdiction. The juvenile court judge, among other things, has vast socio-educational resources, composed of investigative services, (social assistants, psychologists, multi-disciplinary services, etc.) and experts (doctors, psychiatrists). These professionals come mainly from either the public sector, or from the associative sector of legal protection of young people. The magistrate can also call on the list of experts of the jurisdictions.

In Portugal the role of protection of minors (in particular child victims of ill-treatment) is given in priority to the 'Commission for the Protection of Minors' composed of a prosecutor/guardian, social worker, teacher, psychologist, doctor, local government representative, police representative and representative of private associations. The juvenile courts have their own social services and the judge can receive the opinions of other experts.

Thus we observe, in all countries, that the organisations for protection and assistance, judicial and social, have at their disposal social services, can call on medical and psychological experts or benefit from the collaboration of special services to conceive, prepare and implement their tasks.

The creation, in recent years, of specific services for assistance to abusing families to which socio-administrative services and courts make referrals, and from whom they seek advice, shows how great the need is to co-operate with experts.

Measures Removing Minors from the Family

The philosophy which underlies social and legal intervention has changed considerably over time. As is explicitly set out in the most recent statutes, the intention is to assist children and young people in difficulty, as well as their families, and this preferably by means of action in the family environment as a whole.

However, realism forces us to conclude that this is not always possible and that measures of removal, set out in all legislations, are inevitable. They therefore take on a more limited and temporary character than formerly.

Generally speaking, removal is proposed or imposed when the family situation and the educational abilities of the parents do not offer sufficient guarantees for the development of the child, when assistance in an open environment has failed or is not feasible, or again in the case of an emergency to protect the child or young person immediately.

Set out in the framework of voluntarily accepted assistance or of legal assistance, these measures are subject to strict conditions which are in principle observed in the majority of legislations.

The interests of the juvenile should - as for any other measure - guide the choice of an intervention of this type. This interest translates into legislation under different forms, but always tied to threats to the well-being of children (Germany, Austria), their health or development (Sweden) abandonment by parents (Greece), or a deficiency compared to 'regular' upbringing (the former Czechoslovakia).

A measure of removal therefore presupposes a thorough examination of the situation (except in an emergency), possible alternatives and possible effects of separation on the child and on the family. These preliminaries are required in many countries, as well as compulsory contact (in some cases) with the organisation of social assistance before making legal decisions of this kind.

In the framework of measures of assistance voluntarily accepted, the agreement of the parents (or those responsible for the child) is obviously necessary. But several legislations also require the consent of the young person from a certain age (fixed at 14 in French-speaking and Dutch-speaking Belgium) or that the minor be heard below this age (elsewhere, at any age). In some systems, let us remember, the absence of consent causes transfer from the social services to the judicial system (Germany, Austria).

In the judicial context, the agreement of the young person and the family, even if not required, is sought after as much as possible. Thus in the French Community of Belgium, the Director of Assistance to Young People, charged with the implementation of legal measures, is required to involve the young person and the persons composing his or her family environment, including foster parents. In Switzerland also, in practice, the placement of an adolescent will not be carried out without at least partial co-operation of the parties concerned in the measure envisaged.

The duration of a measure of removal is limited, but can be renewed. This renewal is also subject to criteria of frequency, duration, preliminary conditions, etc. However, in Italy, with regard to measures of removal of the juvenile from the family, there is no fixed period of time. The general rule that the situation is reversible is still valid when the situation changes.

The voluntarily accepted measure of placement can be suspended, revoked or replaced with another measure, in particular at the request of the young person having reached a certain age.

A voluntarily accepted placement in a residential environment is followed up by means of supervision in the form of visits by the service responsible for the implementation of the measure, and regular reports on the progress of the juvenile. There is a clear desire in all jurisdictions to avoid at all costs deplorable situations of former years, where a child placed in a residence ran the risk of being 'forgotten' for years by the decision-making organisation or service.

Provisional removal from the family does not mean a breaking of ties between the juvenile and the family. Quite the contrary: many legislations (such as the Children Act 1989 and Belgian decrees) stipulate that - unless the interests of the young person are in conflict with it - the service or individual which has taken the young person into care must maintain family contacts or at least favour them. In addition, in the Flemish Community of Belgium, there exists a general condition linked to placements, according to which action must be taken at the same time with the family (if there is one), with a view to bringing the young person back home as soon as possible.

The same trend can be observed in other legislations. German legislation emphasised measures in an open environment to such an extent that even that shows the tendency to return the child to the family as soon as possible. In many systems (Germany, Greece and Slovenia for example), during the period of separation, the parents retain their rights (and obligations) to take care of the child and his or her property.

In an emergency, the court - in French-speaking Belgium, for example - can only place the child in a residence after having been assured that no close relative of the child, removed from the situation of danger, is in a position to take temporary care of the child. Nevertheless, in emergencies, the most frequent solution often consists of temporary removal of the child, without seeking a relative to take custody: this is the case in Greece.

In Germany, these measures can be taken without the consent of the person legally responsible for looking after the child, under two conditions: the life or the physical safety of the child is in danger and the magistrate confirms this within a very short time (the day after provisional removal).

It is interesting to note that the legislations of former socialist systems (Poland, Czechoslovakia, Slovenia) do not deal with emergency cases.

While no distinction is made according to sex, the age of the young person is usually a factor in requiring consent in the case of voluntarily accepted aid, if the minor has reached a certain age, or for precautions linked to monitoring of the placement (e.g. the number of compulsory visits per year varies according to the age of the child in the French Community of Belgium), or again when it is a matter of authorising the young person to settle in an autonomous or supervised residence.

In several responses to the questionnaire, it is pointed out that the law makes no distinction as to sex, but that in reality, this element often appears in the form of discrimination. In Greece for example the number of young girls placed in institutions is much higher than would be justified by their involvement in delinquency (27% for 3.8% of delinquents in 1990). In Slovenia, it has been observed that the criteria to which reference is made to place a girl in an institution are stricter and have stronger moral connotations than when young males are involved. In Sweden, the difference between the sexes is demonstrated by the fact that young girls are most often placed in institutions due to their evading parental control, while boys are placed for having committed offences or drug abuse.

As for modes of placement, the formulation differs according to legislation. Some legislations require that the placement be either 'appropriate', serving the 'interests' of the child, or chosen according to the treatment, upbringing, education or professional training of the young person. Other statutes, on the other hand, no doubt as a reaction to former times when placement seemed to be a social panacea, carefully list the different modes of placement and their duration.

Everywhere, to our knowledge, measures of removal from the family cover both the entrusting of the young person to an individual or foster family and various kinds of residential accommodation. The latter has undergone notable changes in recent years. In most countries, establishments have adopted a more open character and often reduced dimensions. Thus, in Austria, since 1975, all establishments for children and juveniles have become open and new institutional structures, residence communities (*Wohngemeinschaften*) have been introduced. The same is the case in Germany and Slovenia.

In the case of France, children of an early age for whom a placement is necessary are preferably entrusted to foster families or services of social assistance to children. In the same way, particular modes of treatment concerning young drug addicts (foster families, small specialised residential structures) have been developed. The governing body for legal protection of youth seeks to prevent certain structures from collecting only very heavy cases, which would be likely to favour segregation to the detriment of the minors concerned. Finally, mixing is becoming a general tendency within the establishments.

Statistical data relative to children in danger are much less elaborate in many countries than for juvenile delinquents. This remark is also valid with regard to information on the institutional placement of juveniles in danger. However, the responses obtained to the questionnaire show quite clearly that measures removing the child from the family have declined over the last ten years. This emerges clearly from the Greek report (where the total number of placements in 1990 was 94) and the Slovenian report, likewise the Austrian and German reports. In the former Czechoslovakia, there are no statistics available. In Poland, the Family Courts ordered placements in foster families or in institutions in a third of the cases, while for minors in danger, the juvenile courts have taken this step less frequently (in around 14% of cases). The only country where a reverse tendency appears to be in motion is Sweden.

In the 1980s an increased demand for placements in institutions began to make itself felt. We must also take into account the fact that, in this country, the proportion of these placements has been extremely low. In 1989 (incomplete) information related to socio-administrative services indicates that, for juveniles aged 15 to 17, only 0.3% (N=50) were placed in institutions.

The scarce statistical data which we have been able to obtain for French-speaking Belgium - but which unfortunately also deals with juvenile delinquents - indicates:

- a decrease in recourse to placements (consented to or imposed) over the last decade;
- a particularly marked decline regarding placements in institutions;
- more frequent recourse to placements in foster families, the proportion of which compared to the total number of placements increased from 28.1% in 1980 to 33.8% in 1990.

The protective nature of measures removing the child from the family is very perceptible in systems where the competence of socio-administrative services predominates (Sweden, Slovenia). However we are concerned that this protective tendency does runs the danger of seeing the rights of the child insufficiently taken into account by the competent service. The question has been clearly asked in Slovenia. The preventive aspect of measures of removal is obvious in the Greek system, where they have the purpose of preventing delinquent behaviour on the part of the child. German law places emphasis on the principle of necessity (*Erforderlichkeitsprinzip*). Finally, the Polish system appears to be the only one to provide for a measure of compulsory institutional placement, of a medical nature, for young drug addicts.

Removal of the minor is visibly seen as intended to provide a framework, an institutional support for protective intervention or assistance, and not as a 'custodial' measure. The Swiss report states very clearly: 'There are no custodial sentences without a criminal offence'. It remains that when a placement in a closed or 'secure' establishment can be envisaged, it is surrounded by even stricter reservations, and sometimes prohibited for younger age groups, and must be justified by recurrent absconding behaviour, where the young person is a danger to himself or herself, by the danger posed to others (for example in England) or is only available when it is demonstrated that the juvenile has fled from other forms of placement and that the maintenance of his or her physical safety makes it necessary (for example in the Flemish Community of Belgium).

It is difficult to speak of 'alternative measures' to placement, as we would in the case of juvenile delinquency, given the different philosophy which here underlines the removal of the minor. But it is important to note that placement in a foster family can, in one system, refer to a related family (Austria) while in another (Germany for example), this measure is included in the general category of 'full-time care' (*Vollzeitpflege*) which also covers placement in an

169

institution; however a very clear internal progression is established, since placement in an institution is declared to be a matter of last resort.

A reverse tendency appears to be in progress in Sweden where the number of placements in institutions, compared to placements with foster families, has increased in recent years; but in Swedish tradition the institutions are very open. Perhaps this tendency translates a trend towards a 'family-style' treatment, i.e. treatment of the child and of the family?

Greece and former socialist countries do not appear to stress the importance on placements in foster families, although, in some of these countries, this measure has had a very long tradition (in Slovenia for example).

The maintenance of the y oung person in his or her natural environment is often attempted as a solution before a decision on placement is made and accompanied with significant educational support, or the imposition of directives, for the juvenile and/or for parents. Thus, in French-speaking Belgium, under national legislation which preceded community decrees, legal measures of treatment in an open environment with the obligation to submit to the directives of a centre of educational orientation, concerned, in 32.4% of cases, children for whom proceedings had been initiated regarding parents, and in 40% of cases, juveniles considered to be in danger. A placement followed this final experiment of treatment in an open environment in 19% of cases for proceedings involving parents and in 36% of cases for juveniles in danger.

In England and Wales, programmes of *intermediate treatment* are used for young people who are not delinquents but who are considered to be at serious risk of becoming delinquent, with the purpose of avoiding a placement.

The Polish system also has measures of an 'intermediate' nature, which are not recent, but are of a somewhat different kind. The Family Code provides for 'placement in an organisation or institution of professional training or another part-time institution for the care of minors.'

In some countries, (Belgium for example), residential services more and more frequently practice 'granting of autonomy' to young people entrusted to them. This measure cannot be understood as a real form of treatment of the young person in an open environment, but rather as a partial measure of this kind. Half way between residential placement of juveniles and maintaining them in their usual environment, which means placing them in a supervised residence, this measure presupposes that the juveniles receive educational assistance while at the same time experiencing conditions of life closer to an open environment. The provisions regulating the authorisation and granting of subsidies to services which carry out legal measures have made it possible to develop this measure which can take the form of educational treatment in a residential establishment where the minor has sometimes stayed very briefly, or on the basis of the family environment.

As for any other measure imposed by the legal system, the court makes its choice on the basis of reports, examinations or expertise at its disposal and after having heard the juvenile and the family, the public ministry (where it intervenes) and the lawyer of the juvenile or of the family participating in general in the debate. In England and Wales, when a *guardian ad litem* has been appointed to represent the particular interests of the child, this person can also intervene in the choice of measure.

Treatment in an Open Environment

General considerations

Treatment of children in an open environment has acquired a predominant place in the range of measures available for both young people in danger and delinquents; nevertheless a comparative analysis related to the modes of intervention in an open environment encounters many difficulties.

Legislations do not always set out in a clear manner the possible forms of this treatment - no more than they state all the forms of danger - doubtless because it is almost impossible to do so!

Let us also note that these measures can have varied 'targets' or 'beneficiaries': some of them are exclusively intended for parents, others for juveniles, while a third group targets both. The tendency to treat a family group as a whole is no doubt more accepted in cases where juveniles are in danger than in cases of juvenile delinquency. Another difficulty is linked to the fact that although legislations list measures of treatment in an open environment - and measures removing the child from the family - there are also exceptions, i.e. systems where the legislator has, so to speak, given 'carte blanche' to the competent authority or social service (Slovenia) or the Guardianship or Family Court (Poland, Germany). In Belgium, although voluntary aid organisations have virtually been granted *carte blanche* in the same way, coercive measures at the disposal of the court are precisely defined in legislation.

This distinction between voluntarily accepted aid and imposed aid is significant in many systems (Germany, Austria, Belgium, Sweden) where the consent of the young person (or legal guardians) is considered as a criterion authorising intervention of the social services, while the court is given the task of imposing coercive measures. Elsewhere, such a distinction does not exist (the former Czechoslovakia, Greece, Slovenia) but the legislation contains, at least in theory, the possibility of judicial control over the decisions of the social service (Slovenia).

Among the measures set out, some clearly contain elements of coercion, others elements of assistance. This distinction is purely theoretical here and does not take into account the nuances resulting from the manner in which a measure is actually carried out.

Among coercive measures concerning parents let us mention reprimand (the former Czechoslovakia), restriction of parental rights (Poland), directives (Greece, Poland, Belgium); all systems have some form or other of limitation or removal of parental authority, some the complete removal of parental authority. Measures of assistance to parents, in practice, mostly target the family group itself; let us cite advice, therapy and educational assistance (Austria, Germany, Sweden), various forms of social work, etc. Traditionally

171

in France the educational measure in an open environment for juveniles in danger is 'educational assistance in an open environment' (AEMO), carried out by an educator who provides 'assistance and counselling' to the family. It should be noted that when removal from the family is decided upon, it is not a matter of a punitive measure, but of a measure of 'protection', taken in the interests of the child and of limited duration.

New measures in an open environment are appearing in reforms which are being proposed or are under way. They are based in particular on a model which seeks 'active participation of the community of origin and of the local community' and on new participation of the family in the treatment of these children. New measures of material assistance to families are envisaged.

In Portugal community measures have the purpose of preventing 'the stigmatisation and absence of the family'.

In France the decree of 22 July 1987, introduced in the new Code of Civil Procedure a series of procedural dispositions which remind us of the necessity to involve families in procedures of educational assistance. All recent educational trends lead the services of legal protection of youth to work in close liaison with the families.

Generally speaking, new measures 'in an open environment' are still based on the notion of the interests of the juvenile, depend on local resources and often call on multi-disciplinary and 'multi-category' groups.

Among measures which are intended for young people, some also have a more coercive character than others. For the former, we think of measures of reprimand (Czechoslovakia), directives (Germany, Austria, the former Czechoslovakia) or supervision known in almost all countries under one form or another. More in response to a wish to assist, we note measures of educational guidance, daytime education, assistance in professional training (Germany, Austria, Poland, Sweden), insertion into educational projects (Flemish Community of Belgium).

Evolution

It must be restated that all countries in our study have, for some years now, given priority to the adoption of measures focused on the natural environment of the young person. However it is difficult to state that the principle is effectively put into practice concerning children and young people in difficulty.

Statistical information communicated to us is scarce. When it exists, it is incomplete, imprecise or, unfortunately, does not distinguish measures concerning young people in danger from those reserved for juvenile delinquents. Besides (in French-speaking Belgium, for example) statistics on 'Placements' partially cover the granting of autonomy on some occasions.

Nevertheless in accumulating partial observations, in collecting various indications, in proceeding by successive steps, we think that movement is under way now for young people in difficulty as well as for delinquents.

Without being able to go into detail, we can state the following facts:

- in recent legislation the idea of assistance (which therefore presupposes the giving of advice, opinions, measures of educational support) is overtaking that of protection (which formerly often meant measures of separation from the family); treatment in an open environment is considered a priority; stress is placed on the responsibility of parents and the support to be given them; restrictive rules apply to measures which separate the young person from the environment;
- the training given to new practitioners and the recycling imposed by legislative reform, strive to instil these new trends in intervening parties;
- provisional measures taken in the framework of both procedures concerning parents and those concerning juveniles give a greater place (in Belgium at least) to supervision in the juvenile's natural environment; however, measures of placement, although they are in decline, still remain the most frequent;
- modes of treatment in an open environment are being diversified, with a real effort towards innovation in some regions. Thus in the Flemish community of Belgium experiments have been carried out in recent years which emerge from new possibilities of intensive family guidance, granting of autonomy to the minor with guidance, post-residential measures of accompaniment, diverse educational projects, treatment in day centres (semi-open measure). In England and Wales, let us remember, programmes of intermediate treatment are accessible to juveniles who are not yet delinquents but who are close to becoming delinquent;
- in certain countries - particularly in Belgium - some of the residential establishments are plainly being reorganised with a view to partially transforming their capacity for residential accommodation into a service of assistance, follow-up, and educational support in an open environment. This movement, favourable to treatment in an open environment, requires that changes take place at the same time in modes of subsidising, in factors taken into account to calculate the number of subsidies, the reimbursement of extra costs and the costs of writing off debts.

It must also be recognised that practices on the ground change only slowly. In Belgium for example, a 'relational tradition' which dates back a long time has existed between the juvenile courts and the organisations and resources of the residential sector which does not favour the implementation of a new philosophy based on the open environment. The mentalities of professionals must adapt to new directions of work, new forms of treatment in an open environment and the authorities responsible for policies of assistance to young people in difficulty must translate their intentions into action in encouraging the creation of new services and support for treatment in the environment of the juvenile. Evaluating studies should besides be carried out to 'reveal' the function of various forms of treatment in an open environment and assess their results

External collaboration

In this respect, considerable differences exist between certain groups of countries. In most countries studied - especially those which have recently adopted new legislation - there is insistence on new partners, in particular the various organisations which make up the associative sector. However, former socialist countries are experiencing the reverse situation. Existing structures are of a state nature and are in the process of profound transformation (such as youth organisations and sport associations); the private sector is almost non-existent with the exception of the religious sector, which is however of little importance. In these conditions society is particularly weak and a lot of time and effort will be required before it can develop. Nevertheless two countries, Poland and Slovenia, have a long tradition of recourse to voluntary workers (most often motivated students who are directed by their lecturers). We also find independent groups of people (such as the Association for a Better School in Slovenia), the extension of which could serve as a basis for the associative sector.

The movement of diversion from the court, like the priority given to assistance in the natural environment of the young person, has contributed to expanding the number of parties in collaboration in matters of assistance to young people in danger. Besides, in bringing to the fore principles of the priority given to prevention and voluntarily accepted aid, respect of the fundamental rights of the juvenile and the family, the co-ordination of services of assistance to juveniles, a new role is given to the family, the school, health services, the local community, local elected officials, the associative sector. These parties are given a greater responsibility in the development of young people.

In France the new role of the community has been developed particularly in the framework of city policies and local projects. Decentralisation and new powers transferred to territorial collectives have formed general councils and also, from local government, privileged representatives of jurisdictions can propose new modes of treatment of juveniles in difficulty. In the framework of city policies in particular, inter-ministerial actions are brought into force. Let us note, among other things, that the Ministry of Justice recently developed a policy of access to legal advice which favours education of juveniles and families concerning their rights. In this sense, conventions with the bar and legal associations have been passed with a view to introducing service of legal advice associated with the local community. We must also mention, in the case of France, the important role played by associations which have been granted powers by the Ministry of Justice and which deal with almost two thirds of the educational measures imposed as educational assistance. Thanks to the flexibility of their administrative frameworks and the resources at their disposal, these associations contribute a great deal to the development of new forms of treatment. Finally, a new important partner in matters of legal protection of minors is the national education system. The governing body of the legal protection of juveniles and the jurisdictions multiply contacts with the school in the framework of assistance: for example in procedures of reporting that children are in danger or are being ill-treated, sexually abused or intimidated.

Similar actions are indicated in the Portuguese response, linking the school, the health sector, voluntary institutions, associated organisations from the local community and the court.

In the area which interests us here, social work within and with the family is being developed in all its aspects. The decline in 'residential treatment' in favour of other modes of action – guidance, imposition of directives, socio-educational support – is changing intervention techniques and directing families towards the resources offered by the community to the population as a whole. Supporting parents in their family roles presupposes their participation in solutions to problems of their children (which besides are often seen as family problems) and that they are assisted in gaining access to available social resources. The new role given to the environment of the young person implies that work with the family should be associated with all types of intervention regarding the young person in danger, as required in some legislations.

The preference given to measures of socio-educational support in the family has, on occasion, led to the creation of new specialised services, with a view to carrying out treatment in an open environment, divided into federations or associations. These new structures are acquiring, little by little, a certain weight in their relationships with authorities which mandate them. More flexible, more innovative, they attempt experiments more readily than traditional administrative services can. But these specialised structures themselves can only act in addressing in turn other organisations or community services. How in fact can a project of educational orientation or intensive guidance be realised without establishing links with elements from the environment of the young person (family, school, etc.) which are likely to inform, enlighten and participate in the action?

We must also mention the new, more active, co-operation provided by professional organisations already involved in the protection of young people. Thus in French-speaking Belgium, some new bar organisations have given a particular impetus to new directions in policies of assistance, while supporting in their work recourse to measures in an open environment.

Little by little, it seems that the role of organisations responsible for the protection of young people, and still more, for specialised social assistance which is offered to them, is undergoing change. Rather than intervening singly, by themselves, they act as the driving element, the guide, the compulsory relay and a centre point for a network of individuals and external services. In the centre of the cloth they weave, they direct, control and supervise. It would however be erroneous to believe, insist several reports, that all the potential collaborators 'play the game' and fulfil the role assigned to them. The response of the family (often itself involved in the problems), of the school and of various services concerned is not always adequate and the community is still not always ready to reach out to its members who are most fragile, deviant or in difficulty.

Without limits and without control, calling on the associative sector is in danger of leading to anarchy in interventions and the reduction in responsibility of organisations of protection. Everywhere the contribution of the associative sector is channelled by legal provisions which determine the framework and modes of intervention. It is also limited by routes of private recourse intended for young people. In a more direct manner the action of the associative sector is clearly defined by legal conditions which govern the authorisation and granting of subsidies to individuals and institutions who collaborate in the protection of young people. These provisions are an important element of control in that they fix the conditions which must be met by the intervening parties, determine the specific actions which can be taken, ensure a framework and establish regulations for supervision, as well as educational and financial monitoring.

Recourse to voluntary workers has developed to a lesser extent. It has had a greater success in Poland, Slovenia and Anglo-Saxon countries where the community spirit is an important cultural element. But, in a general manner, the involvement of voluntary workers comes about through their integration in the structure of the associative sector. However, it should not be forgotten that certain individuals are invited to play a particular role, to fulfil certain functions in the system, according to their qualifications, competence and experience such as Scottish Panel Members, Committees of Concern or the Commission of Mediation in the Flemish Community of Belgium. If these individuals are considered 'experts', they nevertheless frequently receive particular training.

It is also accurate to say that more and more importance is being attached to the training of all individuals who collaborate in the assistance of young people in difficulty. This concern is very noticeable in some recent statutes, such as the new law on voluntary work adopted in Italy in 1991, or again the decree of the French Community of Belgium which opens the door to administrative initiatives, intended to inform and train all those who give their support to the application of measures of assistance to young people. But it is also important to underline that the associative sector itself is proving very attentive to the training of its personnel. Programmes of training, interviews, study seminars and conferences have multiplied in the last ten years. Two subjects, in Belgium at least, appear to have been favoured: on the one hand information concerning legislative reform and new provisions for assistance and protection, and on the other hand the formation of new technical and practical professional approaches (the systematic approach and transactional analysis have gained great favour in recent years).

176

Modern Legislation for a Country of Contrasts: The Example of Brazil

Annina Lahalle

The Network wished to extend its study to other countries, with realities different from those of European countries, which have recently adopted in their legislation the principles of international rules and the implementation of new measures in an open environment. This could allow us, in a further stage, to widen our interest to other countries and development outside Europe.

The effective application of international rules and recommendations can only be understood through study of different countries and realities. This is what emerges from our introductory analysis in which we pointed out that the Beijing Rules are intended to apply 'to all minors, with no distinction, in any system of justice, in all parts of the world'. And it is probable that it will be in countries which are less developed economically or in the process of transformation (within or outside Europe) and with a higher demographic concentration of young people that we will find complementary and important elements to answer our original dilemma: is treatment in an open environment a reality or a Utopia?

Justification of the Choice

Brazil was a privileged region for our study. A country of considerable contrasts which had just achieved democracy after more than 20 years of a hard and repressive regime of military dictatorship, it was introducing new social legislation and laws for the protection of minors.

In emerging from dictatorship, two great popular demands were expressed: the right to vote and the right to a new Constitution. And it is certainly in this demand for a new Constitution that we note one of the major characteristics of this renewal of democratic expression. Although the Assembly, elected by the people, has fulfilled its legislative role, the people has also participated in the creation of a 'Magna Carta' with the support of representatives from the most varied classes of society.

Brazilian constitutions, since their origins (the first dates from 1824), have always gone beyond the simple description of the organisation of State institutions, their competence and powers. They raise in detail the rights and responsibilities of citizens and the manner in which the State must guarantee the rights set down.

Thus, for the purpose of our interests here, the Constituent Assembly has not only heard the representatives of different social and educational sectors charged with the treatment of delinquent minors or those in difficulty, including associations of juvenile court magistrates, but has also heard the representatives of populations personally concerned including 'street children' organized into a 'movement'. This participation by part of the civil population, legally considered minors, must be ranked as an important innovation in the process of democratisation of a country where the population aged under 18 makes up 41% of the total. Is it a question of 'the right to speak', as it is envisaged in the Convention on the Rights of the Child?[1] Or a simple adult strategy? It is difficult to answer these questions. But the euphoric climate in which the Constitution of 1988 was voted in, definitely shows the desire, at this historic moment, to 'hear' all the 'speech' coming from the people.

The analysis of Brazilian juvenile justice must take into account two types of standards:

- the *constitutional rules* of 1988 concerning the family, children and adolescents, their rights and the protection of these rights which the State must ensure;
- the 'Status of the Child and the Adolescent' of July 1990.

Political and Administrative Background: Demographic Data

A federal republic since 1889, Brazil is currently governed by the texts of the Constitution of 1988. It is a presidential system: the president is elected by universal suffrage for a term of five years. The senators are elected, by direct vote, for a term of eight years: there are three senators for each State. The Chamber of Deputies is composed of 487 federal representatives elected for four years, in proportion to the number of inhabitants of their respective states and the Federal District (from eight deputies to a maximum of 70). The response to the questionnaire mentions the existence of 37 political parties.

The federation is composed of a Federal District, seat of the capital, Brasilia, and 26 member States. Each State has a great deal of independence regarding its organisation. The States are governed by a governor elected for four years and Secretaries of State make up the executive power. Each State has its own constitution, judicial power and legislative powers exercised by a Chamber of Deputies. The municipality is the basic political and administrative cell of the nation. Each municipality has a mayor and executive power exercised

1. Several articles of the Convention on the Rights of the Child protect this right of expression: 'The member states guarantee the child who is capable of discernment the right to freely express his or her opinion in every question concerning him or her (art. 12) . . . The child has the right to freedom of expression. This right includes the freedom to seek, receive and disseminate information and ideas of all kinds (art.13) . . . The member states recognise the right of the child to freedom of association (art.15) . . .'

by a Chamber of local councillors; judicial power belongs to the State to which the municipality belongs. In 1987 there were 4,257 municipalities and 64 were in the process of creation.

The territory of Brazil stretches out over slightly more than 8.5 million square kilometres (or slightly more than 16 times the area of France). Its population is around 150 million inhabitants, *41% of whom are aged under 18.*

The Brazilian population is concentrated along the Atlantic coast, in particular in the South-East region where the State of São Paulo is situated. This region, which makes up only eleven per cent of the territory, concentrates 43% of the population. It is estimated that 25% of the population lives in a rural environment and 75% in the cities (1990 figures).

As for the population aged under 18, 51.5% are white, 43.3% mulatto or half-caste, 5.1% black and 0.4% oriental. A considerable part of the population lives below the poverty level. In 1988, almost 30% of minors belonged to families with a monthly family income of less than 25% of the minimum wage (the Brazilian minimum wage is equivalent to around US$60). Social and economic differences are most marked between the States of the North-East (poorest) and of the South-East and between the black and mulatto populations and the white populations which are more numerous in the South-Eastern States.

The Street Children

The problem of poor children and their family situation has given rise to definitions drawn up by international organisations (including UNICEF). Two notions are most commonly used: 'street children' and 'children in the streets', who maintain contact with their parents or community but who habitually live in the street either idly or doing minor jobs.

The response to the questionnaire gives several figures originating from Brazilian public organisations. Thus, in 1976, a parliamentary commission of enquiry into the 'Brazilian reality of minors' put forward a figure of slightly more than 13 million children in a situation of 'deficiency' (i.e. whose parents or guardians did not provide the conditions necessary to supply their basic needs) and two million children actually abandoned (by their parents or guardians). The 'programme of governmental action', published in 1987, in turn estimated that in 1984 the number of minors in a state of 'deficiency' had increased to 36 million and that of abandoned children to seven million. However the response to the questionnaire also underlines the fact that all these statistics must be treated with great caution as they are often only estimations of a vast social and economic problem.

Regarding 'children in danger' and 'juvenile delinquents' in the legal sense of the terms, there is no reliable national statistic. Even for the State of São Paulo the statistics are only partial.

Brief History of Juvenile Law in Brazil

Although the Penal Code of the Empire and the first Penal Code of the Republic already contained differences in treatment for minors according to their 'moral responsibility' and their 'discernment', it was only in 1921 that the first courtrooms specialising in juvenile matters were created. [1]

The Penal Code of 1940 established the 'complete lack of criminal responsibility' of minors aged under 18. This principle has been maintained until today and has been the basis of both the Juvenile Code of 1979 and the Status of the Child and Adolescent of 13 July 1990, currently in force. The minor is therefore not subject to any criminal penalty.

The 'Juvenile Code' of 1979 was based on the theory of the 'irregular situation' of minors (situations revealing social pathology such as abandonment, situation of deficiency or of victimisation, perpetrators of criminal offences). The juvenile court judge established the facts and protection was referred to organisations created by the State. In the 1970s a national policy of responding to the problems of minors was drawn up with the creation of the 'National Foundation for the Welfare of Minors' (FUNABEM), on a federal level and Foundations for the Welfare of Minors in member States. The response to the questionnaire defines this Code by its paternalistic aspects.

The new Status of the Child and Adolescent defines minors under 18 as *subjects* of law, eliminating the condition of *object of intervention* either by society or by the State. Still, according to the response to the questionnaire, 'status' is based on the concept of child and adolescent 'citizens', subject to total protection, i.e. protection of fundamental rights to physical, intellectual, emotional, social and cultural development.

The Current Legal Framework in Brazil

The texts currently applicable, both for 'juvenile delinquents' and 'children in danger' are:

- The Constitution of the Federal Republic of Brazil, proclaimed on 5 October 1988;
- the 'Status of the Child and Adolescent' (SEA), law no. 8.069 of 13 July 1990.

The legal texts have their basis in federal authority and apply throughout the national territory. Judicial organisation is, however, the responsibility of each member State. As these texts are very recent, no answers to the questionnaire

1. It must be pointed out that Brazilian law, in all sectors, has always been inspired by European law — the Napoleonic Code in civil matters and the Rocco Code in relation to criminal law. As for practice, in juvenile law, many magistrates and educators have had periods of study in different European countries, including France.

permit us to analyse their effective applicability. What we wish to underline are the peculiarities of this modern legislation in a country of great social and economic contrasts and the concern of legislators to respect the recommendations of international rules and to take into account current trends in matters of criminal policy.

Juvenile Delinquents

The principle of lack of criminal responsibility of minors under 18 is maintained in the texts. The SEA distinguishes the 'child' from the 'adolescent': a 'child' is any person up to the age of 12 and an 'adolescent' the young person from 12 to 17.

The Brazilian system therefore must be analysed alongside those systems which envisage trends towards prevention and education, and which entrust to magistrates the protection of both delinquent and deviant young people, and minors in danger in the same context. Juvenile justice remains specialised, and in districts where there is no juvenile judge, this function is carried out by a judge of instance within the framework of the provisions of the SEA.

Juvenile justice ('justice of childhood and adolescence') has a wider competence than European juvenile justice systems. It is specialised in almost all procedures which concern a minor (civil and criminal majority is fixed at 18): adoption (including international adoption); care and guardianship; termination or modification of parental authority; authorisation of marriage; custody conflicts; food provisions and modification of civil status[1] in addition to procedures concerning juvenile delinquents and minors in danger or difficulty.

Socio-educational structures have been created by the SEA. These structures - 'Municipal Guardianship Councils' - work in close co-operation with the juvenile court judges. They are competent to decide on 'measures of protection' for 'children' (under 12), and can be compared with 'Commissions of Protection' defined in Portuguese law.

Guardianship Councils are defined by article 131 of the SEA as 'the permanent, autonomous, non-jurisdictional organisation, charged by society with monitoring the observation of rights guaranteed to minors by the statutes'. Each municipality will have at least one 'Guardianship Council', 'composed of five members, chosen for three years by the local community' (art. 132 of the SEA) (hence the stress we have put previously on the importance of municipalities in national organisation). These 'Councils' should therefore be the expression of the 'community' in the sense of the United Nations recommendations. The commentators on article 132 of the SEA stress that 'this Council allows the community for the first time to manage questions relative to children and adolescents in situations which make them more vulnerable, demanding an immediate decision on the part of the competent authorities. The

---

1. Many children who come into the juvenile justice system have never been registered in a civil status. The magistrate must correct this situation which is often linked to the poverty of the parent.

181

participation of the community in the elimination of these problems is a new and concrete fact since, working together with professionals who accumulate scientific or empirical 'knowledge' there will be a group of persons chosen for their moral qualities by the community, to assist in the bringing of a solution to the problem'.

The answer to the questionnaire emphasises the role of local elected officials and communities as privileged partners in the functioning of 'Guardianship Councils'.

The various functions of the 'Guardianship Councils' are set out in article 136 of the SEA. They must, among other things, in addition to functions indicated previously of taking measures of protection for children under 12: report to the Public Prosecutor's Department any violation committed by anyone, an individual or an institution, against the fundamental rights of minors, implement the measures of assistance in an open environment applicable to parents in bringing them assistance and advice, and report cases which come under judicial competence.

Analysis of the new Brazilian text makes it apparent that the principal objectives pursued by measures intended for juvenile delinquents do not have a punitive nature: they aim for education and social reinsertion. When the delinquent act causes material loss, the measures can have a retributive and restitutional character (obligation to repair damage and render services to the community).

The measures can be ordered singly or cumulatively and can be modified by the magistrate at any time. The juvenile court judge always takes into account the circumstances of the offence and the personality of the minor. The judge also tries, as far as possible, to ensure that links with the family or community where the minor lives are maintained.

The maintenance of family and community ties appears in several articles of the SEA as a priority, moving in the direction of the recommendations of the United Nations. These articles can be compared with certain articles of recent European laws, such as the Italian law.

'Children' who have committed an offence are subject only to 'measures of protection'; 'adolescents' can be made subject to 'socio-educational measures'.

Measures of protection for children are:

- return to the family; measures of educational orientation and support; programmes of registration in an academic establishment or insertion into a community programme; or a placement in an educational establishment.

Socio-educational measures for adolescents consist of:

- measures which do not involve deprivation of liberty: reprimand, obligation to make restitution;
- community service (generally eight hours per week for a maximum of six months); probation (for a minimum of six months, there is no maximum).

182

The support of the minor is required for all measures of reparation to the victim or community service.

Measures involving deprivation of liberty:

- the regime of semi-liberty, which has a mixed character: an establishment which is closed during the night and academic, working or training obligations during the day. This regime can be an intermediate step after a placement in a closed establishment;

- placement in a boarding school which is the only custodial measure for adolescents. The boarding schools are public and depend on the executive power of each member State. The monitoring of the measure remains the responsibility exclusively of the judicial power. The duration of placement is reviewed by the magistrate every six months and cannot surpass three years in total. This measure is, in the framework of the law, considered exceptional and should not be ordered except for serious offences of a violent nature, when no other measure can be considered. One of the answers to the questionnaire states that these measures should only be applied in the case of infractions which, in the case of an adult, would be punished by six to 30 years' imprisonment. This placement can also be ordered when all other educational measures have proved ineffective due to persistent bad behaviour or dangerous conduct of the juvenile: in these cases the maximum duration is three months; and

- finally, a measure of provisional placement during proceedings is possible: it will not exceed 45 days.

These custodial measures can only be ordered after a procedure before the juvenile court judge, with all the guarantees of defence and appeal. Defence is ensured by a lawyer.

The role of experts is predominant in these procedures: it involves specialists in educational, social and psychological matters who belong to public services for the protection of children and adolescents.

Defence by a lawyer, appeal channels, procedural guarantees, presence of legal guardians and experts are innovations in Brazilian law concerning juvenile delinquents. Likewise the role attributed to the Public Prosecutor's department and the new powers of the police.

The deputy public prosecutor can opt to abandon proceedings. This is in effect a measure of diversion from the (juvenile) court and avoidance of a criminal trial. Only the magistrate can decide on the application of the procedure. The abandonment of proceedings, before the trial, consists of a measure of remedy (legal pardon). The measure must be accepted by the juvenile court judge: refusal is made by referring to the Public Prosecutor. This measure of remedy is inspired by the 'legal pardon' of Italian juvenile law.

This same measure can be judicial and accompanied by conditions. In this case guarantees of procedure and defence will be assured.

As for police authorities, their powers and functions have been redefined in the SEA in order to prevent arbitrary situations. The adolescent arrested after being caught red-handed must be brought as soon as possible to the Guardianship Council or before the juvenile court judge. Parents or guardians must be informed of the arrest and place where the adolescent is being held.

As in most systems of protection, the Brazilian response stresses the fact that the choice of measure, including a custodial measure, is related more to the personality and 'needs' of the minor than to the proportionality between the offence and the decision taken. Thus, among the range of possible measures, a very great importance is given to measures in an open environment. Social work in an open environment has been known for a long time in Brazil and practiced by the associative, religious and lay sectors. It has developed among the most disadvantaged populations, in particular of the shanty towns. Thus, 'programmes' have been set in motion to answer to the needs of 'street children', sometimes with specific features linked to age or sex.

The Constitution of 1988 and the Status of the Child and Adolescent give a new dimension to the open environment in inserting it among legal measures of treatment of young delinquents and children who are abandoned, in danger or in a situation of deficiency.

Children in Danger

As for this second category of juveniles, children in danger and young people in difficulty, the applicable texts are the same as for juvenile delinquents. The competent authorities are also the 'judge of children and adolescents' and the 'Guardianship Councils'. Public or private organisations and the associative sector are widely associated with protection.

The protection of children and young people in difficulty is rooted in the new idea of protection of 'fundamental rights'. The 'fundamental rights' of the child are described in the Constitution of 1988: they are based on the rights protected by the Universal Declaration of Human Rights and the Convention on the Rights of the Child. The idea of 'danger' or 'risk' is an underlying theme in the texts.

The protection of children and young people in difficulty is rooted in the new idea of protection of 'fundamental rights'. The 'fundamental rights' of the child are described in the Constitution of 1988: they are based on the rights protected by the Universal Declaration of Human Rights and the Convention on the Rights of the Child. The idea of 'danger' or 'risk' is an underlying theme in the texts.

The danger or risk is evaluated according to the right 'violated': against the child or by the minor. Likewise, the criterion which determines competence (judge of children and adolescents or 'Guardianship Council') and the measures applicable is that of the 'right violated'.

Violation of the 'fundamental rights', protected by the Constitution and by the SEA (article 98) can be of three types:

- by action or omission by society or by the State;
- by fault, omission or abuse on the part of parents or guardians;
- by the juvenile.

The rights which must be protected by the State are all related to life, education, health, food and shelter, etc.

The questionnaire indicates as examples of violations of the rights of the child by parents 'absence, abandonment, negligence, sexual violence, ill-treatment.'

Finally, still according to the response to the questionnaire, are taken into consideration 'acts of the minor', 'abuse of drugs or alcohol, prostitution, etc.' Delinquent acts, even though they are committed by the minor, are considered separately in the SEA (the former code combined them with other situations). Certain situations, more linked to poverty, such as begging, vagrancy and wandering, are not mentioned in the response. These situations should be resolved by a policy of general assistance; they only become situations of danger if, for example, there is exploitation of the child's begging by an adult.

The aim of measures envisaged is of a protective and educational nature: protection of the child and adolescent, but also education of parents in the carrying out of their family obligations. The juvenile court judge is competent when there is a 'situation which demands a placement in a foster family or a measure which has an effect on the exercise of parental authority'. The 'Municipal Guardianship Councils' are empowered to decide on other educational measures for minors: orientation, medical assistance, inclusion in community programmes or provisional reception in an establishment.

The range of measures applicable to parents is considerable. They can be educational and impose rules of conduct and conditions such as:

- insertion in a community programmeme or one of protection of the family;
- insertion in a programme for the treatment of alcoholism or drug addiction or in programmes of psychological or psychiatric treatment;
- the obligation to supervise children in their schoolwork and to accompany them for any medical or psychological treatment or any other measure decided.

The 'Guardianship Councils' offer measures of assistance to parents on the basis of a measure similar in spirit to French educational assistance in an open environment ('assistance and advice') to ensure that they adhere to the directives imposed.

- insertion in a programme for the treatment of alcoholism or drug addiction or in programmes of psychological or psychiatric treatment;

- the obligation to supervise children in their schoolwork and to accompany them for any medical or psychological treatment or any other measure decided.

The 'Guardianship Councils' offer measures of assistance to parents on the basis of a measure similar in spirit to French educational assistance in an open environment ('assistance and advice') to ensure that they adhere to the directives imposed.

The measures applicable to parents can also have a 'punitive' aspect: cautioning, withdrawal of custody of the child, suspension or termination of parental authority and removal of the parent at fault from the family home in the case of ill-treatment, oppression or sexual abuse.

The text does not mention 'adhesion' of the family. Failure to respect obligations can lead to administrative sanctions, or, for obligations related to parental authority, criminal sanctions.

In the case of children or adolescents at risk there are no 'custodial measures'. Transfer to an establishment or foster family does not 'legally' constitute deprivation of liberty. In practice, the custodial aspect of transfer to an institution is certainly debatable.

No financial aid is envisaged among measures intended for parents. The texts have only one stated aim: to protect and reinsert the minor and educate parents and guardians in the accomplishment of their family duties. Poverty should never constitute a sign of danger or risk for judicial authorities: it is a social problem which as such depends on solutions linked to public social policy.

This obligation of the State to assist parents in raising their children is also set out in article 18.2 of the Convention on the Rights of the Child: 'to guarantee and promote the rights enumerated in this Convention, member states provide appropriate aid to parents and legal guardians of the child in the exercise of the responsibility of raising the child'.

In procedures of protection of children and adolescents in danger or at risk the public ministry is always represented and the minor has the right to the presence of a defence lawyer. The minor will be heard in every case if his or her age permits it. Brazilian law does not mention direct referral to the judge by the minor or adhesion to measures.

Although, for juvenile delinquents, measures in an 'open environment' are characterised by measures of reparation and community work, young people in difficulty are favoured in that they are priorities and all the resources of the community are made available to them.

The response to the questionnaire emphasises the difference between the 'spirit' of the previous law and of the new laws. It is stated that 'the previous law permitted, in practice, the criminalisation and rendering harmful situations of deficiency resulting from poverty and misery. The current law gives priority to the attention which must be paid to the child and adolescent and which is based on the principles of universality and humanisation of treatment . . . in the same sense, current standards indicate that the child and adolescent are no longer simply passive subjects of intervention and legal sanctions'.

Treatment of children and young people in danger or difficulty is envisaged with a unique dimension in the Constitution: 'it is the obligation of the family, society and the State to guarantee to the child and adolescent, with absolute priority, the right to life, health, food, education, leisure, professional training, culture, dignity, respect, liberty and a family and community life, in addition to the obligations to protect them from all forms of discrimination, exploitation, violence, cruelty or oppression'.

The Status of the Child and Adolescent states in turn that it is necessary to 'give preference to measures which tend to reinforce family and community ties'.

The response to the questionnaire stresses two important requirements for the effective application of new statutes: on one hand, a need for an evolution in attitude change (especially in the conservative sector) towards the acceptance of new measures in an open environment which are advocated and towards the non-incarceration of the majority of minors; on the other hand, the continual transformation of former boarding establishments into new structures and the adequate retraining of personnel accustomed to working in a secure environment.

We could conclude by congratulating ourselves on this new law which bases its new orientations regarding the treatment of minors on the protection of all the rights stipulated in international rules and the respect of the recommendations of the United Nations. Ideas which are priorities are emerging: protection of the minor, social reinsertion, maintenance of family ties, the open environment and prevention, etc.

We could also state that the choice of a country like Brazil, where social contrasts are extremely marked, is fully justified in our research and should be particularly interesting for the United Nations and for international organisations.

However, it seems to us, regarding Brazil, that, without wishing to prejudice in any way the applicability of a law so ambitious in its modern aspects and in its apparent rejection of repressive measures, certain questions remain open which invite reflection on our part.

Brazilian society is not accepting of juvenile violence and one viewpoint given wide publicity is advocating a lowering of the age at which young people become subject to the jurisdiction of the adult courts, a more punitive approach (particularly on the part of the police) and a return to structures for the confinement of juveniles whose 'dangerousness' has been demonstrated. This would inevitably require another change in legislation. There was no time limit on incarceration before the introduction of the new laws and no procedural guarantees; the ending of the status of 'dangerousness' depended on the reports of specialists.

Social violence in Brazil often arises in opposition to juvenile violence: murder of delinquent children by 'death squads' is additional evidence. However, despite the violence here and there, there exists, parallel to and opposed to the repressive movement, a movement led by magistrates, educators, social workers and progressive sections of society who truly believe in the value of individualised action in favour of each young person and who wish to provide their country with a modern and humane juvenile justice system. Pious wishes? Utopia? It is impossible to make a prognosis for the future of this country where under-18s represent more than 40% of the population and 'street children' are counted in millions. From there arises the importance of particular attention on the part of international organisations to the implementation (considering both failures and successes) of the new measures envisaged in the Status of the Child and Adolescent and the evolution of juvenile justice.

It seems therefore that it is particularly important to centre these comparative studies, between developed and developing countries, on the application of new laws and the quantitative and qualitative importance of new measures advocated (including their social 'cost'): what kind of justice, what measures for the millions of underprivileged children on the planet? The Brazilian example can serve as an important model and can lead to deep reflection on the effectiveness of international rules.

SECTION V GENERAL CONCLUSIONS

Horst Schüler-Springorum[1]

Usefulness and Limits of Comparison

Comparison is a useful method in itself. Many processes of learning in our daily lives are founded on the recognition of differences by comparison. In criminal policy, comparison is a method which has proven itself for the discovery of different solutions applied to comparable problems, thus making it possible to extend the number of arguments and modes of action. It is exactly on this principle that the questionnaire drawn up by the International Network of Research into Juvenile Law is based. Parallel to a comparison between national statutes, a comparison of their implementation was intended to compare practices.

The perusal of the questionnaires has demonstrated - once more - how difficult it is to obtain responses which can really be compared with one another. It is precisely the questions on actual practices which remained unanswered. It was clear from the beginning that this project did not have the aim of collecting information on the methods used in dealing with particular cases (e.g. 'what should be done with juvenile 'X', in a situation 'Y', in country 'Z'?') The problems posed by the comparison of practices are both methodological and profound. Methodological problems, due essentially to the variety of responses provided to the questionnaires, have already been explained in the introduction. On the other hand the best illustration which can be given to fundamental problems is the comparison of statistical data. Even if the information is extremely 'precise' regarding the number of measures or the number of individuals dealt with in this way in a given country, it teaches us nothing about the application of this measure or whether or not it is uniformly 'distributed' throughout the country. Research carried out on a national level has always shown considerable disparities on this point. This implies that the true situation in the regions of country 'A' can be the same as in country 'B', while the comparison of national statistics had made apparent great discrepancies. This gives rise to even more difficult questions, such as that of knowing what exactly is the reality of a given measure, independently of knowing how it is experienced and lived by the person concerned.

Compared to this problem, the comparison of rights and statutes appears *a priori* more straightforward. But even in this domain, well-known problems are encountered. They begin with *notions* in which superficial similarities may hide deep underlying differences. 'Deprivation of liberty' for example can cover completely different modes of treatment, which again makes difficult

---

1. With the collaboration of Karen Schobloch, assistant researcher at the Institute of Criminology at the University of Munich.

189

the comparison of the degree of seriousness which is in fact felt. These discrepancies are still greater on the level of measures in an open environment. Thus 'mediation-reparation-reconciliation', which has been the subject of many discussions (see *Appendix I*, questions 40 and onward) is still at an experimental stage, leading to a great variety of realities hidden behind the same word (Austrian law and German law define this measure using different words, which would appear to mean that the measure is not the same; on the other hand, in French-speaking countries, where we speak of 'mediation-reparation', the element of 'reconciliation' is not to be found). As another example, let us take simply the abandonment of proceedings (see *Appendix I*, question 17 and onward) and with it the nuances which are found behind the notions of 'abandonment of proceedings, closing of cases, diversion from the court, alternative measures' see *Section II* and further the idea of 'recourse to extra-judicial measures' (Beijing Rules No. 11). If we add the problems posed by a legal comparison to those which have already been mentioned on the subject of the comparison of practices, we note that the declarations made by each country as to legislative priorities do not necessarily mean that they are to be found in practice, especially if it is a matter of a reform process in progress (see *Appendix I*, question 39 and onward).

The inquiry made by the Network has given rise to results which seemed important and determining to the authors. These results draw, for reasons already indicated, essentially on *tendencies*, as they emerge from the answers given to the questionnaire, or the *impressions* which allow them to be generalised. From these tendencies and impressions we derive several answers to the problem formulated in the introduction; they lead us to the general conclusions which are the subject of the current analysis.

General Results

From a global point of view, we note the confirmation of the most important hypothesis of our study: deprivation of liberty concerning juveniles is in the process of decline. However this evolution is not proceeding at the same speed or by the same route everywhere. We have noted essentially two reasons for this. In most Eastern European countries the impetus has come from the change in the political system. For other countries we note that the problem of deprivation of liberty is largely a tributary of the system of dealing with minors. Whatever the case the answers to the questionnaires have shown that this declining movement concerning deprivation of liberty is not a simple trend in criminal policy but a general tendency in policies concerning youth. This is also true regarding the measures applicable to young people in danger which stress that restrictions on the liberty of young people should be kept to a minimum. For this reason this change contains a wealth of nuances. Thus in a country which has adopted a system distinguishing the criminal domain from that of protection it does not seem particularly difficult to decrease deprivation of liberty within the criminal system. For between the act of legislation and its

190

application the route is relatively short: in a schematic fashion, the legislator only has to limit deprivation of liberty in declaring it a 'last resort', to immediately and effectively reach this end. In many countries, so-called alternative measures, including diversion from the court (alternatives to custody) have effectively contributed to reducing deprivation of liberty at an initial stage.

As for young people in danger, the route from the determination of the aims to their realisation is longer. For in this case it is not the justice system which plays the determining role but the administrative system. Administration is in principle organized at different levels: the various competences are divided into central, regional, local and other jurisdictions. It is evident that the risk of bureaucratisation is increasing in parallel; it is therefore interesting to observe that 'decentralisation' appears as a sort of magic word for reforms in matters of assistance to young people. For decentralisation finally leads us into the narrow area of local communities where the 'reservoir' of social services should be the greatest - the 'reservoir of new partners' for young people in danger and their families.

The best illustration of the change concerning assistance to youth is the reference to opposing ideas which have encumbered current and past policy, such as: the *imposition of measures* compared to an *offer of assistance* or *coercion* compared to *voluntary adhesion* or *institutional placement* compared to *assistance in an open environment*. Such oppositions also imply a parallel growth in means and methods of assistance to youth, for the number of measures which can be ordered is in itself less than that of the measures which can theoretically be applied, thus assistance in an open environment implies in itself more possibilities than an institutional placement. The bringing together of such concepts demonstrates well that in the current perspective, social work can only proceed according to the method called 'trial and error'; intervention is associated with the chance that it may help and not the assurance that it will succeed.

Protection and/or education are aims which are found almost everywhere when assistance is 'offered' to young people. The best interests of the minor is the most important criterion of interpretation of these ideas. The concept of protection has a double content: it is not only a matter of protected education, to which every child has the right (art. 13.1 of the International Pact on Economic, Social and Cultural Rights), but also protection from 'victimisation' within and outside of the family. With regard to ill-treatment or even abuse of the minor within the family, there is a possible conflict between the interests of the minor and the rights of the parents, between the rights of parents and the right of the State and society to intervene and even remove children and adolescents from the family. The United Nations directing principles for the prevention of juvenile delinquency (the 'Riyadh Directing Principles'), No. 46, is an interesting attempt to counterbalance this situation of conflict: the placement of young people in an institution should only take place as a last resort and then only for a period of time absolutely vital, with the interests of the child being the essential consideration. It is necessary to strictly define the criteria for recourse to official interventions of this type, which should normally be limited to the following situations:

(a) the child or adolescent has endured suffering inflicted by parents or guardians;
(b) the child or adolescent has been subjected to physical, sexual or emotional abuse by parents or guardians;
(c) the child or adolescent has been neglected, abandoned or exploited by parents or guardians;
(d) the child or adolescent has been exposed to serious physical or psychological danger due to his or her own behaviour and neither the minor, parents or guardians, nor community services outside of institutions can counteract this danger by means other than placement in an institution.

This attempt to find a solution to this conflicting situation does not however answer the question of who should be competent to take the decision. This question will be considered in the next section.

Competent Authorities

This title has been borrowed from No. 14.1 of the Beijing Rules. The notion of competent authority has been variously defined as 'court, tribunal, commission, council, etc.'. This notion, as it has been termed, is destined to encompass as far as possible all classical systems from the model of protection (welfare model) to the justice model. The various models reflect their historical and cultural evolution from the Roman legal tradition, for example, or the Anglo-Saxon tradition. The present research has also permitted such a systematisation; in the part devoted to the historical reminder of juvenile rights (see introduction), we have placed in parallel three systems which have emerged. This method allows us, through the responses provided, to restore the characteristics of a given system in a wider context. In fact these characteristics are much less easy to determine on the sole basis of abstract objectives (as they are assigned to a law or legal system applicable to minors) than on the basis of both interaction between the objectives and the standards which allow the realisation of these objectives and the manner in which these standards themselves are applied.

In attempting to capture in an inter-systematic fashion the legal information related to a country, we encounter two phenomena which we have termed 'interchangeability of ideas' and 'dissimulation of objectives'.

By 'interchangeability of ideas' we mean that the same notion does not necessarily mean the same thing in different countries and that different notions can on the other hand cover the same thing. Thus, regarding juvenile delinquents, a primary role is given to 'education' in Italy, Switzerland, Germany and the former Czechoslovakia, while in Belgium and France it is more a question of assistance, care, reinsertion and acquiring responsibility. In

Belgium, in the absence of criminal sanctions, it is the protection of young people which predominates. However the impression which emerges remains abstract as in this case education is seen as protection and assistance while in Switzerland the notion of education seems to have a more severe content, if one refers to reprimand, work, school detention and institutional placements. In Austria (and in Sweden and Scotland to a lesser extent) a parallel function is taken on by 'individual prevention'. At other times, in Austria, an aim of individual prevention is followed without specifically mentioning education. At the end of the day the two terms ('education' and 'individual prevention') seem in practice to mean the same thing except that there is no intervening detention used as a sanction in Austria when the directives and obligations imposed on the juvenile have not been respected as there is in Germany.

The best illustration of the second phenomenon, termed 'dissimulation of objectives', which can be made on the basis of an intellectual step of an experimental nature is to combine the three models mentioned in the introduction - protection, justice and extra-judicial - with objectives which exclude one another (such as education as opposed to the appropriate penalty as opposed to social aid). In this manner it becomes clear that concrete interventions in concrete cases have many more resemblances than have abstract aims and that behind these measures which exclude one another, there exists in fact the same transformation of an aim into its opposite. A court for family affairs can, under the pretext of education, send a young person to an institution, where he or she cannot harm society. A juvenile court can speak of a deterrent while at the same time envisaging social reinsertion. A council of social action can invoke the necessity to treat and train young people, while estimating in reality that they will only get what they deserve.

The two phenomena thus described can in fact be explained very simply. The real problems caused by deviant behaviour of a young person in society have much more in common than judicial solutions derived from culture and traditions, and each similarity is accelerated by modern techniques and by the economy. It is not therefore very surprising to note that the countries which wish to offer, thanks to their juvenile criminal law, assistance, re-socialisation, and care, are not necessarily those where interventions are less serious; inversely, those which proclaim the protection of the community and sanctions as aims, without excluding the other aims already mentioned, do not necessarily lead to the most serious measures.

As for the following conclusions made on the basis of the inquiry of the research network, not only are these limited to tendencies and impressions, but also these tendencies are derived solely from the information provided.

The Open Environment

Criminological research has always, let us say in a schematic fashion, been primarily concentrated on incarcerated delinquents. Consequently the negative effects of deprivation of liberty are among the results which have been most studied and documented. The effort undertaken to diminish deprivation of liberty now represents the strongest trend in criminal policy. This tendency has been globally imposed in the Beijing Rules (Nos. 19.1, 17.1c, 13.1, 23 and onward, see also no. 2.2a). This research apparently has the same objective with regard to the small number of countries which responded to the questionnaire. Certain ideas emerge: the most disadvantaged minors are the ones most likely to be deprived of their liberty when they are the ones most in need of protection from this measure. Young people have been and still are being incarcerated for reasons which are not due to reprehensible criminal conduct. This is demonstrated in all the different models of treatment of deviant behaviour, whether that behaviour incurs criminal penalties or not. The theoretical models, as outlined to us, have developed in the most diverse fashions in the countries consulted.

The aim pursued by the prioritisation of treatment in an open environment can be generalised in the following ways:

The treatment of young delinquents in an open environment has given rise to a determined number of interventions, presenting a multicoloured table; the measures mentioned in question 40 (*Appendix I*) are only examples. In this respect, it is also important to mention a measure with a great deal of future potential, the guilty verdict without a penalty (see Austria, para. 12 of the law on juvenile jurisdiction), especially the mechanism of abandonment of proceedings, combined with conditions or referral from the judicial sector to the social sector (see *Appendix I*, questions 19 and 20). If the variety of these modes of intervention still seems to be more extensive regarding young people in danger (see *Section III*), what happens in reality for each type of intervention seems on the other hand to be more easily visible for young delinquents. This could be due to the fact that in criminal matters it is a question of developing alternatives to the traditional deprivation of liberty (see *Appendix I*, questions 15 and 42), while in matters of assistance to youth (see *Appendix I*, question 34), it is more a matter of finding a modern system adapted to our era. In this respect, we note that where there exists juvenile criminal law, there is also a system of assistance to youth (but the reverse is not true). The question of alternatives to custody becomes all the more crucial as we approach a system of juvenile 'criminal' law.

It is indeed this last case (predominantly penal model) which teaches us the most about non-custodial interventions, as they are generally linked (among other things) to assistance, treatment, education, etc. This therefore calls on the competence of non-legal professions (see *Appendix I*, questions 16, 43 and 44). These social workers, educationalists, psychologists, etc., think and work in a completely different context from those in the legal profession (judges, prosecutors, etc.). The imperatives belonging to each category are in opposition; authoritarian intervention versus an offer of assistance, coercion versus voluntary co-operation, as well as interests such as the interest in arriving at a disposition of the case compared to the 'progress' or the 'evolution of the individual'. There results a weakening of the traditional criminal justice establishment applicable to minors, which leads to different consequences. In the process of construction of measures in an open

194

environment, we observe a phenomenon of retreat of the justice system in favour of an enlargement of the competence of social workers. Elsewhere, the legal system always appears as 'the strong arm'. It will not intervene unless measures in an open environment, which it has initiated but the implementation of which has been entrusted to the social services, have not brought the desired success.

We find the same relationships, albeit less marked, in the legal system applicable to young people in danger. While social work is at the basis of the sector of assistance to young people, there exists nevertheless mechanisms of transfer towards criminal jurisdictions for serious crimes or for reasons of public or legal interest (as in Scotland or Northern Ireland). In countries such as Belgium, Portugal, Poland and Brazil which do not have juvenile criminal law but special jurisdictions unique to minors in danger and delinquents, problems of conflict between the legal and social sectors are certainly still greater.

Concerning the role of the legal system in an open environment, from previous indications there emerges a tendency which should be reinforced in the future. This tendency is attached to the functions of judicial instances which are to constrain the behaviour of an individual or to guarantee protection. The justification of coercion is obvious in juvenile criminal law. In the sector of assistance to young people the same function appears when a judicial instance has a secondary competence because apparently necessary intervention cannot be implemented on a voluntary basis. The guarantees are more significant when custody requires the intervention of the judge to impose or grant it, either for young people in danger or juvenile delinquents. In juvenile criminal law, the function of a guarantee is also taken on by the principles of proportionality and the secondary nature of detention, as these principles protect the individual concerned from too severe intervention. The expression 'a last resort', very often used, is the most perfect illustration of this idea (see Beijing Rules Nos. 17, 19).

The trends which are linked to this question ensure that coercion should have even less important a role in the future, while guarantees should on the other hand become stronger. With regard to the first part of this affirmation, it is enough to remember that where juvenile criminal law exists the practice of closing proceedings and the increase in competence of the social sector finally leads to an elimination of traditional penal imperatives from the area of juvenile law. The same movement of diversion from the court can be noted in the area of assistance to young people as well as the greater role given to 'voluntarily' accepted intervention (see *Section III*).

A certain number of points lead us to think therefore that the protective function of judicial power will increase. Young people in danger are protected when supervision and monitoring of intervention comes under the authority of the court. The importance of this can be noted in the area of assistance to young people as well as the greater role given to 'voluntarily' accepted intervention (see *Section III*).

A certain number of points lead us to think therefore that the protective function of judicial power will increase. Young people in danger are protected when supervision and monitoring of intervention comes under the authority of the court. The importance of this function logically increases according to the intensity of the measure in question. So what is there a need for guarantees against? It is above all a matter of protection against excessive intervention in the social and personal life of the individual or that of parents or guardians. It is not only interventions which go 'too far' which can be termed excessive, but also those which are unnecessary and which in fact lead to greater social control (net widening). Besides, it is perfectly conceivable that a legal guarantee could be necessary against 'corruption', that is, against measures of assistance to youth which are justified in the name of assistance, education or protection but which in reality serve society to protect it from young people and their behaviour. It is not the fact that a measure of assistance to youth benefits society at the same time which is the problem, but rather its untruthful justification. It is obvious that the risk increases according to the seriousness of the intervention and reaches its greatest degree with an institutional placement.

The proof of the function of guarantees is even more simple in matters of juvenile criminal law. We have already mentioned on this subject the principles of the secondary nature of punishment and proportionality. One can note the same effect concerning fundamental procedural guarantees ranging from the presumption of innocence to professional carrying out of defence (*Appendix I,* question 24; Beijing Rules No. 7).

If this model is put into practice the justice system itself appears as a guarantee of 'last resort' for young citizens.

Deprivation of Liberty

The results of research on this question are almost impossible to dispute. Except for the occasional difference, the answers irrefutably reflect (also questions 3 and 47) - at least concerning the juvenile sector - the effort made in criminal policy to reduce detention.

In this respect the problem already raised regarding social work plays an important role in the explanation of the discrepancies which exist, related to the 'severity' or 'mildness' of each country but also as a condition of progress in criminal policy. We can therefore suppose that a country which does not yet possess differentiated social services (or which cannot finance them) cannot simply abolish closed institutions. For the institutions are also - as has been seen - of service to society, and cannot be done away with without creating a high risk for society. On the other hand, in countries where there are social services which deal with young people in danger or delinquents according to their needs, social work diminishes such risks at the same time. It follows that the construction and development of such services - probation, measures in an open environment, etc. - is indispensable if the currently dominant liberal trend is to continue.

A guarantee that this trend should persist and not go into reverse (whatever the justification) evidently does not exist. Thus after analysis of the questionnaires, the situation in Sweden is in some ways in opposition to the general tendency towards the lessening in severity of measures and interventions. There we observe a reinforcement of the demand for a strengthening of the punitive element, in the areas both of young people in danger and juvenile delinquents. Given that Sweden has always been liberal in the two domains, one could suspect a regression, which could probably also establish itself in other countries. However, it is important to place this tendency in context. The situation in Sweden is characterised by a very high rate of closing of proceedings and by an extremely low number of young detainees or young people placed in an institution. For this reason it is still too early to say if the change observed in Sweden must be considered as the reversal of a liberal policy. Whatever the case in the European context, the example of Sweden (and of Scandinavia in general) calls for vigilance, lest a similar change, for whatever reason - economic recession, change in mentality, etc. - sets in elsewhere.

The advice to be vigilant is not obviously *stricto sensu* the result of the inquiry. It is much more a matter of a postulate of criminal policy which requires justification. This justification is simple since all the best empirically founded studies confirm that deprivation of liberty, for this age group, creates more problems than it solves and is harmful to the person concerned. Hence the need for avoiding detention of young people as much as possible.

Utopia or Reality?

We have not reached 'Utopia'. The 'utopian' situation raised in the title of this work is the treatment of young people in an open environment. Globally speaking, we can affirm on the basis of our research - as has already been mentioned above in the second point - quite a clear result: while the countries consulted are in different states of advancement towards this utopia, there emerges nevertheless an almost general consensus regarding the justice of the direction taken. In this respect, we note a completely different attitude concerning the task which must be accomplished by society with regard to young deviants or delinquents. In a schematic fashion we can say that former marginalisation and exclusion have been replaced by assistance and integration.

We can only speculate on the question of why attitudes are changing (or have already changed) in our time. We could at best explain it in the following manner: with the passage of time the traditional attitude could only generate disappointment and distrust. In fact, marginalisation and exclusion of young delinquents (like the high rates of recidivism which were recorded after the incarceration of juveniles) have brought disappointment in relation to their lack of usefulness to society. As for mistrust, it was simply due to the punitive system itself. We know the characteristics of this system. It is very general definitions which determine deviant behaviour. These definitions are used by individuals with central positions (administration) or positions of power (justice) to have repressive sanctions and interventions imposed; in the case of an institutional placement, they will be carried out by people with the same attitude (personnel in a secure institution, for example). It is indeed the increase in disappointment regarding institutions and mistrust towards personnel in the traditional system which have finally led to a change of attitude, a change which appeared throughout our research and is found in the very title of this work.

Thus, there exist many arguments in favour of this route towards Utopia. We could make two observations regarding the following of this route which stem principally from the study of Brazil, termed a 'country of contrasts'. The first concerns the limits assigned to a reform made by law. It is evident that even a 'good' law which deserves to be described as 'modern' or 'progressive' is not sufficient to engender reform when the gap between the content and the social situation is too great. In such a case, it is essentially the individuals concerned who will find this discrepancy between the good intentions of the legislator and the difficulties in implementation hypocritical. The second observation concerns the economic conditions of active work in an open environment. Economic change (in Europe and world-wide) has already led to a tightening of national, regional or local budgets intended for work with juvenile delinquents or young people in danger. The argument used, that such budget reductions are only the result of badly placed priorities, does not take us anywhere.

On the other hand, we can see a kind of warning not to fall back into the old attitude of marginalisation and exclusion of young people, for this, too, costs a lot of money and is less useful (as has already been seen).

Utopia or reality? Given a general perspective, our research justifies the optimism of envisaging a 'concrete utopia'.

The Background of Europe

Europe is - as research has again shown - a somewhat 'Babylonian' region. Nowhere in the world does one find a greater diversity of traditions and cultures, mentalities and, especially, languages within such a confined space. Changes in the social and cultural environment over a short distance often provoke some confusion in visitors from North America (or China and Australia). 'Europe of 1993' will alter all these differences only slightly.

Although we declared in the introduction that 'research should also respond to the specific needs for knowledge in the European context of 1993', the answers found will be limited, as the specific acquisition of knowledge - specific to the interests of a united Europe - appears rather restricted.

Nevertheless, the theories presented here stem from the hypothesis that a prudent evolution in national law towards a 'European law' is an aim to be followed. Whatever the case, we can make some suggestions, which, to be sure, are not directly linked to the results of the study, but which seem appropriate to show both the obstacles and the chances of achieving this aim.

Procedural law appears to be more suitable for the harmonisation of law than for the law itself. This theory is founded on observations already made on the role of the legal system as an instance of control of interventions and of guarantee. These two functions are in principle assumed by the legal provisions of 'form', i.e. procedure. These provisions should be easier to reconcile than fundamental provisions such as the systems of sanctions applicable to minors or the criteria of intervention in matters of the protection of youth. Certainly, the Swiss example, with a single federal law and a multiplicity of procedural laws on a cantonal level, contradicts this theory, but we can consider whether the historical reasons for the evolution in Switzerland will be repeated in Europe.

The lowest age thresholds are more appropriate than the highest for a harmonisation of rights regarding age categories. This theory concerns in particular legal systems which have autonomous juvenile criminal law. The Beijing Rules are favourable to an lower age threshold which 'should not be too low' (No. 4 with commentary), without however expressly mentioning an age, due to the absence of general agreement on the proposed minimum age of 12. On the other hand, the age of 18 has already almost universally been considered as a threshold of responsibility (19 in Austria) as far as there exists no particular system applicable to young adult delinquents. In addition, according to the Beijing Rules (no. 3.3) 'efforts will be made to extend to young adult delinquents the principles incorporated in this collection of rules'.

The international instruments on the rights of children present elements favourable to harmonisation of laws. The International Convention on the Rights of the Child presents is the most recent evolution in this sector. It was created, like the European Convention on Human Rights and other similar declarations and conventions, with the aim of improving uniformly, through the granting of legal guarantees, the social situation of the individual concerned. In this respect, the Convention on the Rights of the Child has set very high aims, so high that the chances of putting them into practice will, for a very long time, be very different from one country to another. The fundamental provisions of the European Convention on Human Rights seem from this point of view to coincide perfectly with the interests of juvenile delinquents and young people in danger: this is especially due to fundamental procedural rights prescribed in articles 6 and 7 of the European Convention and the guarantee of article 5 concerning illegal deprivation of liberty.

The continuing decrease in deprivation of liberty depends principally on the development of measures in an open environment. This point was the subject of the preliminary discussion related to the importance of social work. In Europe, if we are to maximise the use of measures in an open environment, we must constantly exchange experiences and information in matters of social work. The more we reach such a *connexio* of social services, the better we will be able to remove the obstacles which are often linked to national mentalities, in particular regarding the provision of adequate financial resources.

Finally, we must encourage the mutual recognition by European countries of national decisions as well as their implementation concerning juvenile delinquents and young people in danger. This point appears particularly important when considering the probable increase in the migration of young people in a united Europe. In addition, such a mutual recognition of decisions would allow us to gradually envisage, in juvenile law, recourse to a sort of 'most favoured nation clause', especially concerning detention of minors.

Appendix I: Questionnaire

Country:

Name and function of person filling out the questionnaire:

Introduction

Please give details on:

1. the current political and administrative background of your country;

2 current demographic data;

3. a brief history of juvenile law.

Legal framework concerning juvenile delinquents

4. What are the legal texts currently applicable to juvenile delinquents?

5. What age brackets are involved (problem of criminal majority)?

6. Is there a difference between punishable offences, according to whether juveniles or adults are involved?

7. What jurisdictions or other institutions (e.g. socio-administrative services) are competent?

8. What types of interventions are set out in the texts (penalties, measures, non-intervention)?

9. What are the principal objectives legally pursued by these interventions (punishment, education, retribution, insertion, etc.).

10. What criteria determine the choice of the type of intervention (penalties, measures, etc.): proportionality, gravity and circumstances of the offence, recidivism, legal precedents needs, peculiar to minors, etc?

11. Does the law stipulate different penalties or measures according to the seriousness of the offence?

12 Do legal arrangements regarding minors permit the imposition of heavier penalties and measures on juveniles than on adults (due to the danger represented by them, their educational needs, etc.)?

13. What are the penalties or measures available which do not involve detention?

14. What are the penalties or measures available which involve detention?

> - Is there a minimum or maximum duration?
> - Are there differences according to age groups?
> - Are there differences according to sex?

15. Are there alternative measures to penalties or deprivation of liberty (kinds, duration, choice criteria, competent authority and supervision of the carrying out of these measures)?

16. Who can contribute, and how, to the choice of alternative measures (defence, victim, social services)?

17. Is the abandonment of proceedings possible? At what level (police, Public Prosecutor's office, court)? Does the law impose conditions?

18. Can the abandonment of proceedings be subordinated to the imposition of socio-educational measures (obligations, benefits etc.)?

19. Can abandonment of proceedings be accompanied by a referral either to other legal channels or to non-legal channels?

20. Are there legal possibilities of transfer of cases between juvenile and adult jurisdictions, and vice versa? In what cases? Under what conditions?

21. What provisional measures can be taken before judgement (gradation of measures, time limits, supervision)?

22. Under what conditions (age, time limits, offences, etc.) can deprivation of liberty be ordered? Under what form (prison, secure educational establishment)?

23. Are there possible alternatives to provisional detention?

24. What rights of the juvenile are recognised (defence, guarantees, etc.)?

25. What is the role of experts (psychologists, social workers, etc.) in the proceedings?

Framework concerning young people in difficulty (in danger, in an irregular situation, ill-treated, etc.)

26. What are the legal texts currently applicable to young people in difficulty?

27. To what kinds of situations do these texts apply (e.g. ill-treatment, negligence, moral danger, family conflicts, etc.)?

28. What age groups are concerned?

29. What legal or other institutions are competent (including socio-administrative services)?

30. What criteria justify the competence of a particular intervening authority (characteristics, urgency of the situation, agreement of the juvenile, agreement of the family, etc.)?

31. What types of legal or social interventions are set out in the texts (measures for juveniles, measures for parents, legal non-intervention, etc.)?

32. What are the principal objectives legally pursued by these interventions (protection, education, insertion, welfare, autonomy, etc.).

33. Do legal arrangements permit the removal of a juvenile from the family: motives, conditions, form, duration, etc.? Are there differences according to the age and sex of the minor?

34. In the case of reactions which would deprive the juvenile of liberty, are there alternative measures?

35. Who can contribute and how to the choice of these alternative measures (specialised defence, social services, etc.)?

36. Are there legal possibilities of transferring cases from socio-administrative services to competent jurisdictions, or vice versa? In what cases? Under what conditions?

37. What rights of the juvenile are recognised (seizure, agreement, being heard, etc.)?

38. What is the role of experts (psychologists, social workers, etc.)?

Treatment in an open environment of juvenile delinquents and minors in difficulty

39. What is the importance given, in law and in practice, to treatment in an open environment?

40. During the last ten years, has change taken place in this area, concerning the type of measures, their application, modes of carrying out, etc.)?

203

And this, in particular, for the following measures:

- community service;
- probation (or any other comparable measure);
- intermediate treatment;
- mediation/reparation.

41. For each type of treatment in an open environment, indicate as far as possible its importance, in exact and relative figures, compared to the total number of decisions taken.

42. In practice, has it been noted that one or other of these measures of treatment in an open environment is replacing penalties or detention for juvenile delinquents?

Can you provide supporting statistical indications, in particular on the evolution of measures or custodial sentences?

43. Are new parties participating in the carrying out of these measures of treatment in an open environment? Who? How? In what form and under what conditions?

44. In the carrying out of these measures, is a new role being delegated to the local community? To the family of the juvenile? To the school?

45. What are the legal limits and what are the checks on the intervention of the associative sector?

46. Is training available for voluntary workers? What training?

Reform projects

47. In the framework of the above questions, are reforms being planned or studied in your country?

Appendix II: People Who Responded to the Questionnaire

Germany: Wolfgang Heinz, professor at the University of Konstanz.

England and Wales: Dilly Gask, lay magistrate; member of NACRO council.

Austria: Udo Jesionek, president, Vienna juvenile court; professor, University of Linz.

Belgium: Colette Somerhausen-Pelseneer, lecturer at the Université Libre de Bruxelles; Kristine Kloeck, lecturer at the Vrije Universiteit Brussel.

Brazil: Sergio Adorno, professor, University of São Paolo; Paolo Alfonso Garrido, Public Prosecutor of the Republic, Public Prosecutor's office for juveniles São Paolo; Sabrina U. Heldman, researcher, University of São Paolo; Myriam Mesquita Pugliese de Castro, researcher, University of São Paolo.

Scotland: Stewart Lynch, Association of Reporters to Children's Panels.

France: Michel Allaix, magistrate, Management of Legal Protection of Minors of the Ministry of Justice.

Greece: Angelika Pitsela, criminological researcher at the University of Cologne.

Northern Ireland: Dr. Willie McCarney, juvenile court magistrate, Belfast.

Italy: Luigi Fadiga, president of the juvenile court in Rome.

Luxembourg: Vammille Schneider, Service for the Protection of Youth; François Kimmel manager, Central Service for Social Assistance, Public Prosecutor's Department.

The Netherlands: Anton van Kalmthout, lecturer at the University of Tilburg.

Poland: Zbigniew Holda, professor at the Marie-Curie Sklodowska University, Lublin, Jadellonian University, Krakow.

Portugal: Rosa Maria Clemente, Care Services for Minors, Ministry of Justice.

Slovenia: Alenka Selih, professor at the University of Ljubljana; Natasa Oven, assistant at the University of Ljubljana.

Sweden: Hanns von Hofer, Service of Criminal Statistics, Stockholm.

Switzerland: André Dunant, president of the juvenile court in Geneva; Jean Zermatten, juvenile court judge in Sion.

Czechoslovakia: Helena Válková, Institute of legal science at the Academy of Sciences, Prague.

Appendix III Comparative Table

Germany

Federal republic made up of *Länder*. The Chancellor directs the federal government. The President of the Republic is elected for five years by the Federal Assembly (*Bundestag*) and by certain representatives of the Länder. There are two chambers: the *Bundestag,* elected for four years and the *Bundesrat* appointed by the governments of the *Länder.*

After unification of the FRG and the GDR the total population is around 80 million inhabitants, of whom 17.3% are aged under 15.

Austria

A federal republic made up of nine provinces or *Länder,* of which each has its own Assembly. The President of the Republic is elected for six years. The Chancellor is the head of the parliamentary majority and directs the federal government. There are two chambers: the National Assembly (*Nationalrat*), elected for four years and the Federal Council (*Bundesrat*) appointed by the nine Assemblies of the *Länder.*

Population: 7,500,000 inhabitants, of whom 530,000 are aged between 14 and 19 years.

17.6% of the population is aged under 15.

Belgium

Constitutional monarchy. Originally a unified state, the country has moved towards a kind of federal state by the creation, besides the state, of 'communities' and 'regions'.

Three communities have been established, of which the essential element is the language spoken; the Flemish Community, the French Community and the German-speaking Community. Belgium also has three 'regions', of which the essential element is territory: the Walloon region, the Flemish region and that of the capital, Brussels. Administrative organisation includes: the central administration of the state, divided between national ministries; the administrations of the communities and regions, divided between community and regional executives.

Population: almost ten million inhabitants, of whom approximately 9% are foreigners. Minors under 15 represent 18% of the population and 15 to 25-year-olds 15%.

Division by community: 55% in the Flemish Community; less than 1% in the German-speaking Community (67,000 inhabitants); the rest in the French Community.

Brazil

A federal republic made up of a Federal District, seat of the capital, Brasilia, and 26 member states. A Presidential system with two chambers: the Senate and the Chamber of Deputies. The President of the Republic is elected for five years, the senators for eight years and the deputies for four years. The member states are governed by a governor elected for four years and secretaries of state are the executive power. Each state has its own constitution, judicial powers and legislative authority exercised by a Chamber of Deputies.

Population: almost 150 million inhabitants, of whom 41% are under 18.

France

French institutions are fundamentally fixed by the 1958 Constitution. The President of the Republic, with wide powers, is elected by direct universal suffrage and appoints the Prime Minister and, on the advice of the latter, the members of the government, responsible to the National Assembly. Legislative power rests with two chambers, the National Assembly and the Senate, elected by direct and indirect suffrage respectively. The Constitutional Council is charged with verifying the constitutionality of laws.

The territory is divided into 22 administrative regions, sub-divided into 96 metropolitan départements, besides overseas départements, two territorial collectives and overseas territories.

Population: 56 million inhabitants, of whom a quarter is aged under 18; 20.2% under 15.

Greece

A parliamentary republic. The Head of State is elected for a period of five years by the Chamber of Deputies and nominates the Prime Minister. Unicameral system; the Chamber of Deputies is elected for four years.

Population: around 9,800,000, of whom 908,000 are aged 7 to 12, 758,000 from 13 to 17; 431,000 from 18 to 20. 19.7% of the population is aged under 15.

Italy

A republic. The law particularly favours local autonomy. Decentralisation is considerable and translates into the creation of a regional level of government, quite different from one region to another.

The President of the Republic is elected for seven years by the Parliament (formed by the Chamber of Deputies and the Senate).

Population: 57,600,000. 17.1% of the population is under 15.

Luxembourg

Representative democracy under the form of a constitutional monarchy. The exercise of the executive power belongs exclusively to the Grand Duke and the legislative power jointly to the Grand Duke and the Chamber of Deputies. The exercise of judicial power belongs to courts and tribunals. The legal powers of the Grand Duke are set out in the Constitution.

The Netherlands

Parliamentary monarchy. The Sovereign exercises certain powers, in particular during the formation of governments. The Prime Minister is responsible before the Parliament, composed of a 'First Chamber' (Higher Chamber), which corresponds to the Senate and is elected for six years and a 'Second Chamber' (Lower Chamber), which corresponds to the House of Representatives and which is elected for four years.

Population: 14,500,000 of whom approximately 24.5% are aged under 18.

Poland

A republic. Population: around 38,200,000, of whom 11,320,000 are aged 0 to 17 (around 4,000.000 under 4).

24.9% of the population is aged under 15.

Portugal

Its territory also includes the Archipelagoes of Madeira and the Açores, in the Atlantic. A Republic. The political system is a semi-presidential parliamentary democracy. Power is centralised, except for the autonomous regions of Madeira and the Açores. The territory is divided into eleven provinces.

Population: 10,530,000. Urban population is 29.3% of the total. Children and young people under 19 make up around 16% of the population.

21.2% are aged under 15.

United Kingdom

United Kingdom of Great Britain (England, Wales and Scotland) and Northern Ireland. Parliamentary monarchy. The Sovereign has symbolic authority. The Prime Minister is responsible before the House of Commons. The Parliament is composed of two Chambers: The House of Commons, elected for five years, and the House of Lords, composed of peers nominated for life or with hereditary titles.

Population: 57,200,000 inhabitants, of whom 18.9% are aged under 15.

Switzerland

Federal Republic, composed of 23 cantons (of which three are made up of two half-cantons). Each canton has internal sovereignty and a Constitution. The official languages are German, French, Italian and Rheto-Romanic.

The federal institutions are the 'Federal Assembly' (Parliament), consisting of the 'National Council' elected for four years and the 'Council of States' elected by the cantons. The Federal Assembly is the supreme authority and it elects the executive, the 'Federal Council'.

Population: 6,500,000 inhabitants, of whom 16.4% are aged under 15.

Slovenia

A quite recent pluralist democracy (1990), the country was part of the Federal Socialist Republic of Yugoslavia until June 1991. A parliamentary republic, where the President, elected tor five years, has a limited role. The Parliament is composed of two chambers (the 'State Assembly' - the legislative Chamber, and the 'Council of State' - the consultative chamber), both of which are elected for four years.

Population: almost two million inhabitants, of whom around 207,000 are aged 7 to 13 and 120,000 are aged 14 to 18.

Sweden
Parliamentary monarchy. The Sovereign has symbolic powers. Power is exercised chiefly by the Prime Minister who is responsible before the Parliament, which is composed of one Assembly, the *Riksdag*, elected for three years.

Population: around 8,400,000, of whom 332,000 are aged 15 to 17 and 144.000 are aged 18 to 20. 16.5% of the population is under 15.

Czechoslovakia
A federal republic. System of three Chambers (at the time of the research).

Population: 16,625,000, of whom 741,000 are aged from 15 to 17; in the Czech republic: 10,360,000; in Slovakia: 5,265,000. 23.3% of the population is under 15 years of age.

ENDNOTE to *Appendix III*

1. The information is incomplete for certain countries. Details given are as per the information provided to the Network at the time of its research. Source for information concerning the proportion of children under 15 years in the population: *The Economist, Vital World Statistics 1990.*

Appendix IV: Legal Texts Applicable to Juvenile Delinquents[1]

Germany
Jugendgerichtsgesetz of 1 October 1953 in the version of 30 August 1990, which came into force on 1 December 1990.

England and Wales
Children and Young Persons Acts of 1933 and 1969. Criminal Justice Act of 1991, which came into force in October 1992. [2]

Austria
Jugendgerichtsgesetz, which came into force on 1 January 1989

Belgium
Law for the protection of youth of 8 April 1965.

Scotland
Social Work (Scotland) Act 1968. [3]

France
Ordinance of 2 February 1945.
Law of 1950, which came into force on 1 January 1951 (part of the Penal Code).
Law on criminal procedure of 1950, which came into lorce on 1 January 1951.
Law on penitentiary treatment, which came into force on 1 January 1990.

Northern Ireland
Children and Young Persons (Northern Ireland) Act 1968
Treatment of Offenders Order 1988

Italy
Law of 4 June1967
New Code of Juvenile Criminal Procedure of 22 August 1988

Luxembourg
Law for the protection of youth of 12 October 1971

The Netherlands
Law of 9 November 1961 (Art. 77a-78 of the Penal Code; art. 486-509 of the Code of Criminal Procedure; art. 44 and 56 of the Code of Judicial Organisatlon).

Poland
Law of 26 October 1982, which came into force on 13 May 1983

Portugal	Law of 23 September 1982, which came into force on 1 January 1983
Slovenia	Yugoslav criminal law of 8 October 1976, which came into force on 1 July 1977 and the Slovenian criminal law of 8 October 1976, which came into force on 1 July 1977.
Sweden	Law of 22 December 1962, which came into torce on the 1 January 1965; social law of 1 January 1982.
Switzerland	Law of 18 March 1971, which came into force on 1 January 1974.
Ex-Czechoslovakia	Law of 29 November 1961 reforming the Penal Code and the Code of Criminal Procedure.

Legal texts applicable to minors in danger[4]

Germany	Kinder-und-Jugendhilfesgesetz (1990). Law on assistance to children and young persons, which came into force in 1991. Civil Code.
England and Wales	Children Act 1989.
Austria	Civil Code. *Jugendwohlfahrtsgesetz* (1989) (Laws on the welfare of juveniles). *Außerstreitgesetz* (Law on arbitration) and *Jugendgerichtsgesetz* (Law on the Juvenile Court). Procedural rules.
Belgium	Law of 8 April 1965 relative to the protection of youth. *Besluit van de Vlaamse Executieve tot coördianatie van de decreten inzake bijzondere jeugdbijstand* - 4 April 1990 (Decree of the Flemish Executive of 4 April 1990 coordinating decrees relative to special assistance to young people). Decree of 4 March 1991 relative to assistance to young people. (French Community of Belgium). *Besluit van de Vlaamse Executieve houdende vaststelling van de voorwaarden van erkenning en subsidiëring van centra voor hulpverlening inzake kindermishandeling* - 8 July 1987 (Decree of the Flemish Executive of 8 July 1987 fixing the conditions of consent and subsidising of aid centres for abused children).

211

Brazil	Constitution of the Federal Republic of Brazil ot 5 October 1988. Status of the Child and Adolescent. Law 8.069 of 13 July 1990.
Scotland	Social Work (Scotland) Act 1968.[3]
France	Law of 4 June 1970 modifying article 375 of the Civil Code. Law of 8 October 1966 and decree of 25 April 1969 on guardianship of social services. Decree of 18 February 1975 on legal protection of young adults. Law of 6 January 1986 on decentralisation and transfer of competence. Law of 10 July 1989 on the prevention of ill-treatment of children.
Luxembourg	Law of 12 November 1971 relative to the protection youth.
Greece	Law of necessity on the organisation and functioning of institutions for the re-education of young people (1940). Civil Code (Family law) (1941, in force since 1946).
Northern Ireland	Children and Young Persons Act (Northern Ireland) 1968
Italy	Law no. 1.404 of 20 July 1934 creating juvenile courts (article 25). Articles 330, 333 and 336 of the Civil Code, modified by law no.151 of 19 May 1975. DPR no.616 of 24 July 1977 of decentralisation and transfer of competence. Law no.184 of 4 May 1983 on the adoption and placement of minors. Article 34 of law no.448 of 22 September 1988 (Code of Juvenile Criminal Procedure).
Poland	Family Code (1965). Law on the treatment of juveniles (1983). Law on guardianship (1964). Law on social welfare. Law on drug abuse (1983).

Portugal	Law no.314 of 1978 on the organisation of supervision of minors.
	Law no.189 of 1991 creating commissions for the protection of minors.
Slovenia	Slovenian law on marriage and family relations (1977, amended in 1989).
	Slovenian law on social welfare (1979, amended in 1989).
	Slovenian law on contraventions (1983).
	Slovenian law on the education and training of physically and mentally disabled children and young people (1979).
Sweden	Law on social welfare (Socialtjänstlagen).
	Law on the treatment of minors (*Lagen om vard av unga*).
Switzerland	Civil Code - art. 307 to 317
Ex-Czechoslovakia	Family Code 1963 (as amended).

ENDNOTES to *Appendix IV*

1. Details as communicated to the Network by their correspondents.

2 Since the original French version of the Network's research was published see, for the UK, amendments contained in the Criminal Justice Act 1993 and the Criminal Justice and Public Order Act 1994.

3. Since the original French version of the report was published, see now, for Scotland the Children (Scotland) Act 1995. [Publisher's note: A concise treatment and the more recent position can be located in Kelly A. (1996), *Introduction to the Scottish Children's Panel*. Winchester: Waterside Press. For some further details, *see* p.224]

4. Details as communicated to the Network by correspondents.

Bibliography Part 1

General literature concerning several countries included in the research

Bishop, N. (ed.): *Scandinavian Criminal Policy and Criminology 1986-90.* Stockholm, 1990.

Booth, T. (ed.): *Juvenile Justice in the New Europe.* Sheffield, 1991.

Dünkel, F: 'Réflexions au sujet d'une élaboration de règles minima par les Nations-unies pour la protection des mineurs privés de liberté'. *Revue internationale de criminologie et de police technique* 41 (1988), pp 309-323.

Dünkel, F.: 'La privation de liberté a l'égard des jeunes délinquants. Tendances actuelles dans le cadre d'une comparaison internationale'. In: Sace, J., Van der Vorst, P. (eds.): *Justice et jeunes délinquants. Aspects institutionnels et criminologiques.* Actes de la Journée d'étude organiseé en hommage à L. Slachmuylder. Brussels 1989, pp. 127-146 (mise à jour in: Junger-Tas, J., Boendermaker, L., van der Laan, P.H. (eds.): L'avenir du système pénal des mineurs. Leuven 1991, pp. 385-400).

Dünkel, F.: 'Legal Differences in Europe relevant to Juvenile Criminology'. In: Booth, T. (ed.): *Juvenile Justice in the New Europe.* Sheffield, 1991, pp. 1-29.

Dünkel, F.: *Les législations en vigeur relatives aux jeunes adultes délinquants.* 10ème colloque de criminologie. Council of Europe. Strasbourg, 1993 (also in English translation).

Dünkel, F. and Rossner, D.: 'Law and Practice of Victim/Offender Agreements'. In: Wright, M., Galaway, B. (eds.): *Mediation and Criminal Justice. Victims Offenders and Community.* London, 1989, pp. 152-177.

Dunkel, F. and Zermatten, J. (eds.): Nouvelles tendances dans le droit pénal des mineurs. Médiation Travail au Profit de la Commlmauté et Traitement Intermédiaire. Freiburg im Breisgau, 1990.

Eliaerts, C., et al. (Eds.): Van jeugdbeschermingsrecht naur jeugdrecht? Arnhem, 1990.

Jung, H.: 'Structural Problems of Juvenile Justice Systems'. In: *The Journal of the Law Society of Scotland 1982,* pp. 315-318.

Junger-Tas, J., Boendermaker, L., van der Laan, P. H. (Eds.): *The future of the juvenile justice system.* Leuven, Amersfoort, 1991.

Klein, M.W. (ed.): *Western Systems of Juvenile Justice.* Beverly Hills, 1984.

van der Laan, P., Giller, H.: 'Comparative juvenile justice systems analysis. An Anglo-Dutch initiative'. In: Junger-Tas, J., et al. (eds.): *The future of the juvenile justice system.* Leuven, Amersfoort, 1991, pp. 377-383.

Lahalle, A.: *Les règles internationales et les grands systèmes de droit des minelos en Europe occidentale.* Vaucresson, 1990

Sace, J., van der Vorst, P. (eds.): *Justice et Jeunes Délinquants. Aspects institutionnels et criminologiques.* Brussels, 1989.

Snare, A. (ed.): 'Youth, Crime and Justice'. Oslo, *Scandinavian Studies in Criminology,* vol. 12, 1991.

Tutt, N.: 'Law and Policies on Juvenile Offending in England and Wales, Scotland, Northern Ireland and the Republic of Ireland'. In: Kerner, H.J. et al. (eds.): Jugendgerichtsbarkeit in Europa und Nordamerika - Aspekte und Tendenzen - Munich, 1986

Literature in French or English in various countries

Germany

Dünkel, F.: 'L'influence de la Défense Sociale sur la réforme du droit pénal des mineurs et de leur détention en RFA. Comparaison entre des pays européens'. *Revue de droit pénal et de criminologie* (Brussels) 65 (1985), pp. 507-528.

Heinz, W.: 'La diversion (déjudiciarisation) dans le droit pénal des mineurs en République féderale d'Allemagne. Resultats de recherches empiriques'. *Revue internationale de criminologie et de police technique* 64 (1991), pp. 485-510.

Mérigeau, M.: *Le droit pénal des mineurs et des jeunes adultes en République Fédérale d'Allemagne.* Ed. Pedone, Paris, 1987.

Mérigeau, M., Dünkel, F.: 'Etat actuel et perspectives d'évolution du droit pénal des mineurs en République fédérale d'Allemagne'. In: Eliaerts, C., *et al.* (eds.): *Van Jeugdbeschermingsrecht naar Jeugdrecht?* Antwerp, 1990, pp. 231-252.

Mérigeau, M.: 'Evolution du droit pénal des mineurs et des jeunes adultes en République fédérale d'Allemagne. Réflexions sur le projet de réforme de septembre 1989'. *Revue internationale de criminologie et de police technique* 44 (1990), pp. 309-325.

Schüller-Springorum, H.: 'Jeunesse, crime et justice', *Revue internationale de criminologie et de police technique* 39 (1986), pp. 339-352.

Belgium

'L'aide à la jeunesse. Anatomie du décret du 4 mars 1991'. Actes du colloque organisé le 25 octobre 1991. Editions du Jeune Barreau de Liège, 1991.

Moens, J., Verlynde, P.: *Les mesures à l égard des mineurs. Les mesures à l égard des parents.* Brussels, Bruylant, 1988.

Verhellen, E., Cappellaere G.: 'L' assistance spéciale et judiciaire aux jeunes en Communauté flamande'. In: *Journal du droit des jeunes* Liège, 1990, no. 1, pp. 11.

Walgrave, L.: 'La repénalisation de la délinquance juvénile: une fuite en avant'. *Revue de droit pénal et de criminologie* 65 (1985), pp.603-620.

France

Barre, M. D., Tournier, P., Leconte, B.: *Le travail d'intérêt général. Analyse statistique des pratiques.* Paris, CESDIP, 1986

Barrere, C.: *Les expériences récentes réalisées pour améliorer l'exercice par les mineurs de leurs droits judiciaires.* Reims, CERAS, 1991.

Bongrain, M.: *La loi au secours de l'enfant maltraité.* Vanves (CTNERHI) 1987.

Callu, E., Caquil. G., Lahalle, A.: *La tutelle aux prestations socialfamiliales. Etude des stratégies des acteurs institutionnels.* Vaucresson, 1991.

Chauviere, M.: *Enfance inadaptée, l'héritage de Vichy.* 2ème edition, Paris, Ed. ouvrières, 1987.

Chaillou, P.: *Le juge et l'enfant.* Toulouse, 1987.

CTNERHI: Analyse économique du système de protection judiciaire de la jeunesse (note de synthèse par Marie-Eve Joël et Suzanne Charvet-Protat) Paris, 1991.

Dessertine, D., Maradan, B.: *Pratiques judiciaires de l'assistance éducative* (1889/1941). Paris, MIRE, CNRS. 1991.

Dubet, F.: *La galère: jeunes en survie.* Fayard, 1987.

Fenet, F., Sagotduvauroux, D.: *Enfants placés, pourquoi?,* Lille, ADNSEA, 1987.

Fize, M.: La démocratie familiale . *Evolution des relations parents-adolescents.* Paris, Presses de la Renaissance, 1990.

Carapon, A., *et al.: La justice des mineurs en région parisienne.* Universite Paris-I, 1985.

Gorny, V.: *Vos enfants et la loi.* Hachette, 1987.

Lahalle, A., *et al.: Les procédures civiles de protection des mineurs (mesutes d 'assistance éducative).* Approche de sociologie judiciaire comparée. Vaucresson, 1987.

Lahalle, A.: *L'assistance éducative dans le dispositif de protection judiciaire de la jeunesse.* Vaucresson, 1992.

Lenoel, P.: *Moins de 18 ans: vos droits.* Lieu commun, Paris, 1987.

Mazerol M. T.: *Image et choix d'une profession: la magistrature parmi les professions du droit.* Vaucresson, 1987.

Mecheri H. F.: *Prévenir la délinquance.* Paris, Ed. l'Harmattan, 1986.

Messerschmitt, P.: *Les fugues de l'enfant et de l 'adolescent.* PUF, 1987.

Michard, H.: *De la Justice distributive à la Justice résolutive.* Vaucresson, 1985.

Padeu, C.: *La prise en charge des enfants par l'aide sociale à l'enfance* ODAS, 1993.

215

Peyre, V., Pineau, J., et al.: *Politique de prévention et acteurs de la protection judiciaire de la jeunesse* (1983- 1986). Vaucresson, 1987.

Renucci, J.F.: Enfance délinquante et enfance en danger. Paris, CNRS, 1990.

Renucci, J.F.: *Le droit pénal des mineurs. Que sais je?* Paris, PUF, 1991.

Robertis, C., Pascal, H.: L'intervention collective en travail social L'action auprès des groupes et des communautés. Le Centurion, 1987.

Rugo, A.: *Le milieu ouvert le tournant*:1983/1988. Lyon, AERPS, 1988.

Thevenet, A.: L'aide sociale aujourd 'hui après la décentralisation. Paris, ESF, 1986.

Vial, M., Burguiere, E.: Les institutions de l'éducation spécialisée. Paris, INRP, 1985.

WEISS, J.: Ces enfants meurt1iers. Garancière, 1986.

The Netherlands

Junger-Tas, J.: 'Le traitement intermédiaire aux Pays-Bas'. In: Dünkel, F., Zermatten J. (eds.): Nouvelles Tendances dans le droit pénal-des mineurs. Freiburg, 1990, pp. 193-209.

Van der Laan, P.M.: 'Innovations in the Dutch juvenile system -alternative sanctions'. In: Junger-Tas, J., Block, R.L. (eds.): *Juvenile Delinquency in the Netherlands*. Amstelveen, 1988, pp. 203-239.

Portugal

Gersao, E.: 'Le Portugal entre les pièges de la "protection" et de la "justice" des mineurs. In: Junger-Tas, J., et al. (eds.): *The future of the juvenile justice system*. Leuven, Amerstoort, 1991, pp. 261 -273.

Slovenia

Ancel, M.: *Le droit pénal de la Yougoslavie*. Institut de droit comparé de l'université de Paris. Paris, 1962.

Dekleva, B.: 'Renewal of residential treatment institutions in Slovenia'. In: Junger-Tas, J. et al. (eds.): *The future of the juvenile justice system*. Leuven, Amersfoort, 1991, pp. 401-410.

Selih, A.: 'Children's Rights in Slovenia. Summary'. In: Selih, A. (ed.): *Pravni vidiki otrokovih pravic*. Uradni list RS, Ljubljana, 1992.

Stewart, U. L. (ed.): *The Changing Faces of Juvenile Justice*. New York, 1978, pp. 111-134.

Bibliography Part 2

The following comprehensive bibliography was prepared by Frieder Dünkel for the purposes of her contribution, *Current Directions in Criminal Policy*, in *Section II* of this book: see pp. 38-74.

Albrecht, H.-J.: Entwicklungstendenzen des Jugendkriminalrechts und stationärer Freiheitsentziehung bei jugendlichen Straftätern in den USA. In: Dünkel, F., Meyer, K. (Eds.): Jugendstrafe und Jugendstrafvollzug. Vol. 2, Freiburg 1986, pp.1211-1305.

Albrecht, H.-J.: Kriminologische Perspektiven der Wiedergutmachung. Theoretische Ansätze und empirische Befunde. In: Eser, A., Kaiser, G., Madlener, K. (Eds.): Neue Wege der Wiedergutmachung im Strafrecht. Freiburg 1990, pp.43-72.

Albrecht, P.-A., *Schüler-Springorum*, H. (Eds.): Jugendstrafe an Vierzehn - und Fünfzehnjahrigen. München 1983

Arbeitskreis deutscher, schweizerischer und österreichischer Strafrechtslehrer: Alternativ-Entwurf Wiedergutmachung (AE-WGM). München 1992.

Bondeson, U.: Die Effizienz unterschiedlicher Formen der Strafaussetzung zur Bewährung - Bericht über ein Forschungsprojekt in Schweden. In: Dünkel, F., Spieß, G. (Eds.): Alternativen zur Freiheitsstrafe. Freiburg 1983, pp.148-164.

Bondeson, U.: Innovative Non-custodial sanctions. In: Bishop, N. (Ed.): Scandinavian Criminal Policy and Criminology 1986-90. Stockholm 1990, pp.19-29.

Booth, T. (Ed.): Juvenile Justice in the New Europe. Sheffield 1992.

Bosch, J.: Die Freiheitsstrafe und ihre Surrogate in Italien. In: Jescheck,H.-H. (Ed.): Die Freiheitsstrafe und ihre Surrogate im deutschen und ausländischen Recht. Baden-Baden 1983, pp.327-372.

Bundesamt für Justiz (Ed.): Vorentwurf und Bericht der Expertenkommission zum Allgemeinen Teil und zum Dritten Buch des Strafgesetzbuches und zu einem Bundesgesetz über die Jugendstrafrechtspflege. Bern 1993.

Bundesministerium der Justiz (Ed.): Schlußbericht der Jugendstrafvollzugskommission. Köln 1980.

Bundesministerium der Justiz (Ed.): Arbeitsentwurf eines Gesetzes zur Fortentwicklung des Jugendstrafvollzugs und zur Eingliederung junger Straffälliger. Stand: 30.6.1980. Bonn 1980a.

Bundesministerium der Justiz (Ed.): Schadenswiedergutmachung im Kriminalrecht. Bonn 1988.

Bundesministerium der Justiz (Ed.): Jugendstrafrechtsreform durch die Praxis. Bonn 1989.

Bundesministerium der Justiz (Ed.): 'Diversion' im deutschen Jugendstrafrecht. Thesen, Empfehlungen, Bibliographie. Bonn 1989a.

Bundesministerium der Justiz (Ed.): Täter-Opfer-Ausgleich. Bonner Symposium. Bonn 1991.

Busch, M., *Hartmann,* G., *Mehlich,* N.: Soziale Trainingskurse im Rahmen des Jugendgerichtsgesetzes. 3rd ed. Bonn 1986.

Cavadino, M.: Persistent Young Offenders. Journal of Child law 6 (1994), pp. 2-7

Cornils, K.: Freiheitsstrafe und Strafvollzug bei Jugendlichen in Schweden. In: Dünkel, F., Meyer, K. (Eds.): Jugendstrafe und Jugendstrafvollzug. Vol. 1, Freiburg 1985, pp.497-534.

Cornils, K.: Schweden. In: Eser, A., Huber, B. (Eds.): Strafrechtsentwicklung in Europa 3. Freiburg 1991, pp.961-1002.

Cotic, D.: Jugendstrafe und die Vollziehung von Strafsanktionen gegenüber Minderjährigen in Jugoslawien. In: Dünkel, F., Meyer,K. (Eds.): Jugendstrafe und Jugendstrafvollzug. Vol.2, Freiburg 1986, pp.1081-1109.

Council of Europe: Prison Information Bulletin No.12, June 1988. Strasbourg 1988.

Council of Europe: European Rules on Community Sanctions and Measures. Recommendation No. R (92) 16 and Explanatory Memorandum. Strasbourg 1992.

Deutsche Vereinigung für Jugendgerichte und Jugendgerichtshilfen e.V. (Ed.): Die jugendrichterlichen Entscheidungen - Anspruch und Wirklichkeit. München 1981.

Deutsche Vereinigung für Jugendgerichte und Jugendgerichtshilfen e.V.: Für ein neues Jugendgerichtsgesetz. Vorschläge der DVJJ-Kommission zur Reform des Jugendkriminalrechts. DVJJ-Journal 3 (1992), No. 1-2, pp.4-39.

Dolcini, E., *Paliero,* C.E.: Alternativen zur kurzen Freiheitsstrafe in Italien und im Ausland. ZStW 102 (1990), pp.222-246.

Dünkel, F.: Täter-Opfer-Ausgleich und Schadenswiedergutmachung. Neuere Entwicklungen des Strafrechts und der Strafrechtspraxis im internationalen Vergleich. In: Marks, E., Rössner,D. (Eds.): Täter-Opfer-Ausgleich. Vom zwischenmenschlichen Weg zur Wiederherstellung des Rechtsfriedens. Bonn 1989, pp.394-463.

Dünkel, F.: Zur Schädlichkeit von 'schädlichen Neigungen'. Neue Kriminalpolitik 1 (1989a), No. 4, pp.34-37.

Dünkel, F.: Freiheitsentzug für junge Rechtsbrecher. Situation und Reform von Jugendstrafe, Jugendstrafvollzug, Jugendarrest und Untersuchungshaft in der Bundesrepublik Deutschland und im internationalen Vergleich. Bonn 1990.

Dünkel, F.: Was bringt uns der Jugendarrest? ZfJ 77 (1990a), pp.425-436.

Dünkel, F. Zur Situation des Jugendarrests in der Bundesrepublik Deutschland vor und nach der Vereinigung. DVJJ-Journal 2 (1991), pp. 23-34.

217

Dünkel,   F.: Das deutsche Jugendgerichtsgesetz im europäischen Vergleich. In: Bundesministerium der Justiz (Ed.): Grundfragen des Jugendkriminalrechts und seiner Neuregelung. 2. Kölner Symposium. Bonn 1992, pp.92-122.

Dünkel,   F.: Thesen zu einer Neukonzeption freiheitsentziehender Sanktionen im deutschen Jugendstrafrecht. Neue Kriminalpolitik 4 (1992a), No. 3, pp.30-34.

Dünkel,   F.: Brauchen wir ein Jugendstrafvollzugsgesetz? ZRP 25 (1992b), pp.176-181.

Dünkel,   F.: Heranwachsende im (Jugend-)Kriminalrecht im westeuropäischen Vergleich. ZStW 105 (1993), pp.137-165.

Dünkel,   F.: Untersuchungshaft als Krisenmanagement? Daten und Fakten zur Praxis der Untersuchungshaft in den 90er Jahren. Neue Kriminalpolitik 6 (1994), No 4, pp. 20-29.

Dünkel,   F.: Current legislation as regards young adult offenders. 10th Criminological Colloquy. Council of Europe. Strasbourg 1994a (also in French translation).

Dünkel,   F.: Les législations en vigueur relatives aux jeunes adultes délinquants. 10ème colloque de criminologie. Conseil de l'Europe. Strasbourg 1993a (also in English translation).

Dünkel,   F., Mérigeau, M.: Les expériences de médiation délinquant-victime en République fédérale d'Allemagne. In: Dünkel, F., Zermatten, J. (Eds.): Nouvelles tendances dans le droit pénal des mineurs. Médiation, travail au profit de la communauté et traitement intermédiaire. Freiburg 1989, pp.95-124.

Dünkel,   F., Meyer, K.: Die Reform von Jugendstrafe und Jugendstrafvollzug - Gegenstandsbereiche und Ziele eines internationalen Vergleichs. In: Dünkel, F., Meyer, K. (Eds.): Jugendstrafe und Jugendstrafvollzug - Stationäre Maßnahmen der Jugendkriminalrechtspflege im internationalen Vergleich. Vol. 1, Freiburg 1985, pp. 2-41.

Dünkel,   F., Rössner, D.: Law and Practice of Victim/Offender Agreements. In. Wright, M., Galaway, B. (Eds.): Mediation and Criminal Justice. Victims, Offenders and Community. London et al. 1989, pp.152-177.

Dünkel,   F., Vagg, J (Eds). : Waiting For Trial. International Perspectives On The Use Of Pre-Trial Detention And The Rights And Living Conditions Of Prisoners Waiting For Trial. Freiburg 1994.

Dünkel,   F., Zermatten, J. (Eds.): Nouvelles Tendances dans le Droit Pénal des Mineurs. Médiation, Travail au Profit de la Communauté et Traitement Intérmédiaire. Freiburg 1990.

Dünkel,   F., van Kalmthout, A, Schüler-Springorum, H. (Eds.) : Entwicklungstendenzen und Reformstrategien im Jugendstrafrecht im internationalen Vergleich. Bonn 1996 (in print).

Dupont,   L., Walgrave, L.: Jugendschutzgesetz und stationäre Unterbringung delinquenter Jugendlicher in Belgien. In: Dünkel, F., Meyer, K. (Eds.): Jugendstrafe und Jugendstrafvollzug. Vol. 1, Freiburg 1985, pp.537-563.

Eisenberg, U.: Jugendstrafrecht und Jugendstrafrechtspflege im internationalen Vergleich. In: Bundesministerium der Justiz (Ed.): Jugendstrafrechtsreform durch die Praxis. Bonn 1989, pp.45-73.

Eisenberg, U.: Jugendgerichtsgesetz. Kommentar. 6th Ed., München 1995.

Eliaerts,   C., et al. (Eds.): Van jeugdbeschermingsrecht naar jeugdrecht? Arnhem 1990.

Feld,   B.C.: The Juvenile Court meets the Principle of the Offense: Legislative Changes in Juvenile Waiver Statutes. Journal of Criminal Law and Criminology 78 (1987), pp.471-533.

Handler,   J.F., Zatz, J. (Eds.): Neither Angels nor Thieves: Studies in Deinstitutionalization of Status Offenders. Washington/D.C. 1982.

Heine,   G., Locher, J.: Jugendstrafrechtspflege in der Schweiz. Freiburg 1985.

Heinz,   W.: Jugendgerichtsbarkeit in der Bundesrepublik Deutschland. Empirische Bestandsaufnahme der Sanktionspraxis, gegenwärtige legislative Reformtendenzen und Perspektiven für die innere Reform. In: Kerner, H.-J., Galaway, B., Janssen, H. (Eds.): Jugendgerichtsbarkeit in Europa und Nordamerika - Aspekte und Tendenzen. München 1986, pp.527-641.

218

Heinz,   W.: Neue ambulante Maßnahmen nach dem Jugendgerichtsgesetz: Forschung und Forschungslücken. In: Bundesministerium der Justiz (Ed.): Neue ambulante Maßnahmen nach dem Jugendgerichtsgesetz. 2nd ed. Bonn 1986a, pp.162-195.

Heinz,   W.: Jugendstrafrechtsreform durch die Praxis - eine Bestandsaufnahme. In: Bundesministerium der Justiz (Ed.): Jugendstrafrechtsreform durch die Praxis. Bonn 1989, pp.13-44.

Heinz,   W.: Jugendliche Wiederholungstäter und Jugendstrafrechtspraxis. Das jugendstrafrechtliche Konzept der 'schädlichen Neigungen' im Spiegel empirischer Befunde. INFO (Landesgruppe Baden-Württemberg in der Deutschen Vereinigung für Jugendgerichte und Jugendgerichtshilfen e.V.) 1/89a, pp.7-62.

Heinz,   W.: Der Regierungsentwurf zur Änderung des Jugendgerichtsgesetzes. Ein wichtiger, aber auch nur ein erster Schritt in die richtige Richtung. RdJ 38 (1990), pp.133-149.

Heinz,   W.: Die Jugendstrafrechtspflege im Spiegel der Rechtspflegestatistiken. Ausgewählte Daten für den Zeitraum 1955-1988. MschrKrim 73 (1990a), pp.210-226.

Heinz,   W.: Abschaffung oder Reformulierung des Erziehungsgedankens im Jugendstrafrecht? In Bundesministerium der Justiz (Ed.): Grundfragen des Jugendkriminalrechts und seiner Neuregelung. 2. Kölner Symposium. Bonn 1992, pp.369-414.

Heinz,   W.: Diversion im Jugendstrafverfahren. ZStW 104 (1992a), pp.591-638.

Heinz,   W.: Flucht ins Prozeßrecht? Verfahrensrechtliche Entkriminalisierung (Diversion) im Jugenstrafrecht : Zielsetzungen, Implementation und Evaluation. Neue Kriminalpolitik 6 (1994), No. 1, pp. 29-36.

Heinz,   W., *Spieß*, G.: Reaktionsalternativen im Jugendstrafrecht: Determinanten und Auswirkungen unterschiedlicher Strategien der Strafverfolgung bei jugendlichen Erst- und Bagatelltätern. 1. Zwischenbericht für die Deutsche Forschungsgemeinschaft. Konstanz 1984.

Hinrichs, K.: Der Ungehorsamsarrest - Repressive Antwort auf schwierige Fälle? Wege zu seiner Vermeidung. In: Deutsche Vereinigung für Jugendgerichte und Jugendgerichtshilfen e.V. (Ed.): Mehrfach Auffällige - Mehrfach Betroffene. Erlebnisweisen und Reaktionsformen. Bonn 1990, pp.330-343.

Huber,   B.: Jugendstrafe und Jugendstrafvollzug im Umbruch -Stationäre Maßnahmen in der Jugendkriminalrechtspflege in England und Wales. In: Dünkel, F., Meyer, K. (Eds.): Jugendstrafe und Jugendstrafvollzug. Vol. 1, Freiburg 1985, pp.669-754.

International Penal and Penitentiary Foundation (Ed.): Standard minimum rules for the implementation of non-custodial sanctions and measures involving restriction of liberty. Deventer 1989.

Jesionek, U.: Jugendgerichtsgesetz 1988. Wien 1994.

Jung,   H.: Das schottische Children's Hearing System. In: Herzberg, R.D. (Ed.): Festschrift für D. Oehler. Köln u.a. 1985, pp.705-727.

Junger-Tas, J.: Le traitement intermédiaire aux Pays-Bas. In: Dünkel, F., Zermatten, J. (Eds.): Nouvelles Tendances dans le Droit Pénal des Mineurs. Freiburg 1990, pp.193-209.

Junger-Tas, J., *Boendermaker*, L., *van der Laan*, P.H. (eds.): The future of the juvenile justice system.Leuven, Amersfoort 1991.

Junger-Tas, J., *Kruissink*, M.: Ontwekkling van de jeugdriminaliteit: periode 1980-1988. Arnhem (WODC) 1990.

Kaiser,   G.: International vergleichende Perspektiven zum Jugendstrafrecht. In: Schwind, H.-D. et al. (Eds.): Festschrift für G. Blau. Berlin, New York 1985, pp.441-457.

Kaiser,   G.: Die Behandlung junger Rechtsbrecher zwischen informeller Konfliktregelung und defensivem Formalismus -Erziehungsstrafrecht ohne

Chancen? In: Wolff, J., Marek, A. (Eds.): Erziehung und Strafe. Bonn 1990, pp.62-82.

Kaiser,   G.: Erfahrungen mit dem Täter-Opfer-Ausgleich im Ausland. In: Bundesministerium der Justiz (Ed.): Täter-Opfer-Ausgleich. Bonner Symposium. Bonn 1991, pp.40-50.

Kerner,   H.-J.: Jugendkriminalrecht als 'Vorreiter' der Strafrechtsreform? In: 40 Jahre Bundesrepublik, 40 Jahre Rechtsentwicklung, ed. by the members of the Law Faculty of the University of Tübingen. Tübingen 1990, pp.347-379.

Kerner,   H.-J., Marks, E., Rössner, D., Schreckling, J.: Täter-Opfer-Ausgleich im Jugendstrafrecht. BewHi 37 (1990), pp.169-176.

Klages,   J.: Freiheitsstrafe und Strafvollzug bei Jugendlichen in Dänemark. In: Dünkel, F., Meyer, K. (Eds.): Jugendstrafe und Jugendstrafvollzug. Vol. 1, Freiburg 1985, pp.391-423.

van der Laan,   P.M.: Innovations in the Dutch juvenile system -alternative sanctions. In: Junger-Tas, J., Block, R.L. (Eds.): Juvenile Delinquency in The Netherlands. Amstelveen 1988, pp.203-239.

van der Laan,   P.M.: Experimenten me alternatieve sancties voor jeugdigen. Arnhem, 1991.

Lahti,   R.: Freiheitsstrafe und Jugendgefängnis in Finnland. In: Dünkel, F., Meyer, K. (Eds.): Jugendstrafe und Jugendstrafvollzug. Vol. 1, Freiburg 1985, pp.425-461.

Lopes Rocha, M.A.: Die Reform des Jugendstrafrechts in Portugal. In: Dünkel, F., Meyer, K. (Eds.): Jugendstrafe und Jugendstrafvollzug. Vol. 2, Freiburg 1986, pp.891-903.

Mair,   G., Nee, C.: Electronic monitoring. The trials and their results. London (HMSO) 1990.

Mérigeau, M.: La justice pénale des mineurs en RFA - Evaluation du compromis entre le pénal et l'éducatif. Thèse de droit. Université de Bordeaux I. Bordeaux 1988.

Mérigeau, M.: Frankreich. In : Eser, A., Hubber, B. (Eds.) : Strafrechtsentwiicklung in Europa 4, Teil 1. Freiburg 1993, pp. 467-541.

Ministère de la Justice (Ed.): Réponses à la délinquance des mineurs. Paris 1990.

Ministère de la Justice (Ed.): Rapport sur l'exercice 1991. Paris 1992.

Ostendorf, H.: Wider die Verselbständigung des sog. Ungehorsamsarrests zu einer zusätzlichen jugendgerichtlichen Sanktion. ZblJugR 70 (1983), pp.563-576.

Ostendorf, H.: Zukunft des Jugendstrafrechts. In: Bundesministerium der Justiz (Ed.): Jugendstrafrechtsreform durch die Praxis. Bonn 1989, pp.325-337.

Ostendorf, H.: Jugendgerichtsgesetz. Kommentar. 3nd ed. Köln et al. 1994

Peters,   K.: Strafprozeß. Ein Lehrbuch. 4th ed. Heidelberg 1985.

Pfeiffer,   C.: Kriminalprävention im Jugendgerichtsverfahren. Köln u.a. 1983.

Pfeiffer,   C.: Jugendkriminalität und jugendstrafrechtliche Praxis - eine vergleichende Analyse zu Entwicklungstendenzen und regionalen Unterschieden. Hannover (Expertise zum 8. Jugendbericht) 1988.

Pfeiffer,   C.: Diversion - Alternativen zum Freiheitsentzug, Entwicklungstrends und regionale Unterschiede. In: Bundesministerium der Justiz (Ed.): Jugendstrafrechtsreform durch die Praxis. Bonn 1989, pp.74-100.

Pfeiffer,   C.: Wird nach Jugendstrafrecht härter gestraft? Strafv erteidiger 11 (1991), pp.363-370.

Pfeiffer,   C.: Neuere kriminologische Forschungen zur jugendrechtlichen Sanktionspraxis in der Bundesrepublik Deutschland - eine Analyse unter dem Gesichtspunkt der Verhältnismäßigkeit. In: Bundesministerium der Justiz (Ed.): Grundfragen des Jugendkriminalrechts und seiner Neuregelung. 2. Kölner Symposium. Bonn 1992, pp.60-90.

Pfeiffer,   C.: Täter-Opfer-Ausgleich - das Trojanische Pferd im Strafrecht? ZRP 25 (1992a), pp.338-345.

Pfeiffer,   C., Strobl, R.: Abschied vom Jugendarrest? DVJJ-Journal 2 (1991), No. 1, pp.35-45.

220

Picotti,   L., *de Strobel*, G.: Freiheitsentziehende Maßnahmen gegenüber Minderjährigen und Jugendstrafvollzug in Italien. In: Dünkel, F., Meyer, K. (Eds.): Jugendstrafe und Jugendstrafvollzug. Vol. 2, Freiburg 1986, pp.905-996

Pieplow,   L.: Erziehung als Chiffre. In: Walter, M.: (Ed.): Beiträge zur Erziehung im Jugendkriminalrecht. Köln u.a. 1989, pp.5-57.

Rössner,   D.: Jugendstrafvollzug bei 14- bis 18Jährigen -Problemanzeige und Perspektiven. In: Kerner, H.-J., Kaiser, G. (Eds.): Kriminalität. Persönlichkeit, Lebensgeschichte und Verhalten. Festschrift für H. Göppinger. Berlin u.a. 1990, pp.523-536.

Rössner,   D.: Strafrechtsfolgen ohne Übelszufügung? NStZ 12 (1992), pp.409-415.

Roxin,   C.: Die Wiedergutmachung im strafrechtlichen Sanktionensystem. In: Badura, P., Scholz, R. (Eds.).: Festschrift für P. Lerche.München 1993, pp.301-313.

Sace,   J., *van der Vorst*, P. (Eds.): Justice et Jeunes Délinquants. Aspects institutionels et criminologiques. Bruxelles 1989.

Sagel-Grande, I.: Einige Reformansätze im niederländischen Jugendstrafrecht. ZfJ 73 (1986), pp.281-289.

Schöch,   H.: Vorläufige Ergebnisse der Diskussionen zu einem Alternativ-Entwurf Wiedergutmachung (AE-WGM) im Arbeitskreis deutscher, österreichischer und schweizerischer Strafrechtslehrer. In. Eser, A., Kaiser, G., Madlener, K. (Eds.): Neue Wege der Wiedergutmachung im Strafrecht. Freiburg 1990, pp.73-82.

Schöch,   H.: Empfehlen sich Änderungen und Ergänzungen bei den strafrechtlichen Sanktionen ohne Freiheitsentzug? Gutachten C zum 59. Deutschen Juristentag. München 1992.

Scholten, H.-J.:, *ten Siethoff*, F.G.A.: Jugendstrafe und Jugendstrafvollzug in den Niederlanden. In: Dünkel, F., Meyer, K. (Eds.): Jugendstrafe und Jugendstrafvollzug. Vol. 1, Freiburg 1985, pp.565-666.

Schreckling, J.: Täter-Opfer-Ausgleich nach Jugendstraftaten in Köln. Bericht über Aufbau, Verlauf und Ergebnisse des Modellprojekts 'Waage'. Bonn 1990

Schreckling, J., *et al.*: Bestandsaufnahmen zur Praxis des Täter-Opfer-Ausgleichs in der Bundesrepublik Deutschland. Bonn (Bundesministerium der Justiz) 1991.
Bundesrepublik Deutschland. Bonn (Bundesministerium der Justiz) 1991.

Schreckling, J., Pieplow, L.: Täter-Opfer-Ausgleich. Eine Zwischenbilanz nach zwei Jahren Fallpraxis beim Modellprojekt 'Die Waage'. ZRP 22 (1989), pp.10-14.

Schüler-Springorum, H.: Critical Comparison of the British Detention Centres and the German 'Jugendarrest' System. International Journal of Criminology and Penology 1975, pp.201-211.

Schüler-Springorum, H.: Die Mindestgrundsätze der Vereinten Nationen für die Jugendgerichtsbarkeit. ZStW 99 (1987), pp.809-844.

Schumann, K.F. (Ed.): Jugendarrest und/oder Betreuungsweisung. Bremen 1985.

Schumann, K.F.: Der Jugendarrest - (Zucht-) Mittel zu jedem Zweck. Zentralblatt für Jugendrecht 73 (1986), pp.363-369.

Schwaighofer, K.: Ausgewählte Fragen zum Strafrechtsänderungsgesetz 1987. ÖJZ 43 (1988), pp.587-594.

Snare,   A. (Ed.): Youth, Crime and Justice. Oslo (Scandinavian Sudies in Criminology, Vol. 12) 1991

Stangeland, P.: Freiheitsentziehende Reaktionen und Alternativen zur Freiheitsstrafe bei Minderjährigen in Norwegen. In: Dünkel,F., Meyer,K. (Eds.): Jugendstrafe und Jugendstrafvollzug. Vol.1, Freiburg 1985, pp.463-496.

Stettler,   M.: Avant-projet de loi fédérale concernant la condition pénale des mineurs et rapport explicatif. O.O. 1986.

Stettler,   M.: Die Grundzüge des Vorentwurfs für ein Bundesgesetz über die strafrechtliche Stellung von Kindern und Jugendlichen. SchwZStrR 105 (1988), pp.138-155.

Stile,   A.M.: Neue italienische Kriminalpolitik nach dem Strafrechtsreformgesetz von 1981. ZStW 96 (1984), pp.172-187.

221

Tiffer-Sotomayor, C., *Dünkel*, F.: Das Jugendstrafrecht in Lateinamerika unter besonderer Berücksichtigung des Jugendrechts und der Sanktionspraxis in Costa Rica. ZStW 101 (1989), pp.206-228.

Tracy,   P.E., *Wolfgang* M.E., *Figlio*, R.M.: Delinquency in Two Birth Cohorts. Executive Summary. Washington D.C. (U.S. Department of Justice) 1985.

Tutt,   N.: Law and Policies on Juvenile Offending in England and Wales, Scotland, Northern Ireland and the Republic of Ireland. In: Kerner, H.J. u.a. (Ed.): Jugendgerichtsbarkeit in Europa und 37Nordamerika - Aspekte und Tendenzen - München 1986, pp.469-502.

Tutt,   N., *Giller*, H.: The Elimination of Custody. Unpublished paper of a lecture at the Max-Planck-Institut für Strafrecht. Freiburg 1987.

United Nations (Ed.): The United Nations and Crime Prevention. New York 1991.

Vestergaard, J.: Dänemark. In: Eser,A.,Huber,B. (Eds.): Strafrechtsentwicklung in Europa 3.Landesberichte 1986/1988 über Gesetzgebung, Rechtsprechung und Literatur. Freiburg 1990, pp.41-89.

Viehmann, H.: Anmerkungen zum Erziehungsgedanken im Jugendstrafrecht aus rechtschaffender Sicht. In: Walter, M. (Ed.): Beiträge zur Erziehung im Jugendkriminalrecht. Köln et al. 1989, pp.111-153.

Walter,   M.: Über die Bedeutung des Erziehungsgedankens für das Jugendkriminalrecht. In: Walter, M. (Ed.): Beiträge zur Erziehung im Jugendkriminalrecht. Köln u.a. 1989, pp.59-89.

Wasik, M., *Taylor*, R. : Criminal Justice and Public Order Act 1994. London 1995.

Wiesner,   R., *Zarbock*, W. (Hrsg.): Das neue Kinder- und Jugendhilfegesetz (KJHG). Köln et al. 1991.

Zipf, H.: Kriminalpolitische Schwerpunkte der Strafrechtsreform 1987. ÖJZ 43 (1988), pp.439-449.

Expanded List of Contents of Sections I to V 223

Readers of *Juvenile Delinquents and Young People in Danger* may also be interested in two other publications from Waterside Press, both new in 1996:

Introduction to
The Youth Court
incorporating 'The Sentence of the Youth Court'

Winston Gordon, Michael Watkins and Philip Cuddy

Produced under the auspices of the Justices' Clerks' Society, this handbook contains a straightforward outline of the youth court and current youth justice practice. It incorporates sections on sentencing which follow the successful format of *The Sentence of the Court: A Handbook for Magistrates* (published by Waterside Press in 1995).

Direct mail price: £12.00 (add £1.50 p&p) ISBN 1 872 870 36 8

Introduction to
The Scottish Children's Panel
Alistair Kelly

This book describes in plain language the Scottish children's panel, its philosophy of care and advocates reform of the system taking account of the Children (Scotland) Act 1995 and the demand for a proper respect of children's rights in Scotland within a European context. It will be of interest to practitioners inside and outside Scotland - and is believed to be the first basic account of this topic for 20 years.

Direct mail price: £12.00 (add £1.50 p&p) ISBN 1 872 870 38 4

Also still in print
The Youth Court: One Year Onwards
Bryan Gibson *et al.*

Well received on publication in 1994, this practitioner level work (in contrast to the more basic treatment of the newer *Introduction to the Youth Court,* above) takes stock of the law and practice of the youth courts in England and Wales 18 months after their creation.

Direct mail price: £15.00 (add £1.50 p&p) ISBN 1 872 870 14 7

All from Waterside Press, Domum Road, Winchester SO23 9NN
Tel or fax 01962 855567. E-mail INTERNET:106025.1020@compuserve.com